SMOOTH OPERATING
and Other Social Acts

SUNY series in Multiethnic Literatures
―――――――
Mary Jo Bona, editor

SMOOTH OPERATING
and Other Social Acts

Roland Leander Williams

Cover image: *Phillis Wheatley, Negro servant to Mr. John Wheatley, of Boston* by engraver Scipio Moorhead, active 1770–1779, available through the Library of Congress.

Published by State University of New York Press, Albany

© 2022 State University of New York

All rights reserved

Printed in the United States of America

No part of this book may be used or reproduced in any manner whatsoever without written permission. No part of this book may be stored in a retrieval system or transmitted in any form or by any means including electronic, electrostatic, magnetic tape, mechanical, photocopying, recording, or otherwise without the prior permission in writing of the publisher.

For information, contact State University of New York Press, Albany, NY
www.sunypress.edu

Library of Congress Cataloging-in-Publication Data

Name: Williams, Roland Leander, 1953– author.
Title: Smooth operating and other social acts / Roland Leander Williams.
Description: Albany, NY : State University of New York Press, [2022] |
 Series: SUNY series in multiethnic literatures | Includes bibliographical references and index.
Identifiers: LCCN 2022005689 | ISBN 9781438489476 (hardcover : alk. paper) |
 ISBN 9781438489483 (ebook) | ISBN 9781438484969 (pbk. : alk. paper)
Subjects: LCSH: American fiction—19th century—History and criticism. |
 American fiction—20th century—History and criticism. | African Americans in literature. | Stereotypes (Social psychology) in literature. | Role playing in literature. | Race relations in literature. | Slavery in literature. | LCGFT: Literary criticism.
Classification: LCC PS374.B635 W55 2022 | DDC 813.009/896073—dc23/eng/20220331
LC record available at https://lccn.loc.gov/2022005689

10 9 8 7 6 5 4 3 2 1

With our eyes closed, we see best,
Every odd soul favors the rest.

For the love that Hazel poured into her daughter.

Contents

Acknowledgments	xi
Prologue: On the Sly	1
Birth of Cool	13
Standards and Practices	27
Two of Kind	45
Game of Charades	61
Old Black Magic	83
Lost in Translation	103
Learning the Ropes	117
Blind Man's Bluff	131
Dress for Success	143
Postscript: On One's Game	155
Works Cited	165
Index	171

Acknowledgments

A single hand never produces a book. It takes a village. The encouragement of many friends, including Renie and David Campbell, Marsha Levell, and Victoria McGuigan, made a critical difference. I tip my hat to my grandfather, Leander Roland Williams, for the example that he set. My nieces Tiffany and Teralyn filled me with inspiration. I am indebted to David Bradley for blazing the trail that I followed. Andrea Allison made sure that I stayed the course. Challenges from my colleagues at Temple University kept me going to the end. My graduate student, Christian Rupert, helped me think through the work. I owe Tamara Nopper thanks for broadening my view. Ike Newsum motivated me to draw on my imagination. Most of all, I am grateful to the team at SUNY Press, especially my editor, Rebecca Colesworthy, who did more than a hand's turn with kindness and consideration.

Prologue

On the Sly

Judge not folks by an outward show;
Feathers float while a pearl lies low.

When my grandfather passed, people remembered him as a polite and principled person. Family and friends reminisced about how he left his father's farm in the South to work for the Pennsylvania Railroad in Philadelphia. He won the heart of a devout woman with whom he raised five children in a home that he bought. Members of his congregation paid him tribute for becoming a pillar of their church when it was getting off the ground. His neighbors held nobody more helpful and honest. A subtle side that he owned, which I discovered during my boyhood one day when he took me shopping for a pair of sneakers, went unnoticed by the unsuspecting.

Named Leander, my grandfather came to life as one of nine children whose father was born to an enslaved woman named Blanche Graham and an unnamed father in rural Virginia on the same day that Confederate General Robert E. Lee surrendered his sword to Union General Ulysses S. Grant at Appomattox. His forebear based his conduct on morals taught by native Virginian Booker T. Washington, commending faithfulness to industry, integrity, and intelligence within the bounds of reason. My grandfather picked up his manners from his parent, inclining him to maintain that no matter how fashions change, a ruffled temper will never be in style. He kept a mellow air about him. I never saw him lose his cool.

At twenty, in 1926, Leander departed from Roanoke on the flatbed of a train that he rode to Philadelphia. He made the move in response to a call for Pullman porters to work for the Pennsylvania Railroad operating out of the bustling 30th Street Station. His job had him haul assorted bags aboard cars for white passengers. He also shined the travelers' shoes. In addition, he tended and tidied up sleeping berths for the fares. Leander remained on the job for thirty-five years, became a leader of the local chapter of the Brotherhood of Sleeping Car Porters, and hosted union confabs in his home attended by A. Phillip Randolph, the founder and president of the organization, which was the first African American labor union in the United States.

My grandfather earned a modest salary that exceeded the average for most African American men lucky enough to find employment in Philadelphia. The meat of his bread and butter came from tips handed to him by passengers, whom he pleased with a smile. Customers whom he greeted at depots along the Broadway Limited line running between the City of Brotherly Love and the Windy City, Chicago, must have regarded him as a model servant. They likely showered him with gratuities. On countless occasions, I saw him pull a wad of cash from his pants pocket.

With the income that he earned, he purchased a four-bedroom house. The residence sheltered his family through the Great Depression. While countless households in the city hungered for food, Leander watched his spending to make sure his children never missed a meal. His earnings stood his offspring in good stead through the hard times. He managed his money well enough to contribute a tithe of his income to support the New Bethlehem Baptist Church, where he acted as a lay officer. The church came to install a stained-glass window dedicated to his memory.

Before Labor Day and my first day of first grade, as a favor to my father, my grandfather volunteered to take me to the Thom McAn shoe store and buy me a pair of Chuck Taylor All-Stars by Converse, the sneakers that were all the rage among the boys in my neighborhood at the time. I had a hole in the bottom of my PF Flyers; therefore, as athletic shoes, they were useless for use in sports after school, and they were old hat to my friends, none of whom wanted to be caught dead with the brand on their feet. Stepping into the store with my grandfather filled me with excitement. We were both dressed in our Sunday best, as was always the case when anyone in my family went shopping in Center City, since we never wanted any whites selling or buying merchandise around the commercial strips to doubt that we were respectable and had cash. My grandfather was a short man. Still, greeting the white shoe salesman who met us a few feet inside the door, Leander looked like a giant, ready to perform magic for me.

PROLOGUE

The salesman wore a dingy gray polyester suit with a crumpled white shirt and stained black tie. He was a good bit taller than my grandfather, but he appeared younger than my father. Patting the shoulder pad of my grandfather's brown herringbone jacket, he asked, "How's it going, Pops? Can I do something for you and your boy? Looking for a bargain, I guess," he said.

My grandfather flinched before he nodded, stammered, and flashed a smile. In a gradual and quiet fashion, he explained our mission. He let the white man know that he wanted to purchase me a new pair of sneakers. My grandfather pointed out that I had my heart set on wearing the Chuck Taylor All-Stars brand. He issued a polite request to see the type in my size.

The salesman questioned whether the Converse shoes fell within our price range. They were the most expensive sneakers in stock, he informed us. He asked, "Sure you can afford it, Pops?" Then he directed us to some PF Flyers displayed on a side shelf. Each of them looked worn out of shape from being tried on lots of times. The salesman offered to let my elder have the shoes for up to twenty percent off the sticker price. With a swear word, the white man insisted that the shabby shoes were a real bargain.

My elder hemmed and hawed for a minute. He grinned and shook his head and checked the tag on the PF Flyers. "Wow," he blurted out with bulging eyes. "This could break the bank. Tell me, sir, do you have cheaper shoes in the back? I hate to trouble you, but if you could find some samples that cost a little less, you will help me stay out of the poorhouse."

"Sure, Pops. I have some clearance items that might fit your budget. If you like any of them, I'll let you take them off my hands at the manufacturer price. You could save a fortune on any set of them. Have a seat. I'll bring out three or four boxes. You can have your pick on me for peanuts."

The salesman disappeared into the stockroom. Confusion and disappointment consumed me until my grandfather said, "Let's get out of here. Fool blew his commission. I'll spend my money elsewhere." We were gone before the salesman had a clue.

We hiked to the Father and Son shoe store on South Street, where a Black franchise owner who looked around my grandfather's age sold him the sneakers that I wanted without a word about my elder's ability to pay. I learned a priceless lesson that day about "smooth operating." The full meaning of the moment exceeded my grasp until I had a literature class in college where I read the novel *Invisible Man* (1952) by Ralph Ellison. My elder's performance in the shoe store was clarified by the deathbed speech of the grandfather in Ellison's novel. The fictional figure to his dying day has been known as "the meekest of men." He shocks his family at the end of his life when he bears a subtle side while speaking to his heir:

> "Son, after I'm gone, I want you to keep up the good fight. I never told you, but our life is a war and I have been a traitor all my born days, a spy in the enemy's country ever since I give up my gun back in the Reconstruction. Live with your head in the lion's mouth. I want you to overcome 'em with yeses, undermine 'em with grins, agree 'em to death and destruction, let 'em swoller you till they vomit or bust wide open. . . . Learn it to the young'uns." (Ellison 13–14)

The passage led me to conclude that my grandfather Leander was carrying on a tradition. He was engaging in a form of roleplaying with deep roots in African American culture propagated by the practice of Black bondage that trained white people to look down on Black folk; at the Thom McAn shoe store, Leander was teaching me how to turn an interaction with an imperious white man to my advantage; he was putting on a show, an exhibition of deft dissembling, which had spared African Americans from humiliation and hardship since slavery started.

Leander maintained a regimen, routine, and role that permitted him to make a decent living as a Pullman porter. Richard Wright illustrated the behavior in "The Ethics of Living Jim Crow" (1937) by recounting his time as a porter in a hotel where he "had to exercise a great deal of ingenuity to keep out of trouble" (Wright 14). This book affirms that my grandfather had a sly side that represents a mode of behavior adopted by Black people to counteract the indignities posed by the past slave system. Through accounts of slave narratives and analyses of neo-slave narratives, this volume establishes that an archetypal hero in African American literature puts on false fronts and makes swift uses of improvisation. "Smooth operating" is an expression that attests to the character of the cited act.

Scholars have suspected that Blacks were beaten and broken by bondage and accustomed to act full of folly from fright fostered by the slave system. Their perspective denies that African Americans who suffered slavery possessed the capacity to read a room and conjure up ways to preserve dignity and improve their lot. From the given view, it follows that slavery subjected the enslaved to a reign of terror that traumatized them and left them dumbed down into a pack of cards good for comic relief. The position at issue evokes an image of African Americans, bound by bondage, as mere puppets dangling from strings controlled by hands above their heads. *Scenes of Subjection* by Saidiya Hartman (1997) supports the notion of Blacks as beings bent by slavery into the laughingstock of the land. The ensuing pages of this book show that Hartman and her fellows failed to recognize the resourcefulness and resilience that bondage stirred in the souls of Black folk and carried them away from slavery as well as above barriers raised to keep them cornered in a state of second-class citizenship.

Oppression arouses resistance because persecution chafes the human spirit, whose heart is set on freedom. The history of uprisings against tyranny, beginning long before slaves revolted around Egypt and Rome, persisting well beyond the American Revolution to the struggle against Apartheid in South Africa, and continuing to erupt where despots reign, like volcanoes impelled by nature to blow their stack, tells that people are not born ready for any of their fellows to saddle them, straddle them, and spur them as if they were beasts of burden. Societies have ranked women below men throughout recorded history to the sorrow of the subordinated body. Patricia Hill Collins nevertheless in "Learning from the Outsider Within" (1986) renders it a mistake to assume that African American women, on whom the institution of Black bondage impinged, lived like marionettes at the disposal of white hands empowered by an entrenched social code to manhandle dark members of the "opposite sex." Collins generates trust that enslaved Black females developed a complex culture conceived to afford them ways to define their worth and defend their honor. In her eyes, African American women represent "outsiders within," marginalized members of a social order propelled by their subordination to perform creative acts of resistance to subjection. Her research advocates recognizing "race" and "gender" as partial constructions formed by misconceptions drawn from conditions that situate some without cause above others in society. Collins suggests that Black females represent targets of persecution from different directions. The community faces discrimination stirred by prejudice about their shade and sex on top of their class, allows Collins. Still, in effect, she counts the group as typical of resident underdogs stuck in a hierarchy under the weight of an ideology that denies them the right to climb the ranks. Her findings make it sensible to suppose heroic figures in the minds of African American women favor Harriet Tubman, who rose out of slavery in the antebellum South and became legendary by using her wits to free herself and carry dozens of her people to freedom afterward on the Underground Railroad. The book unfolding here lays grounds for regarding model Black women as consummate practitioners of an act designed to save face and derive power in an oppressive system, a swift sort of performance rating high praise in the opinion of Blacks who dwelled in bondage and took measures to pass their minds and manners to their progeny.

Channeling the ghost of Karl Mannheim haunting *Ideology and Utopia* (1936), Collins leaves room to count Black women in concert with Black men as bits of waves at sea with their sights set by their place in their surroundings. With a seeming sixth sense, she suggests people pick up parts to play through the direction of their background. She brings forth Black feminist thought as a special stream of consciousness engendered by opposition to undue limits on the rights of Black women. Collins could note two genres of African American literature to prove her point. The slave narrative is one and the neo-slave narrative is the other one, where Black female figures star as epic characters quickened beyond male mates.

Slave narratives were the first Black tales of epic proportions that appeared in the country. They hit bookstores and flew off their shelves before Thomas Jefferson thought to write "all men are created equal." Their protagonists start out caught in slavery. The system rubs them the wrong way. In search of understanding, they gain knowledge that teaches them to put on a show for imperious white men while looking to advance their own interests through mind games. By means of a conscious charade, they slip out of slavery and skip into freedom. The conduct of the protagonists who surface in slave narratives is born again in the heroes of neo-slave narratives, as the succeeding pages demonstrate.

A Black woman stars as an artful dodger armed with useful knowledge in the slave narrative *Running a Thousand Miles for Freedom* (1860). Her name is Ellen Craft. She works with her mate to pull off a ploy that permits the couple to escape the scourge of slavery. Craft acted as a team with her partner to capture the details of their flight to freedom in print. The result is a book that stands as an excellent example of how breaks from bondage in slave narratives involve creative charades.

Masters of improvisation occupy the center of classic slave narratives. It is evident in the case of *The Interesting Narrative of the Life of Olaudah Equiano, or Gustavus Vassa, the African* (1789), where a native of Benin, stolen from his village home and sold into the Atlantic Slave Trade, runs a business on the sly from which he saves enough funds to surprise his master with a payment for his freedom. Quick thinking in the *Narrative of the Life of Frederick Douglass, an American Slave* (1845) leads Douglass to assume a false identity, which he employs to take his leave of bondage.

PROLOGUE

In *Incidents in the Life of a Slave Girl* (1861), the hero resorts to a series of ruses on the way to emancipation from slavery, which she describes as a swamp of snakes that lie in wait to spew poison into enslaved women. The heroes of the classic slave narratives face awful oppression. They never lose heart for more than a moment. Persecution motivates them to sharpen their wits and use their heads to resist subjugation.

Frederick Douglass planted the heroic ideal of classic slave narratives in African American fiction through the publication of his novella *The Heroic Slave* (1852), featuring a protagonist who plays up to expectations with a plan to exceed them. *The Conjure Woman* (1899) from Charles Chesnutt, starring a wily Black servant, constitutes an addition to a tradition primed to introduce neo-slave narratives, alleged firsthand accounts of Black bondage from figures whose personal histories affirm that underdogs who live to tell tales grow quick. Neo-slave narratives sprouted around the time of the Black Arts Movement that arose in the wake of Dr. Martin Luther King Jr.'s assassination during the spring of 1968. They reflected an exploding African American drive to debunk stereotypes foisted on them by a way of seeing born out of Black bondage that classified people as colors and stamped the brightest shade the best sort. *Flight to Canada* (1976) by Ishmael Reed gave a jolt to the literary convention through its deployment of absurd situations overcome by magical schemes. Earlier, Ernest Gaines's *The Autobiography of Miss Jane Pittman* (1971) made a significant contribution to the evolution of the neo-slave narrative genre by using the lens of a male gaze to picture a former Black female slave as a marvel who finds discretion is the better part of valor. Octavia Butler's *Kindred* (1979), preceding Sherley Anne Williams's *Dessa Rose* (1986), joined the field with a discerning portrait of an enslaved Black woman who comes under mortal fire from a few different angles, yet survives the barrage by learning to improvise. James McBride's *The Good Lord Bird* (2013) belongs to the genre of the neo-slave narrative as much as *Yellow Wife* (2021) by Sadeqa Johnson, whose main character, evoking fabled Br'er Rabbit caught in the clutches of Br'er Fox, conjures up swift ways to act for the sake of life and limb.

"Birth of Cool," a chapter below, leading to the heart of this book, explores the social conditions that prompted African Americans to develop a habit of concealing their true motives, feelings, and beliefs in public arenas. In truth, slavery in a land sold on liberty was a harsh system, which spurred the enslaved to become "smooth operators," seeking to promote their general welfare through subtle schemes. As Ellison implied in his collection of essays *Shadow and Act* (1964), Black bondage furnished fertile grounds for maestros of improvisation to flourish. "Birth of Cool" proves that the slave system fostered white mindsets orientated to think that Black people come to life short on sense. The misperception induced enslaved African Americans to adopt wily behavior that became an engrained part of their culture; accordingly, African American literature has given prominence to characters that practice dissembling for personal gain.

Next in line, "Standards and Practices" recalls the fates of three individuals enslaved by President George Washington. The trio served in the Philadelphia house that he occupied after the American Revolution. They were named Billy Lee, Hercules, and Oney Judge. Their histories establish that manners taken by slaveholders as evidence of loyalty on the part of the enslaved masked a readiness to implement subversive designs. In essence, the lives of the three slaves manifest "smooth operating." They attest, as Equiano intimated, that the American slave system constituted "a new refinement in cruelty" (58) compelling the enslaved to stay all eyes with an ear to the ground and the teeth to wing it.

Then "Two of Kind" illustrates that an odd white man, disaffected by conventional wisdom, awoke to the realization in the antebellum age that considering enslaved Blacks witless was a fallacious assumption. The chapter reveals that Herman Melville's work *Benito Cereno* (1855) holds a Black protagonist whose temperament matches that of the main character in *The Heroic Slave* (1852) by Douglass. It attests that Melville in harmony with Douglass understood that Black bondage drove the enslaved to mask sneers with smiles and grimaces with grins as they sought to turn the tables on their masters. The connection drawn between the stories, which are both novellas, shows that seeing color as a sign of character placed the fortunes of white slaveholders on top of Black slaves in jeopardy. Together, the tales issue a common caution. They demonstrate that despots who see their subjects as fools become easy prey for underdogs with the mentality of a wolf in sheep's clothing.

Subsequently, "Old Black Magic" refers to Black folktales transported from Africa through the Middle Passage to America, where enslaved blacks adapted them for use in defense of their dignity. Communicated by word of mouth, the stories star little animals who get the better of bigger beasts by virtue of clever schemes. Blacks in bondage developed a brand of the lore, as ancient Africans did, to amuse and also advise. An old Black slave enchanted Joel Chandler Harris with the fables and inspired the white writer to invent Uncle Remus who entertains an adoring white boy with animal tales. *Uncle Remus: His Songs and His Saying* (1880) won Harris great fame and fortune, but his rendition of the tales that he borrowed from the slave who told them to him failed to capture their sly sides. Instead, the white writer's social position conditioned Harris to portray his Black invention Uncle Remus as a figure indisposed to present a false front for his benefit. Alternatively, identification with former Black slaves, relates "Old Black Magic," disposed Chesnutt to paint a vivid picture of a smooth operator, masked by smiles, in his portrait of Uncle Julius, the hero of *The Conjure Woman*.

"Game of Charades" testifies that Mark Twain, akin to Melville, picked up the fact that enslaved Blacks used improvisation to raise their fortunes. Twain's novel *The Adventures of Huckleberry Finn* (1884) presents the region of the Mississippi Delta as the site of a maddening society that works like a masquerade where most participants maintain a blind allegiance to a script that decides their lot by their shade and sex. Top billing goes to white men; white women are ranked second, a rung above Black men, two levels higher than Black women. *The Adventures of Huckleberry Finn* instructs that, in reality, training is everything; it colors Pap, Colonel Grangerford, and the Duke and Dauphin as mistitled figures turned cocky and cruel by the parts ascribed to them, and it foretells the character Tom Sawyer is trained to develop, which sets the boy apart from Huck Finn. "Game of Charades" makes it apparent that "nigger" Jim is a heroic Black figure who imparts a creed, shared by his enslaved fellows, endorsing putting on shows to escape oppression. After the trouble in the fog that occurs in the middle of Twain's novel, the faith of the slave on the run secures the full trust of Huck; it leads the boy to keep a cool head and tolerate Tom when he believes he needs the other kid's help to set Jim free. In effect, Jim turns Huck into a smooth operator through excellent examples, the novel hints, which model a mode of behavior not foreign to female communities.

"Lost in Translation" explains that the discrete social perspective peculiar to African American literature, which extols smooth operating, cool conduct subversive of a cruel social order, goes missing from the film adaptation of the novel *The Autobiography of Miss Jane Pittman*. This chapter attributes the neglect to the position in society of the film director that left him blind to the capacity of Black women for what Collins calls in her book *Black Feminist Thought* "intellectual activism in the face of . . . suppression" (3). On the other hand, the novel by Gaines, reflecting the sway of his grandmother, draws on the mythic symbolism of an oak tree to characterize the protagonist as a person who has grown in strength and gained the wisdom to overcome hardships imposed by racism on top of sexism. By implication, her development pins Black hopes on a commitment to sharpening their wits. The film version just credits Miss Pittman with a capacity for endurance like a tree in want of understanding, a simple organism endowed with a gift for staying power. Therefore, the motion picture in contrast to the novel fails to uncover a knack for exercising ingenuity that slavery drew out of Black women.

In "Learning the Ropes," it becomes clear that *Kindred* characterizes people as products of places in time. The novel, in agreement with *Up from Slavery* (1901), equates Black bondage with a school that inculcated an imperious attitude in the minds of whites to the detriment of Blacks. Through the trials of Dana Franklin drawn back in time from the Bicentennial to the antebellum age, *Kindred* relates the hardships that the slave system posed for Black women. Pulled back in time by mysterious means from the era of the Black Power movement to the period of Black bondage before the Civil War, Dana discovers a need to wise up quick and act soft in the head to reduce the power of the system over her well-being. Butler's *Kindred* underscores Collin's assertion that "Oppression describes any unjust situation where, systematically and over a long period of time, one group denies another group access to the resources of society" (*Black Feminist Thought* 4). A form of science fiction, *Kindred* bears out that Black bondage entailed a type of domination that drove enslaved women to engage in intense intellectual activity.

The eighth chapter in this book, "Blind Man's Bluff," takes a look at *Dessa Rose*. It recounts how haughty white men in the novel have their expectations shattered as they take it for granted they know what is best for women. The Black title character joins forces with an anxious white female named Ruth, who has been regarded as a simple plaything for white men with a sense of entitlement to have their way with members of the "opposite sex" despite their shade. From Mammy, their Black female elder, Dessa and Ruth pick up a trade that permits them to trick the imperious men. Together, the women exploit male impressions of them to dupe men into doing their bidding. "Blind Man's Bluff" asserts that *Dessa Rose* confirms the finding of Judith Butler in "Performative Acts and Gender Constitution" (1988) that "gender is in no way a stable identity or locus of agency from which various acts proceed; rather, it is an identity tenuously constituted in time—an identity instituted through a *stylized repetition of acts*" (519). With varied forms of intellectual activism, the novel suggests, generations of women have undermined domination by men dismissive of their depth and determination.

The final chapter, "Dress for Success," establishes that *The Good Lord Bird* renders the notion of "gender" as well as "race" an absurd idea. Historical fiction, exemplary of a neo-slave narrative, the novel by McBride treats race in the way that Butler thought of "gender," which is as "a constructed identity, a performative accomplishment," an act constituting "a compelling illusion" (Butler 520). Like *The Adventures of Huckleberry Finn*, McBride's work of fiction depicts the world of Black bondage as a bizarre masquerade where roles depend on shades and sex and the majority of players take their parts to heart. The circumstances call for Blacks to stay "two steps ahead of white folks," whom they strive to keep "subject to trickeration" (McBride 60), a form of double-dealing, which came "natural to all Negroes during slave time," seeing that "no man or woman in bondage ever prospered stating their true thoughts to the boss" (53). Henry Shackleford, the hero, who assumes the identity of a Black girl, according to the prevailing definition of such a person, swears that "much of colored life was an act" (53). As Shackleford carries out a charade acting the part of a Black girl, the boy leaves entitled white figures in the dark, but enslaved Black characters recognize the pretense and thus betray a familiarity with a form of performance, involving guile that the past system of slavery bound African Americans to bring into play.

In the main, the chapters that follow uncover a culture brought to life through the birth of Black bondage. Taking into consideration real and imaginary Black figures who find it smart to play dumb, this book affirms that an archetypal African American literary hero amounts to an artful dodger who acts in opposition to an assigned social identity that demands acquiescence to oppression. The coming segments affirm that sly conduct akin to the behavior of my grandfather back in the shoe store constitutes a kind of social act produced for white audiences and staged for the benefit of Black actors. Taken as a whole, this book is a testament to the fact that my ancestor was a good example of an African American who became a smooth operator in public affairs. Leander lived along the lines of an idol set in black letters.

Birth of Cool

Like music, a wise cat surmised,
Life is sweet when improvised.

The birth of Black bondage, which occurred in 1661, when the Virginia assembly authorized the practice, advanced a novel form of social classification. Older societies were partitioned along lines of clan, creed, or culture. Slaves were captured foes or convicted felons. But Black bondage changed the scheme as it divided the land into bands of color. The social order directed African Americans to play subservient roles with a submissive air. Simultaneously, it inflicted white people with a sort of blindness that induced them to eye Blacks with compassion or contempt. Black bondage became a cruel regime that called for a cool response from captives.

Like a pyramid, past societies have had a narrow top and wide bottom divided by a stack of middle grades. Ancient social orders based their ranks on strict rules that linked lots to luck. The cultures pressed people to live at the level of their ancestors. In antiquity, ordained guardians of communal standards foresaw doom for individuals who dared to rise above the rung of their forerunners. By design, the bottom part shored up the upper echelon. The configuration rendered conditions ripe for the cultivation of underdog designs around the rings of the underpinning masses.

The United States was supposed to be different. At birth, it professed to offer "all men" a fair chance to climb to the top or collapse at the bottom of society depending on their own determination. Its founding document, the *Declaration of Independence* (1776), denied that any person was born to stand on the back of anyone else. The original vision of the nation appeared without room for fixed fortunes. In the beginning, the desire of underdogs for a fair chance to improve their lot animated the land. Calling for a fluid society where waves of individuals, unchecked by cultural bars, rise or fall in accord with their resolve, the national development nailed a dream of the downtrodden since the start of the first hard and fast human hierarchy. The nation was not supposed to erect any social structures that denied the children of people who had little status in society a fair chance to rise from the ranks of their parents.

The country had to turn a blind eye to a glaring contradiction to maintain its image of itself as a society without an order that condemned a person to spend a lifetime under the weight of another. Wishes for cheap labor, though, saddled the land with Black bondage long before Thomas Jefferson put pen to paper. The nation was born with an embedded paradox: slavery in a land sold on liberty. Whites trained to have Blacks under their thumb grew to believe it was their natural right; the former came to resent having their rank called into question. The practice of Black bondage produced a state of schizophrenia, which brought on the bloody Civil War over whether "all men," regardless of their shade, deserve an equal opportunity to rise or fall in society. Undoubtedly, the conflict stemmed from the preexisting condition of Black bondage at the birth of the nation, contradicting the Declaration of Independence, causing dissembling to have an appeal to the enslaved, and converting scores of slaves into smooth operators.

Since the establishment of the slave system, African Americans have faced a steady stream of bias and brutality capable of causing enough emotional distress and physical injury to drown them in a sea of sorrow. Celebrated cultural critics depict Blacks as dark bodies that have fallen into dire straits and struggle in desperate need of help to stay afloat. "Trauma" circulates as a buzzword in contemporary Black social studies. Researchers have postulated that generations of oppression have left Black people in a poor mental state with feelings of helplessness, hostility, and hopelessness. They imply that Sethe in Toni Morrison's *Beloved* (1987), a figure rendered dysfunctional by trauma, captures the souls of Black folk.

The drift of the current conversation about African Americans is centered on criticism of racism in effect as a scourge that impairs and dispirits Blacks. It overlooks their creative designs forged to promote their welfare. The prevailing narrative backed by scholars such as Saidiya Hartman, who authored *Scenes of Subjection*, paints Blacks in the bosom of the country as bodies lacking the ability or strength to adopt a mode of behavior that could enable effective resistance to degradation. It fails to witness a resolve to make a way out of no way, which Black churches began urging during the dark days of Black bondage. Some Black studies have missed how much resilience has marked Black culture. In reality, a dedication to weather threats to their dignity, triggered by terrible designs woven into the social system, has marked heroic Black figures in the eyes of their fellows.

Slavery started in need of a pardon because it broke the basic rule on which the nation stood. Black bondage violated the imperative that everyone receive equal treatment. There had to be an excuse for the practice to continue in the wake of the American Revolution fought to free the country from everlasting subjection to the British Crown. The faith of the Founding Fathers that "all men" are born the same made it a sin to place whites over Blacks. It was necessary to count the latter as a breed, species, "race" distinct from white bloodlines. Approval of the system warranted the conversion of African Americans into a lot inferior to whites by nature. "Blacks" needed to signify "not men" in white minds. Belief that color signified character had to take hold.

Scientific conceptions of race that emerged in the eighteenth century offered cover for Black bondage in a nation that railed against tyranny. Arguments for monogenesis, the theory that humans come from a single pair of ancestors, gave way to avowals for *polygenesis*, holding humanity consists of diverse sorts from different sources. Thinking of people as members of races characterized by their complexion spread like a virus through the country. Benjamin Franklin in his *Observations Concerning the Increase of Mankind* (1751) generally split the world into three separate shades: white Europeans, Black Africans, and tawny Asians. *Crania Americana* (1839), written by Samuel George Morton, a pioneering advocate of *polygenesis*, professed that humanity was composed of different groups with uneven degrees of intelligence, discernible by the size of their skulls, the biggest of which belonged to whites and the smallest to Blacks. In 1848, Charles Pickering published *Races of Man and Their Geographical Distribution*, postulating the existence of eleven types of humans. Later, concurring with Morton, Josiah Clark Nott collaborated with George Gliddon to co-edit a collection of articles, titled *Types of Mankind* (1854), arguing that there are different races with unequal crania and that Black skulls were close in size and sense to those of chimpanzees.

Michael Omi and Howard Winant in *Racial Formation in the United States* (1986) described racial categories as social constructs whose substance and significance are determined by socioeconomic and political influences. The authors wrote, "Race consciousness, and its articulation in theories of race, is largely a modern phenomenon" (13). They added, "The social sciences have come to reject biologistic notions of race in favor of an approach which regards race as a *social* concept" (14). Omi and Winant observed, "In the United States, the racial category of 'black' evolved with the consolidation of racial slavery" (18). Their findings sustain the conclusion that Black bondage instigated the racial category of "white" and propagated the development of personalities prone to bedevil Blacks and push them to practice dissembling. Classic slave narratives divulge that the slave system trained white men to see themselves as messiahs or masters in relation to Black people.

John C. Calhoun represents a good example of a white man who developed a messiah complex. Scion of a slaveholder and senator from South Carolina, where the shipping industry lived off the import of Africans seized for sale into slavery, he professed ahead of the Civil War that the slave trade was a "positive good" for everyone involved in the business. His boyhood contacts with Black people, pinned under his weight, primed him to argue, during a session of Congress in 1837, whites and Blacks are tantamount to "two races of different origin, and distinguished by color, and other physical differences, as well as intellectual." Calhoun said, "The relation now existing in the slaveholding States between the two, is, instead of an evil," a godsend; he asserted, "There never has yet existed a wealthy and civilized society in which one portion of the community did not, in point of fact, live on the labor of the other." The senator held that the riches of every affluent civilization has been "unequally divided" with a meager "share" being "allotted to those by whose labor it was produced, and so large a share given to the non-producing classes." In the view of Calhoun, prosperous sites outside the Southern States perpetuated inequality by means of "brute force and gross superstition" or "subtle and artful fiscal contrivances." He swore that a "direct, simple, and patriarchal mode" marked the management of Black bondage; the senator insisted that a rare social system left as much "to the share of the laborer," and "exacted" as "little" in return from their workers as Southern slavery; a "kind superintending care" by whites permitted Black slaves to fare better than "the tenants of the poor houses in the more civilized portions of Europe" (Calhoun 224–25).

In substance, Calhoun drew from his background a picture of African Americans that painted them close to children in need of parental guidance. Of course, as a rule, parents and children are separated by "physical differences, as well as intellectual." The upbringing of the senator trained him to regard young and old Blacks as identical scraps of whole cloth covered with pitch and clear of prudence. His opinion implied that Black bondage was a commendable enterprise because it made good use of Black lives that otherwise would have suffered the trials of orphan youths on their own in the streets. The white slaveholders in the United States, the senator suggested, deserved pats on their backs for producing great wealth by enslaving childish Blacks in a fatherly manner.

Calhoun's heritage blinded him to the propensity of the slave system to engender cruelty by accustoming whites to look down on Blacks. Slavery made slaves favor livestock in the minds of slaveholders who took to heart a sense of themselves as men born to be masters of Blacks. Deep in the heart of Dixie, generations of white males descended from the owners of slaves fell heir to notions that they were born to whip Blacks into shape for their use. The mindset inclined the enslavers to subject the enslaved to lechery, lashing, and lynching on a whim. Babies were snatched from their mother's breasts and sold at auction to slave traders. Black slaves who chafed at the impositions of slaveholders had their bare backs flogged until streams of blood ran from their flesh. Blacks in bondage judged unruly were strung up on a tree over a bonfire to choke and burn to death.

In sum, the slave system fostered two sorts of white attitudes toward Blacks. Both of them believed whites and Blacks represented "two races of different origin, and distinguished by color, and other physical differences, as well as intellectual." Slaveholders like Calhoun possessed a genteel persuasion that prompted them to show slaves compassion. His counterparts had a rustic perspective that provoked disdain for Blacks. Calhoun's view blocked out the reality of contemptuous enslavers who abused Blacks without a second thought. With his fellow traffickers in the practice of involuntary servitude, the senator nevertheless forever shared the common trust of slaveholders that whites rank above Blacks in worth.

Narrative of the Life of Frederick Douglass (1845), chronicling his life and times trapped in the bowels of Black bondage, renders stark portraits of a few contemptuous racists. The slave narrative offers the author's original master, Captain Anthony, as the first example of a racist slaveholder with a lecherous streak who regards Blacks with disdain. Douglass recounts how Captain Anthony was enraged because Aunt Hester, an enslaved "woman of noble form, and of graceful proportions" with "very few equals, and fewer superiors, in personal appearance, among the colored or white women" in the region, saw another slave against the master's wishes. In reaction, the slaveholder "stripped her from neck to waist, leaving her neck, shoulders, and back, entirely naked." Captain Anthony bound Aunt Hester's hands "with a strong rope, and led her to a stool under a large hook in the joist" where he propped her on the chair. Tethering her hands on the peg, he extended her arms "so that she stood upon the ends of her toes." Then, the white man rolled "up his sleeves" and "commenced to lay on the heavy cowskin, and soon the warm, red blood (amid heart-rending shrieks from her, and horrid oaths from him) came dripping to the floor" (Douglass, *Narrative*, 41–42).

On another occasion in Douglass's slave narrative, the author remembers Mr. Austin Gore, whom he credits with "possessing, in an eminent degree, all those traits of character indispensable to what is called a first-rate overseer," that is, a superb manager of slaves. Mr. Gore was disposed to eye "the slightest look, word, or gesture, on the part of the slave" as an expression of "impudence." Bidding "the most debasing homage of the slave," the white man "committed the grossest and most savage deeds upon the slaves under his charge" with "consummate coolness." One day the overseer declared a slave named Demby "unmanageable" because the vassal fled a whipping and "plunged himself into a creek, and stood there at the depth of his shoulders, refusing to come out." In response, "without consultation or deliberation with any one," Mr. Gore "raised his musket," took "deadly aim at his standing victim," and discharged his weapon. In a second, the body of Demby "sank out of sight, and blood and brains marked the water where he had stood." Defending his misdeed, Mr. Gore "argued that if one slave refused to be corrected, and escaped with his life, the other slaves would soon copy the example; the result of which would be, the freedom of the slaves, and the enslavement of the whites" (51–52).

Mr. Edward Covey is a third fiend depicted in *Narrative of the Life of Frederick Douglass*. He was not a "pious" master "who [held] slaves for the very charitable purpose of taking care of them." The figure "was a professor of religion" as well as a "member" and "leader" of a Christian congregation. He gained renown and remuneration as a " 'nigger-breaker,' " a handler who took on obstinate slaves with an aim to transform them into obliging servants for their owners. Douglass in his teen years had differences with his second master, Captain Auld, which caused his owner to lease him to Mr. Covey for a year. The writer recounted how one week passed "before Mr. Covey gave [him] a very severe whipping," which slit [his] back, "causing the blood to run, and raising ridges on [his] flesh as large as [his] little finger." Douglass testified, "During the first six months, of that year, scarce a week passed without [Mr. Covey] whipping [him]," and so leaving him "seldom free from a sore back" (72).

The novel *Uncle Tom's Cabin* (1852) illustrates that past slaveholders came in two styles. Author Harriet Beecher Stowe drew figures in the work from a fair knowledge of slavery in Kentucky across the border from her Ohio family home in Cincinnati. She also gathered ideas from the life story of Douglass along with the *Life of Josiah Henson* (1849), detailing a crippling beating that Henson suffered at the hands of a cruel master before the slave took flight to Canada. In *Uncle Tom's Cabin*, Stowe featured Augustine St. Clare, who favors the type of paternal slaveholder whom Calhoun had in mind when the senator called Black bondage a "positive good." *Uncle Tom's Cabin* presents Simon Legree in contrast to St. Clare, who cares for the novel's enslaved such as Uncle Tom and Topsy in a fatherly manner. Akin to Mr. Covey, Legree projects limitless piety while the slaveholder molests and mauls slaves at his mercy.

Subjection to Black bondage exposed to Harriet Jacobs the two types of slave owners that Stowe described in her novel. *Incidents in the Life of a Slave Girl* (1860), recording the fortunes of Jacobs in slavery, shows that the system posed an awful dilemma for her at a tender age. She faced a choice between serving as a courtesan for a gentleman given to sympathy or living as a concubine for a degenerate gripped by heartlessness. Each of the options in effect required Jacobs to trade sex for the prospect of security. The merciless man identified as Dr. Flint was her designated master. A surrender to his wishes promised to leave Jacobs without a shred of dignity since he had a habit of degrading Black women under his control. The kind man named Mr. Sands was a neighboring slaveholder with the air of a messiah. He seduced the slave girl with flattery before he left her with two children and moved with a blushing white bride to the nation's capital after he was elected to represent his state as a senator in Congress.

While in general Jacobs and Stowe agreed that the kinds of slaveholders amounted to two sorts, the women disagreed about the respectability of the paternalistic type. *Incidents in the Life of a Slave Girl* illustrates a want of appreciation by slaveholders for the true humanity of African Americans, regardless of whether or not the enslavers appeared compassionate or acted cruel in their relationships with Blacks. Jacobs offered assurance that the slave system spread an imperious mentality among whites that disposed them to imagine Blacks as a distinct species with the intellect of children or cattle. Thus, as a rule, slaveholders caused her to feel like a kid in a charity school for juveniles with brain damage or a cow stuck in a swamp full of snakes. Jacobs disapproved of fatherly slaveholders comparable to Mr. Sands right along with perverse owners of slaves similar to Dr. Flint.

Although Jacobs agreed with Stowe about the two types of slaveholders, she disagreed with the white woman about the nature of Black people. The difference of opinion stemmed from the fact that Stowe as much as Calhoun credited African Americans with owning little if any more sense than a child. *Uncle Tom's Cabin* implies that Tom as well as Topsy are better off in the custody of a benevolent white master such as St. Clare. The omniscient narrator of the novel expresses certainty that Blacks and whites are dissimilar in essence. For instance, she says, "Uncle Tom" possesses "truly African features," which incline him to open his heart to others with a "humble simplicity" (Stowe 18). She attributes to the slave an "impassioned and imaginative" (25) temper that she feels is typical of Blacks. The narrator also intimates that St. Clare is praiseworthy for inducing his cousin Miss Ophelia to serve as a guardian for Topsy committed to teaching the Black girl to behave as an obliging ward.

Under the weight of the slave system, sustained by false impressions of Blacks, African Americans were pressed to crouch, cringe, and cower in the presence of whites. Douglass captured the most wretched possible impact of Black bondage on the enslaved in his account of his stay with Covey. He wrote, "I was somewhat unmanageable when I first went there." In "a few months," though, the heartless fiend "succeeded in breaking me." The writer reflected on being "broken in body, soul, and spirit." Douglass confessed, "The cheerful spark that lingered about my eye died," as "the dark night of slavery closed in upon me." He exclaimed, "Behold a man transformed into a brute" (74).

Nonetheless, Douglass was human, all too human. Therefore, he was no more prone in his life to take the demeaning subjugation of Black bondage lying down than Jefferson was prepared in his time to stomach the tyranny of the British Crown. The African American adopted a course of action based on a mode of reasoning aroused by his humanity. A passion to preserve his dignity moved him. He developed an aptitude for underdog scheming, a frame of mind accountable for a form of subterfuge, employed by a person who has little social status in an effort to ease, if not escape, the dehumanizing burden of living under the weight of other people. The slave system pushed Douglass to assume the guise of a "smooth operator," a deft dissembler, given to the deployment of deception for the sake of a real improvement in his lot. Masking his feelings and intentions came to free him from a lifetime of indignity imposed on him by whites who looked down on him.

Douglass took an approach that was common among Blacks in bondage. *Incidents in the Life of a Slave Girl* brings to light the fact that Jacobs choose the given course of action. She resorted to smooth operating in order to mitigate the degrading effects of Black bondage. Hundreds of published narratives recounting the fortunes of African Americans enslaved in the land reveal that deft dissembling became part and parcel of the culture that the slave system sowed among Blacks stuck in the bowels of the social structure. The noted literature demonstrates time and again that it became routine for Blacks to put on a show that seemed to meet white expectations while it gave them the slip as far as possible within the confines of the social order.

The institution of slavery, in sum, governed by whites convinced that Blacks were born to occupy the lowest rank on the social hierarchy fostered a determination among African Americans to live by their wits. It raised a spirit that prompted Blacks to take after fabled Br'er Rabbit caught in the clutches Br'er Fox. Black bondage, declared a "new refinement in cruelty" (Equiano 58) by Olaudah Equiano, the eighteen-century African native sold into the business, no doubt provoked the enslaved to use their heads. Under the circumstances, the slaves hatched a heroic ideal that commends being able to read a room and size up a situation. The subjects of the system set their sights on finding a way to make a way out of no way. Blacks in bondage schemed to triumph over a tragic situation. Smooth operating became their model modus operandi.

It is ironic that the justification for Black bondage rested on belief that Blacks lacked the sense of whites. Slaves had to put considerable smarts to swift use to preserve their dignity. Living their best life depended on staying all eyes with an ear to the ground and the teeth to wing it. They had the human intelligence to see how whites saw them as if they were simple children or stupid cattle. Every Black person who survived bondage in the land with pride learned well that underdogs who live to tell tales grow quickly. Mastering their masters was their key to relief from dishonor and degradation. At the end of the day, in order to maintain their self-esteem, the enslaved had to sharpen their wits beyond those of their masters who rated them dumb.

Some studies of Black bondage dispute this assessment. The research at issue sustains the opinions of former slaveholders who supposed that African Americans amounted to a species separate in color as well as character from whites. For the most part, these accounts of the slave system came from scholars who were apologists for the institution. They contended that Blacks were docile and submissive in nature. Historian Ulrich Bonnell Phillips was a celebrated advocate of the bias. He produced the first acclaimed analysis of Black bondage in the twentieth century. In *American Negro Slavery* (1918), Phillips wrote that Blacks harbored a "racial quality" that rendered them "submissive rather than defiant, light-hearted instead of gloomy, amiable and ingratiating instead of sullen," and their makeup "invited paternalism rather than repression" (Phillips 770). On the whole, *American Negro Slavery* upheld the notion that Blacks had little more sense than children, and so Black bondage was a benign institution that promoted the welfare of the enslaved.

Phillips's work stood as the authoritative study of Blacks in bondage until the middle of the twentieth century when Stanley Elkins wrote *Slavery: A Problem in American Institutional and Intellectual Life* (1959). Overall, Elkins rejected the idea that Blacks were inherently as unsophisticated as children. He granted observers cause to find African Americans inclined to behave in an infantile manner. Elkins argued that slavery produced a "Sambo" mentality, an infantile psychology among Blacks that made them depend on whites for guidance. He hypothesized that "the typical plantation slave" was "docile, irresponsible, loyal but lazy, humble but chronically given to lying and stealing." Insisting that the average slave was "full of infantile silliness" and his "relationship with his master was one of utter dependence and childlike attachment," Elkins attributed the alleged "Sambo" personality to stupefying repression incorporated in the management of the slave system that inhibited the mental maturation of the enslaved (Elkins 131).

The Peculiar Institution (1956), written by Kenneth Stampp, arrived three years before Elkins's *Slavery*. Stampp put forward a thorough refutation of *American Negro Slavery*. He repudiated the racist belief that Blacks were endowed with little more intelligence than children. Moreover, he asserted that Black bondage was an iniquitous institution devoid of redeeming value. He provided evidence that enslaved Blacks fought against their enslavement through various forms of subterfuge including dragging their feet on the job and stealing their masters blind. Stampp faulted previous studies of Blacks in bondage for taking to heart the slaveholders' perspective and failing to take into account the slaves' point of view.

John Blassingame made an explicit point of relating the slaves' side of the story. He studied a fair number of books written by former slaves. The list included the *Narrative of the Life of Frederick Douglass* and *The Interesting Narrative of the Life of Olaudah Equiano* (1789) along with the *Narrative of William W. Brown, a Fugitive Slave* (1847), plus *Twelve Years a Slave* (1853) by Solomon Northup and *Behind the Scenes: Or, Thirty Years a Slave and Four Years in the White House* (1868) by Elizabeth Keckley. In *The Slave Community* (1972), Blassingame presented his findings after he remarked that "historians have never systematically explored the life experiences of American slaves" (xi). He stated, "Rather than identifying with and submitting totally to his master, the slave held onto many remnants of his African culture, gained a sense of worth in the quarters, spent most of his time free from surveillance by whites, controlled important aspects of his life, and did some personally meaningful things on his own volition" (xii). Aiming to discredit Elkins, Blassingame wrote, "The Sambo stereotype was so pervasive in antebellum Southern literature that many historians, without further research, argue that it was an accurate description of the dominant slave personality" (226). As a matter of fact, the disputant submitted, "There is overwhelming evidence, in the primary sources [i.e., slave narratives], of the Negro's resistance to his bondage and of his undying love for freedom" (192). By any means necessary, Blassingame indicates, enslaved Blacks sought to preserve their dignity.

The subjects of slave narratives prove "Sambo" was little more than a figment of the white imagination divorced from reality. The central figures of the stories engage in masquerades that afford relief from abuse. Deliberate plots against the wishes of their masters empowered real-life slaves such as Brown, Keckley, and Northup to escape bondage. It's the same story in the case of Douglass and Equiano. *Running a Thousand Miles for Freedom* (1860) by Ellen and William Craft provides a perfect example. The narrative records the couple's flight to freedom by way of a ruse in which Ellen Craft exploited her fair complexion to pretend to be a young white man traveling to Philadelphia for medical treatment with a devoted slave who in truth was her dark-skinned spouse. The married Crafts were animated by underdog thinking stirred by a wish to rise in society.

Prissy the simple maid played by Butterfly McQueen in *Gone with the Wind* (1939) evokes Topsy in *Uncle Tom's Cabin* and also shows that white people were hanging onto the Sambo myth four-score years after President Abraham Lincoln issued the Emancipation Proclamation in 1863. The role assumed by McQueen in the motion picture obscures the actuality that the slave system induced the development of a discreet disposition displayed by the Crafts. Supposedly McQueen's performance as Prissy in *Gone with the Wind* bothered her conscience. If Paul Laurence Dunbar had lived to witness McQueen play the simple maid, he would have seen that the scripting of her role left out the spirit that saved Blacks in bondage from being consumed by dejection and despair. Dunbar was born a free native of Ohio in 1872. Before he died in 1906, he achieved renown as a poet, praised by William Dean Howells in *Harper's Weekly*. Dunbar grasped the spirit of Blacks stirred by the slave system. By means of the poem "We Wear the Mask" (1896), he gave readers an inkling of the heroic Black psyche induced by slavery that occasioned a certain coolness in the face of demeaning compassion and deadly contempt. Dunbar wrote:

WE wear the mask that grins and lies,
It hides our cheeks and shades our eyes—
This debt we pay to human guile;
With torn and bleeding hearts we smile
And mouth with myriad subtleties.
(*Lyrics of Lowly Life* 197)

African American literature contains ample proof that Black bondage ingrained smooth operating in Black culture. Since the publication of *The Heroic Slave* (1852), Douglass's novella, Black fiction has featured heroes who mask their feelings and aims from the white world. The approach is taken by the main character in Brown's novel *Clotel* (1853). Fiction about Black fortunes outside slavery, beginning with Harriet Wilson's *Our Nig* (1859), indicate that Black bondage established conditions that turned dissembling into an African American trait. *Iola Leroy* (1892) by Frances Harper as well as *The Conjure Woman* (1899) by Charles Chesnutt make certain that in the wake of slavery, Blacks engaged in deception for the sake of their welfare. Following the outlawing of Black bondage, honored members of the Black community went on hiding sneers behind smiles and grimaces beneath grins, as Nat Turner did as a slave before he led the slave rebellion that shocked the slaveholders of Virginia in 1831.

Neo-slave narratives in particular verify that smooth operating represents a mode of behavior adopted by Blacks to avoid mortification and molestation. The genre consists of fiction involving themes and settings typical of the slave narratives written in the eighteenth and nineteenth centuries by enslaved Blacks. Such fiction, full of underdog designs, flourished late in the twentieth century. Margaret Walker's *Jubilee* (1966) is given credit for initiating the development. Her book, appearing at the inception of the Black Arts movement, preceded works such as Ernst Gaines's *The Autobiography of Miss Jane Pittman* (1971), Ishmael Reed's *Flight to Canada* (1976), Octavia Butler's *Kindred* (1979), David Bradley's *The Chaneysville Incident* (1981), and Sherley Anne Williams's *Dessa Rose* (1986). Although the phenomenon is thought to have peaked with the publication of Toni Morrison's *Beloved* (1987), noteworthy neo-slave narratives have appeared in the twenty-first century, such as Edward Jones's *The Known World* (2003), James McBride's *The Good Lord Bird* (2013), Colson Whitehead's *The Underground Railroad* (2016), and *Yellow Wife* (2021) by Sadeqa Johnson. All of the novels support the conclusion that the pursuit of happiness for African Americans since the birth of Black bondage has depended on the achievement of a cool style, featuring skill at reading a room and sizing up a situation with underdog reasoning intent on turning tragedy into triumph.

No doubt, African American literature includes Black figures beaten and broken by white men with superiority complexes. Sethe, who loses her mind in *Beloved*, represents the sort of figure who is shattered by the horror to which slavery exposes her. Still, she stands in contrast to heroes in neo-slave narratives and related works. Sethe cannot hold a candle to resilient Janie in *Their Eyes Were Watching God* (1937) by Zora Neale Hurston, resourceful Ida in *Another Country* (1962) by James Baldwin, or resolute Dana in *Kindred* by Octavia Butler. Idols of Black letters use their imagination to make the best of a bad situation. As Booker T. Washington recalls doing in *Up from Slavery*, they exercise ingenuity to overcome "miserable, desolate, and discouraging surroundings" (Washington 1).

Close readings of selected neo-slave narratives follow below. Beforehand, examinations of classic slave narratives occur. The ventures uphold that slavery furnished fertile grounds for maestros of improvisation to emerge and exploit beliefs holding Blacks inferior to whites. Below, proof surfaces that a cool style came to life on the heels of Black bondage. The upcoming pages convey that thinking of race as a biological condition gave rise to impressions that prompted Blacks to seem reconciled to being an underdog while engaging in acts of resistance to the social position.

Standards and Practices

Still stars shine in the dark of night.
An hour never strikes without light.

The United States originated as a daring enterprise. It began in 1607 when a band of Englishmen landed on the banks of the James River in Virginia. The venture got off to a rough start. Hardship and hunger beset the colony until the native Algonquian people taught the settlers how to plant and harvest tobacco. The knowledge allowed the immigrants to cultivate a cash crop and export it to Europe, where it fed a substantial demand and returned profits that permitted the settlement, christened Jamestown, to become a thriving agrarian business with a steady need for help to handle the harvest. In an effort to recruit hands from abroad, Captain John Smith, a leader of the settlers, pitched the community as a rare undertaking that afforded commoners a fair chance to escape from living under the weight of others by the sweat of their brow.

On the last day of January in 1620, settlers in Virginia petitioned the English Crown to ship orphans to Jamestown so the colony could augment its labor force. The request was made to King James I, a year after the settlers set free close to two dozen Dutch prisoners of war from Angola and put the Africans to work as indentured servants. It showed that the need for labor far exceeded the supply. From the launch of the Jamestown, most of the immigrants who came ashore arrived as hired hands on contracts with fixed terms. The settlement billed itself as an enterprise dedicated to equal opportunity for every person, irrespective of their hue or history. Voluntary service was regarded as the pathway to independence, as it offered a payoff worth in the vicinity of forty acres and a mule, which allowed the indentured to start their own businesses. For three generations, the deal remained in effect until cupidity pardoned by chauvinism raised grounds for a color bar; after that, Blacks faced the need to act like a rabbit caught in the clutches of a fox. In essence, they had to become canny characters.

By means of indentured servitude, diverse shades and stripes reaped dividends that enabled them to become independent businesspeople and set aside a nest egg for their posterity. Yet, since the contracts of the hired hands lasted only four to seven years, the colony faced frequent labor shortages, so new workers, no matter their color or circumstances, remained in demand. Sundry individuals benefited from indentured servitude until 1660, when the attendant fluctuations in the workforce gave rise to cries for a new deal. In the span of a year, the Virginia legislature enacted a law that introduced into the cradle of American society the oldest source of labor in the annals of human history. Copying Egypt, Greece, and Rome, the English colonists resorted to involuntary servitude, that is, slavery, with a historic twist that based the practice on color. American slavery became a distinct brand, best labeled "Black bondage."

Because slavery in theory was out of bounds for "mankind" in a society sold on liberty for "everyman," enslavement could not pass muster in the region unless the populace counted the enslaved out of "mankind." A human proclivity for partiality, conceded in *Observations Concerning the Increase of Mankind* (1751) by Benjamin Franklin, disposed whites to favor their own complexion and subdued opposition to Black bondage. Roused by the profit motive, chauvinism persuaded "whites" to picture "Blacks" as spooky sorts, driven by instincts that rendered them unfit for freedom. Color prejudice stretched through the fabric of the social order. It manufactured a landscape embedded with whites filled with pride or pity in relation to Blacks.

Encapsulating the color prejudice that took hold during the gestation period of the nation, in his *Observations Concerning the Increase of Mankind*, Franklin remarked:

> That the Number of purely white People in the World is proportionably very small. All Africa is black or tawny. Asia chiefly tawny. America (exclusive of the new Comers) wholly so. And in Europe, the Spaniards, Italians, French, Russians and Swedes, are generally of what we call a swarthy Complexion; as are the Germans also, the Saxons only excepted, who with the English, make the principal Body of White People on the Face of the Earth. I could wish their Numbers were increased. And while we are, as I may call it, Scouring our Planet, by clearing America of

Woods, and so making this Side of our Globe reflect a brighter Light to the Eyes of Inhabitants in Mars or Venus, why should we in the Sight of Superior Beings, darken its People? why increase the Sons of Africa, by Planting them in America, where we have so fair an Opportunity, by excluding all Blacks and Tawneys, of increasing the lovely White and Red? But perhaps I am partial to the Complexion of my Country, for such Kind of Partiality is natural to Mankind. (Franklin 475)

Franklin's native tongue made it easy to take dark skin as evidence of inferiority to white people. To him, along with his fellow English speakers, the word "black" suggested darkness, disease, and death. Franklin and his companions were disposed to describe an African as a "Negro," a term derived from a Spanish word with a Latin root, meaning "dark." Through a terrible bastardization that occurred in the colonies, the word "Negro" morphed into "nigger." Meanwhile, Franklin's tongue cast "white" as a signifier for beauty, brilliance, and blessedness. It welcomed settlers with light skin to see themselves as "whites" with a natural right to liberty and deference from Blacks. Thus, Franklin came of age seeing no point in returning to indentured servitude for Blacks.

Earlier societies enslaved convicted felons and conquered foes. The trade was part of the ancient African empires of Ghana, Mali, and Songhay, which lit the Dark Ages with ingenious breakthroughs and yielded the bulk of the Africans trafficked in the international Atlantic Slave Trade. Basing slavery on complexion counted as a significant innovation in the chronicles of compulsory labor. It converted skin color into a social status symbol that would become fixed in the dominant imagination. The slave system rested on feelings that reduced the worth of "Blacks" to three-fifths of "whites." Through the latter part of the seventeenth century, Black bondage spread from Maryland to Maine. The system accustomed whites to assume an imperious attitude toward Blacks. It became customary to base the worth of Blacks on their usefulness to whites.

The "Kind of Partiality" Franklin realized "is natural to Mankind" promoted and pardoned disregard for African Americans. Through his question "why increase the Sons of Africa, by Planting them in America," because the exclusion of "all Blacks" allows "increasing the lovely White," he manifested contempt for Blacks. Born in a poor Boston household forty-five years after the establishment of Black bondage, he came of age used to seeing enslaved Blacks serving at the beck and call of whites rich enough to have slaves work in their homes as domestic servants. The abject servility required of the enslaved likely convinced Franklin that Blacks belonged under whites for want of the brains to benefit from liberty. In his midlife, he would admit trusting that whites were brighter than Blacks.

When Franklin entered publishing in Philadelphia, Black bodies were bought and sold on a street corner two blocks from the address of his print shop. He profited from fees paid to him to run advertisements for slave auctions in the *Pennsylvania Gazette*. As soon as he could afford servants, he purchased slaves. He kept some Blacks in bondage for forty years. A couple, Peter and Jemima, served his family along with a boy named Othello. The printer traveled overseas with black valets named King and George. His treatment of Blacks during the first half of his life indicates that he felt Black lives mattered less than his own.

Franklin changed his mind following a visit to a Philadelphia school opened to educate "Negro" grade schoolers. It was close to a hundred years after the birth of Black bondage. The intelligence of the children struck him as unsurpassed by their white peers. Then, feeling ashamed, he confessed to having believed that Blacks were short on sense. Afterward, to his dying day, he sought to end the subjection of Black bodies to white wills. Franklin allowed King to go free in London before he released the rest of his household slaves. He assumed leadership of the Pennsylvania Abolition Society. In 1790, he petitioned the United States Congress to ban slavery and afford African Americans adequate education and employment. Unfortunately, he proved to be the exception rather than the rule among three of the nation's most prominent Founding Fathers.

Though Franklin reformed his opinion of African Americans, George Washington and Thomas Jefferson clung to the white imagination of Blacks that pardoned slavery. The latter two Founding Fathers were proud sons of Virginia trained to believe whites were born brighter than Blacks. Washington and Jefferson felt burdened with the care of people descended from African roots. While, in the wake of the American Revolution, Franklin protested against Black bondage and pitched the practice as a social and moral blight on the land, the initial two presidents of the United States remained convinced that African Americans were an inferior lot. Both heads of state moved Black slaves from their Virginia estates into the District of Columbia mansion due to became known as the White House.

A slaveholding father sired by a slaveholder raised Jefferson to perceive the enslavement of Blacks as a social practice in the best interests of all parties. Jefferson expressed assurance in *Notes on the State of Virginia* that

Blacks were near baboons in nature. Unlike whites, he felt, they possessed imagination without ingenuity. In his opinion, the Creator packed Blacks with emotion in lieu of reason. Like his father, Jefferson enjoyed the company of a Black woman for the better part of his life. Regardless of such intimacy, in a missive to Benjamin Banneker, the African American polymath, who designed the layout of Washington, DC, Jefferson insisted there was a lack of proof that Blacks were equal to whites. Holding Blacks a good bit less than him in intelligence, the third president passed on July 4, 1826, the fiftieth anniversary of the *Declaration of Independence*.

In *Notes on the State of Virginia* (1785), Jefferson offered the following assessment of Blacks in relation to whites:

> They seem to require less sleep. A black after hard labour through the day, will be induced by the slightest [amusements] to sit up till midnight, or later, though knowing he must be out with the first dawn of the morning. They are at least as brave, and more adventuresome. But this may perhaps proceed from a want of fore-thought, which prevents their seeing a danger till it be present. When present, they do not go through it with more coolness or steadiness than the whites. They are more ardent after their female: but love seems with them to be more an eager desire, than a tender delicate mixture of sentiment and sensation. Their griefs are transient. Those numberless afflictions, which render it doubtful whether heaven has given life to us in mercy or in wrath, are less felt, and sooner forgotten with them. In general, their existence appears to participate more of sensation than reflection . . . Comparing them by their faculties of memory, reason, and imagination, it appears to me, that in memory they are equal to the whites; in reason much inferior, as I think one could scarcely be found capable of tracing and comprehending the investigations of Euclid; and that in imagination they are dull, tasteless, and anomalous . . . They astonish you with strokes of the most sublime oratory; such as prove their reason and sentiment strong, their imagination glowing and elevated. But never yet could I find that a black had uttered a thought above the level of plain narration; never see even an elementary trait of painting or sculpture. In music they are more generally gifted than the whites with accurate ears for tune and time . . . Whether they will be equal to the composition of a

more extensive run of melody, or of complicated harmony, is yet to be proved. Misery is often the parent of the most affecting touches in poetry.—Among the blacks is misery enough, God knows, but no poetry. Love is the peculiar œstrum of the poet. Their love is ardent, but it kindles the senses only, not the imagination. Religion indeed has produced a Phyllis Whately; but it could not produce a poet. The compositions published under her name are below the dignity of criticism. (Jefferson 148–51)

Jefferson never imagined the extent to which the fortunes of Monticello, his beloved Virginia plantation, depended on logic no less than labor applied by African Americans around the manor. Blacks kept the place in good working order. They sowed the fields and raised the crops that they reaped and lugged to the market for sale. Around the house, they cooked the meals, cleaned the quarters, and changed the sheets. Slaves served Jefferson as nannies as well as nurses, millers besides maids, and carpenters on top of cooks, in addition to blacksmiths and bookkeepers, plus butlers who became buddies. With music and mirth, the enslaved at Monticello lifted Jefferson's spirits when they drooped. The estate would have sunk into a shambles without the thoughtful labor of Blacks around the place.

The predicament of Trueblood in *Invisible Man* when the figure must move without moving signifies the sticky situation faced by the enslaved at Monticello who functioned with the weight of a janitor tending a generator that runs a factory. The slaves knew that Jefferson thought "all men" are born alike. They also recognized that he rated them exceptions to the rule. Naturally, they realized, he counted them as chattel and compared them to baboons. Likewise, they saw, the system that authorized their enslavement denied them civil rights under the law, leaving them no form of legal protection and laying them open to meanness and misery. The best any of them could do for their own good, they understood, was to gain the goodwill of their master with an obliging demeanor. For positive results, it was necessary for the slaves to be deliberate, but appear docile. In relation to the impact on their character, their environment amounted to an incubator of ingenuity. The situation was ripe for the cultivation of resourcefulness.

Monticello Blacks had to be proficient and perceptive to promote their private interests. Their master was a patrician who meant to maintain superb help. The plantation slaves had to be good, if not great, at their jobs. As their boss was inclined to regard them as if they were akin to monkeys, they had to improvise schemes to indulge Jefferson without indignity. It was wise for them to stay on their toes, two steps ahead of Jefferson. The third president of the United States gave Blacks too little credit for thinking to pick up signs of the common sense owned by the slaves who stayed in his good graces.

Washington, the nation's first president, kept more than three hundred Blacks in bondage at his Mount Vernon estate. The fates of his slaves, like those of Jefferson, depended on their use of skill and smarts. Washington employed the best help that he could get. The Founding Father had misgivings about the morality of the slavery; still, Washington never credited any Blacks with intellectual depth. After the American Revolution, he claimed to wish to get rid of Black bondage. Yet he declined to convert his slaves into hired hands because the move would have stripped him of their value as property and decreased his wealth. Hence, for Washington, extending the original benefit of indentured servitude to eighteenth-century African Americans was out of the question. He exploited the labor of enslaved Blacks until the day he died.

Sure of their own humanity, Washington's slaves tended to keep their wits about them. More than three hundred in number, they devised ways to act with dignity despite his unflattering opinion of their worth. They operated as a crack business staff. The slaves looked after Washington's orchards of fruit, along with his fields of wheat, corn, and hemp. Several of them manufactured cotton, wool, and silk wares, while others worked as clerks. Their labor put the balance sheet of Mount Vernon in the black.

Following the signing of the *United States Constitution* (1787), Washington moved into a Philadelphia residence. It sat a block away from Independence Hall. He lived there as the nation's first president. The stories of three slaves who accompanied him from Mount Vernon uncover the canny character that sprouted among African Americans. Washington assigned the management of his Philadelphia house to nine trusted slaves. A valet, chef, and seamstress warrant particular note.

The valet was known as Billy Lee. He earned ample respect by becoming a cherished companion and confidante, a loyal sidekick, to Washington. Lee was so dear to the president that he was welcome to pose for a portrait with him and his family. The valet is thought to have crossed the Delaware River beside Washington and stayed at his side through the last battle of the American Revolution. By contemporary standards for a Black man, Lee had a deal that was hard to beat. It afforded him considerable creature comforts denied the average slave. He won Washington's favor with a servile disposition, which likely was a rather shrewd act under the circumstances. Lee in all likelihood warrants recognition for smooth operating as if he were a loyal shepherd's dog. He never fell on the wrong side of Washington, unlike the noteworthy chef and seamstress who were slaves in the president's City of Brotherly Love home.

The president's chef, Hercules, known as Uncle Harkless around the Mount Vernon estate, was the toast of the town in Philadelphia. Diners at Washington's presidential residence gushed about the exquisite dishes that Hercules served. With pleasure, he pocketed a pretty penny by selling leftover portions of his meals to patrons around the city. Along with Billy Lee, the acclaimed chef enjoyed a charmed life by the standards of the day for a Black slave. Hercules showed Washington unquestioned loyalty until the day that the chef's son fell out of favor with the president because of an unconcealed expression of resistance to Black bondage. Thereafter, Hercules and his boy were dismissed from the Philadelphia house staff. They were sent back to Mount Vernon, where they were put to work in the fields. The relocation maddened the chef; it pushed the African American past the limits of his tolerance for indignity. Hercules took flight from Mount Vernon; afterward, Washington saw neither hide nor hair of him again.

The third notable enslaved person was a teenage girl who was the offspring of a white indentured tailor and enslaved Black dressmaker. Oney Judge was the name of the slave girl. Like her mother, she was an expert at needlework. Judge sewed for Washington's family and shopped with his wife. The enslaved teenager acquired a fair taste of the liberty known to free Blacks congregated in a ward south of Independence Hall, yet Judge daily displayed devotion to serving Washington. She attended the president's household without a hint of discontent until the first lady, Martha Washington, offered her as a wedding gift to her granddaughter. Offended, Judge slipped out the backdoor early one evening while the president and the first lady had supper in the dining room. She headed to a station on the Underground Railroad from which she made tracks for New Hampshire.

Billy Lee, Hercules, and Oney Judge prove that Blacks subjected to bondage preserved their dignity as much as possible with skill and smarts. The heroic spirit of the enslaved lies behind the invention of jazz, a form of music that fiddles with convention. Slavery drove slaves to conjure up ways to exploit expectations. They hit upon paths around insurmountable obstacles. Their trials elicited talent that lies dormant in souls at ease. While the institution of slavery accustomed whites to hold Blacks in want of intellectual acuity, it trained African Americans to cultivate a swift character. To a great degree, subjection to being treated as a dense peon inclined Blacks to act smart.

In the eighteenth century, slave narratives appeared as a sui generis convention. The publications were blockbusters through the nineteenth century and flew off bookshelves until the first quarter of the twentieth century. In general, the genre stars a hero with the outward demeanor of Billy Lee, Hercules, and Oney Judge under the gaze of Washington. Models of the literature remove doubt that the inequality inherent in Black bondage engendered a frame of mind that took skin color as signifier of a suitable slot for a shade in society. American slavery constructed and cemented the mentalities of slaveholders besides slaves. Narratives from former slaves stand in good stead enslaved figures who operate with the swiftness of a rabbit poised never to let a fox make a meal out of it. They guarantee that the approach to slavery enacted by Lee, Hercules, and Judge was common among successive generations of enslaved African Americans. They make it obvious that Blacks in bondage put on improvised shows for white men at the drop of a hat.

The Fugitive Blacksmith (1849) proves that enslaved Blacks projected false fronts. The book is the memoir of James Pennington. He was an African American born into slavery on a Maryland plantation. The heart of his narrative contains an account of his improvised escape from Black bondage. He achieved the feat while still in his teens. On his own, Pennington made his way to Philadelphia. Then he headed to New Haven where he found a way to become the first Black student enrolled in Yale University. Through passages of *The Fugitive Blacksmith*, the author bares the soul of a smooth operator. Introducing his story, Pennington implies that slaves played with slaveholders. He wrote in reference to the enslavers, "They are not masters of the system. The system is master of them" (Pennington vii).

The narrator recalls that his father and mother were skilled and self-respecting spouses. Their bond is tested when Pennington is four. His master gives his mother, older brother, and him to a son as a wedding gift. The crass gesture places Pennington's father at a distance of two hundred miles from his family. Because the enslaved father was a talented artisan, the slaveholder, who received the wife and children from his elder as a gift in honor of his marriage, decided to buy Pennington's father and unite the Black man with his family. The transaction illustrates that white slaveholders perceived the Black slaves as property instead of people. It shows too that those skillful slaves were better off because their crafts afforded them some leverage, as the reunion of Pennington's father with his wife and children proves.

Following in the footsteps of his father, Pennington grew into an invaluable carpenter and blacksmith and thereby staved off the most inhumane afflictions of Black bondage. Witnessing one of the cruelest hardships imposed on slaves by the system hardened a resolve in him to flee the business. As *The Fugitive Blacksmith* recounts, an overseer stripped a Black man, strung up the figure in a shed, and lashed his back with a cowhide, causing streams of blood to drench his skin before the eyes of the poor slave's six-year-old daughter. The whipping was a penalty for a display of resistance to the rule of whites over Blacks.

After the brutal scene, Pennington stood certain the slave system kept African American dignity at risk of extinction. He thought up a secret plan to reach Philadelphia, where he had heard Blacks enjoyed freedom from bondage. He avoided stirring suspicion about his disregard for the system while he took time to work out his escape. Pennington left his parents and siblings unaware of his goal. His master saw him as a loyal slave up to the Sabbath day that Pennington packed some provisions and took flight.

Trudging through dark forests and dismal swamps, guided at night by the light of the North Star, he fought famine and fright. Along the way, he confronted white men who suspected he was a runaway. The fugitive was quick to make up a story that tricked the whites into believing that he was a free person going about his own business. His swift response enabled him to continue his journey to freedom. Days later, he crossed the southern of border Pennsylvania. He was lucky to stumble upon a fair Quaker who led him to housing and work among the Society of Friends in the City of Brotherly Love.

Subsequent to Pennington's personal history, *Running a Thousand Miles for Freedom* (1860) conveys a rather excellent display of smooth operating. Again, the latter work relates the story of Ellen and William Craft, the enslaved couple who resided on a plantation in Macon, Georgia. They thought up and pulled off a ruse that permitted them to flee bondage. In the main, they performed a marvelous masquerade for the sake of their dignity.

Running a Thousand Miles for Freedom tells that the minds of slavers induced them to see Blacks as senseless creatures for whites to keep at their disposal. The slaveholders gave Blacks credit for meager natural abilities. They assumed a Black man could handle tools and heave loads. Black women were credited with a talent for domestic service and carnal pleasure. Slaveholders counted slave babies as newfound capital. They assumed that the ability to chart a sound course to follow laid beyond the power of Blacks. Realizing the false impressions of the slaveholders, Ellen and William Craft schemed in secret to chart and conduct a smooth flight.

Being the offspring of a Black slave and her white slaveholder, Ellen inherited a complexion that was a shade of pink. William on the other hand had a dark brown hue inherited from his two enslaved parents. Seeing that Black bondage converted skin color into a status symbol, the Crafts took advantage of the myth to turn the tables on the system. Ellen donned the suit of a young white gentleman. Pretending to be in poor health and heading to Philadelphia for treatment, she traveled north by steamboat and train. Her husband, William, accompanied her. He played the part of a devoted slave at the beck and call of his master. With money William earned from moonlighting as a cabinetmaker, the Crafts had enough cash on hand to ride in style with a succession of white travelers. The spouses traversed a thousand miles and rejoiced when they reached the city of Philadelphia on Christmas Day. In the end, they gave sincere thanks "to God, for his goodness in enabling [them] to overcome so many perilous difficulties, in escaping out of the jaws of the wicked" (51).

An earlier work likewise conveys an instance of the smooth operating. It is *The Interesting Narrative of the Life of Olaudah Equiano, or Gustavus Vassa, the African* (1789). The text recounts the fortunes of a man born in Africa as the son of a tribal chief. It begins in an eighteenth-century village nestled in a fruitful valley that is a part of the Benin kingdom. The local population consists of pious and productive people whose prime occupation is farming. Their sole cause for warfare is self-defense. Leading members of the community such as Equiano's father have the privilege of owning many slaves. In any case, slavery is not treated as a hereditary fate. The enslaved come from the ranks of convicted felons and captured foes, and they are granted civil rights. By custom, village slaves confront little lawful reason to fear a total loss of their dignity.

After circumcision, Equiano waits for puberty to have a weal lanced across his forehead to mark him a cut above his mates with a duty to someday fill his father's shoes. The ritual demonstrates that inequality dwelled among ancient African folk. By divine decree, not physical features, it was held, a chosen few are born to reign over others. Equiano takes the unfairness in stride until hostile natives snatch him from his home and dump him in the local slave traffic, leading to his deposit, some months later, in the belly of an English ship holding dozens of Blacks chained and stacked on racks like livestock in layered pens. The African is dumbstruck by the pale complexions and profound cruelty of the vessel's crew. Engulfed in shame through his voyage to the "New World," he surmises, unlike his people who conceded the humanity of their slaves, that the crew aboard the ship place him and his fellows out of the human race. He says, "Surely this is a new refinement in cruelty, which, while it has no advantage to atone for it, thus aggravates distress, and adds fresh horrors even to the wretchedness of slavery" (58).

In the New World, Equiano hears the word "nigger" spoken plenty in reference to him by individuals without his complexion, who are identified as "free white people." Under the circumstances, Equiano grows aware of a need to dissemble in the face of an imperious lot blind to his true identity. He neither sees himself as a Black man nor suffers without indignation the handling of a farm animal until he encounters the men who picture themselves as whites. The African has to exercise a deal great of ingenuity to improve his lot. He makes up his mind to learn from his white masters their tongue, tenets, and trades while he presents an obliging character for their satisfaction. Through his behavior, Equiano intends to help whites help him free himself from them for the sake of his dignity.

Because he spends the bulk of his days as a slave working on a merchant ship, knowing how to navigate a boat could facilitate his exit strategy. But the white captains and crews whom he serves withhold the knowledge. From them, Equiano should just learn how to read and write and count well enough to carry out orders and toe the line. Their refusal to teach him navigation renders the prospect of an escape from bondage on his own by way of a seafaring vessel rather risky business, especially in light of the fact that he has never learned to swim. Regardless, Equiano sharpens his wits well enough to steer a ship "by dint of reason" (124). Proving himself well-endowed with brains, when the chief officer of a ship and his first mate fall ill in the midst of a stormy sea, stunning a shaky crew, Equiano saves the day. Through a swift application of reason, without reference to a compass, he guides the boat, none the worse for wear, to a dock in Montserrat. His recollection of the episode supports his wish that his story "may tend . . . to remove the prejudice that some conceive against the natives of Africa on account of their colour" (45). In his narrative, he implores:

> Let such reflections as these melt the pride of their superiority into sympathy for the wants and miseries of their sable brethren, and compel them to acknowledge, that understanding is not confined to feature or colour. (46)

Equiano secures his freedom by means of his private enterprise. He studies the commercial practices of Robert King, his third and final master, who is a prosperous Philadelphia wholesaler of livestock and produce. Becoming adept at the white man's business, Equiano launches his own trade on the side. He makes enough money retailing goods to purchase his liberty from King, and he leaves the white man surprised that he has the mind and means to buy his independence. *The Interesting Narrative of the Life of Olaudah Equiano, or Gustavus Vassa, the African* certifies that discrete mentalities extraneous to physical traits set Blacks and whites at odds during the era of Black bondage. The "peculiar institution" cultivated in Blacks a penchant for dissemblance, as in whites it planted a predilection for dominance. The state of mind for neither color was innate; the mentalities were bred by the slave system. Equiano establishes that Black bondage had the effect of closing white minds and opening Black ones with regard to the scope of humanity. Slavery in the country programmed whites to function with an imperial air in accord with terms that compelled Blacks to defend their dignity through veiled acts against white monopolies of power. It put Equiano in the position of a poker player stuck into a crooked game where his fortunes depend on his winning the pot with a bad hand by seeming to play without a full deck, keeping his cards close to his chest, and not missing a single trick.

Reasons for the kind of swift maneuvers that win Equiano freedom course through the *Narrative of the Life of Frederick Douglass*. They start with Douglass noticing a deep-seated difference between the way Black lives matter in Black and white minds. He watches his master have the enslaved Black woman named Aunt Hester beaten as if she were a stray cow that he needs to have whipped home. Douglass also witnesses his mother serving at the pleasure of their master. Under thick cloaks of darkness, his mother must steal moments and food from the white man to care for her son. The slaveholder feeds slave women and children troughs of mush made for pigs. He cares more for his horses than for the Black stable hands that groom and guard his colts. By sharing the story of Mr. Gore, the heartless white overseer who declares Demby, a Black slave, "unmanageable" and shoots the poor slave dead in a pond for opposing a beating, Douglass makes plain that slavery in the land, to the regret of African Americans, cheapened their lives in white minds. "It was a common saying," the author reports, "even among little white boys, that it was worth a half-cent to kill a 'nigger,' and a half-cent to bury one" (53).

Douglass was relocated from a Maryland plantation to a household in Baltimore. In the new place, he detects a link between learning and liberty once his second master, Mr. Auld, scolds his spouse, Mrs. Auld, for seeking to teach the Black boy how to read and write. The husband orders the wife to cease and desist from offering the youth further instruction in literacy because the skill. The white man swears:

> "If you give a nigger an inch, he will take an ell. A nigger should know nothing but to obey his master—to do as he is told to do. Learning would spoil the best nigger in the world. Now," said he, "if you teach that nigger (speaking of myself) how to read, there would be no keeping him. It would forever unfit him to be a slave. He would at once become unmanageable, and of no value to his master. As to himself, it could do him no good, but a great deal of harm. It would make him discontented and unhappy." (57)

Black bondage is new to the Mrs. Auld. She has come down South from a Northern state to wed her husband, a hereditary slaveholder. Prior to her marriage, Mrs. Auld has followed her own mind, supported herself as a weaver, and never kept a slave. Still, she honors her wedding vow to obey her husband. The white woman transforms into a diehard slaveholder. She develops fierce opposition to Douglass learning anything beyond obedience.

From the experience, Douglass determines to become literate because he guesses that the ability will pave his way from slavery to freedom. Considering that the goal goes against his master's policy in addition to the law, he has to employ a variety of clever tactics to achieve his end. He befriends poor white boys who hang around a Baltimore shipyard and know how to read. Plying them with bread from his master's cabinet, he persuades them to help him decipher books. Once he is able to read, he obtains *The Columbian Orator* and scours it for lessons on writing. The primer is loaded with rhetoric that advocates liberty from bondage and bias. An exchange with a master and slave who wins the latter liberty stiffens the resolve of Douglass to achieve self-emancipation. Dreaming of drafting someday a counterfeit pass with which to slip away from bondage, he commits to becoming proficient at penmanship by betting schoolchildren, whom he knows can write, that he can draw letters of the alphabet better than they can; of course, he loses the wagers, but afterward he practices copying the winners' handwriting with bits of chalk on fences, walls, and streets. Douglass secures a copy of *Webster's Spelling Book* and studies it, along with grade school textbooks belonging to the son of his master. Through years of deception and discipline, Douglass turns himself into a tolerable English writer.

In the *Narrative of the Life of Frederick Douglass*, critics maintain, the author reveals his most liberating feat when he relates his skirmish with Mr. Covey that causes the slave-breaker to get off his back. Regardless, the open resistance fails to free Douglass from bondage. In reality, it takes a discreet application of defiance for him to gain his independence. Following the publication of his slave narrative, Douglass reported, he escaped from Black bondage by donning the uniform of a sailor, borrowing the papers of a free Black seaman, and traveling in the style of the Crafts by train and steamboat to Philadelphia. His clever charade got him out of slavery. He achieved the coup without violence, which made him a prime example of a smooth operator.

Incidents in the Life of a Slave Girl (1861) shows that Harriet Jacobs cultivated ingenuity to escape the fate of a concubine valued as much as a prized lamb. Under the pseudonym of Linda Brent, Jacobs had her slave narrative published. She recalled that her mother as well as her father came from an enslaved mother and slaveholding father. At first, she was trained to work as a domestic servant for slaveholders who allowed her to become literate and respected her human rights. The author reviled the day she became the property of a dirty old white man who wanted her groomed to satisfy his sexual desires. She was just a teenager when the disgusting creep began putting the make on her behind the back of his wife.

The Jacobs book laments that the abuse of Black women is a standard practice among slaveholders. Kids with brown faces who favor their master drive his wife into maniacal fits of rage during which the madwoman terrifies and tortures Black women in her house on whom her husband has designs. The second master of Brent, named Dr. Flint, inflicts corporeal punishment on an enslaved maid because she has let her enslaved husband get wind of her master's liaison with her. Afterward, the fiendish slaveholder sells the couple to separate buyers in order to be rid of their bickering. Over and over, before the slave girl turns sixteen, Dr. Flint corners her in rooms and badgers her with lewd propositions.

The slave system renders it impossible for slave girls to hold off the advances of their masters. Slaveholders and their sons regard the Black females as fair game for sexual exploitation. Brent laments:

> No pen can give an adequate description of the all-pervading corruption produced by slavery. The slave girl is reared in an atmosphere of licentiousness and fear. The lash and the foul talk of her master and his sons are her teachers. When she is

fourteen or fifteen, her owner, or his sons, or the overseer, or perhaps all of them, begin to bribe her with presents. If these fail to accomplish their purpose, she is whipped or starved into submission to their will. She may have had religious principles inculcated by some pious mother or grandmother, or some good mistress; she may have a lover, whose good opinion and peace of mind are dear to her heart; or the profligate men who have power over her may be exceedingly odious to her. But resistance is hopeless. (Jacobs 51–52)

In her memory, Jacobs compares the status of a slave girl to the plight of a creature stuck in a swamp, swarming with poisonous snakes. The predicament has a noxious effect on her soul. She dreads that her sole recourse is sex in exchange for security. The situation causes her to turn down a marriage proposal from a free Black man. She understands that custom denies the Black suitor the right to protect her from sexual assaults by white men. Brent recalls making a deliberate choice to grant her favors to Mr. Sands, a local white patrician, a future United States senator, who happens to be her senior by several years. He warms her heart with kind words that stoke her hopes and dreams. By means of their relationship, she aspires to find shelter from a descent into depravity proposed by Dr. Flint.

Mr. Sands has a boy and girl with Brent. Then the local white patrician leaves the slave girl in a lurch. She stays in the household of Dr. Flint by the Inner Banks of North Carolina, while he goes to Washington, DC, to launch his career in Congress, accompanied by a white bride from a reputable white family. Brent plays tricks on Dr. Flint to keep him off her as she remains by him in order to keep an eye on her children. She retreats to a crawl space in the roof above the house of her grandmother, Aunt Marthy. A hole in the wall allows her to take peeps at her offspring. She hides in the narrow refuge for seven long years.

With the ability to write, she throws Dr. Flint off her tracks by drafting letters and forwarding them to him with postmarks from New York and Boston by way of an underground network composed of Blacks committed to the betterment of their fellow African Americans. Brent's correspondences dupe the licentious Dr. Flint into believing that she is far from his sight. In actuality, she watches him over his head in her hideout. The ploy affords her a chance to slip downstairs from her perch, stretch out her limbs beyond the limits of the crawl space, and steal real good looks at her children.

The slave girl writhes in great agony through lonesome hours in her nook. In any event, she never succumbs to despair. Brent never amounts to a passive victim of oppression. A desire to escape Dr. Flint's plantation rises in her soul. She enlists the assistance of the Black network that has handled her letters to Dr. Flint. In time, she secures passage on a boat that transports her to the city of Philadelphia, where Reverend Jeremiah Dunham welcomes her into the bosom of the Mother Bethel A.M.E. Church.

The motifs that occupy classic slave narratives like *Incidents in the Life of a Slave Girl* make it a small wonder that white stories of Black bondage misrepresent African Americans. *Uncle Tom's Cabin* (1852) owns the distinction of being the most renowned and read book about the slave system. Black figures that appear in Harriet Beecher Stowe's novel are marked by a single trait. They are deferential like Tom, defiant like Eliza, or derelict like Topsy. White characters in the novel such as Augustine St. Clare and Miss Ophelia have the capacity to grow and change. It is typical of Blacks in the book to have a flat persona. Classic slave narratives, at odds with *Uncle Tom's Cabin*, attest that Black bondage inclined the enslaved to hide the depths of their humanity from white eyes. The grounds for the slave system developed a divide that left Blacks in a spot where they faced the need to check terrible impositions by improvised means, as Brent does in her distressing story. Epic figures among the enslaved, captured in slave narratives, kept whites in the dark concerning their true abilities and aims through the discipline of smooth operating.

During the seven years that Brent hides in the crammed garret of her grandmother's home, Dr. Flint never gets wind of her presence. Her entire family and fellow slaves keep her dodge secret. The truth of the matter reveals a dedication to smooth operating shared by the African Americans in her old neighborhood. In unison to the best of their ability, the Black community in effect puts on a show for whites to protect a group member who in their eyes was heroic. Their conduct debunks the belief of Jefferson that Black lives "participate more of sensation than reflection." The reality that they hold their tongues about Brent's ruse testifies that they are guided by thought more than by feeling. Given a fair chance to work as an indentured servant with civil rights and earn a payoff in the vicinity of forty acres and a mule, Brent's collaborators could have become prosperous entrepreneurs on par with Franklin.

Two of Kind

One drawn to coats that others wear,
A wolf in sheep's clothing can snare.

A rare white writer realized how slavery sowed the seeds of the heroic ideal that took root in the souls of Black folk and sprouted the buds of Black culture. During the years of Black bondage, whites who wrote about Blacks were incredulous of the African American ability to deliberate. From such authors as William Gilmore Simms and John Pendleton Kennedy to Harriet Beecher Stowe, white writers produced literature that portrayed Black characters ruled by emotion. So reports in 1805 of a slave mutiny at sea on the *Tryal* startled the authors. And in 1841, they were shocked by news of an uprising by slaves aboard the *Creole*. The events disturbed the writers, for they were indisposed to credit the mutineers with sufficient smarts to muster the cunning and conviction to take their captors by surprise.

Among his peers, Herman Melville was an outlier. His novella *Benito Cereno* (1855) paints a picture of a Black slave distinguished by a knack for introspection and improvisation. Identified as Babo, the character exhibits neither the glaring defiance of Abe in Kennedy's *Swallow Barn* (1832) and George Harris in Stowe's *Uncle Tom's Cabin* (1852) nor the gracious deference of Lucy in the former novel and Uncle Tom in the latter work. Babo maintains a cool demeanor that masks a determination to achieve freedom. With considerable thought, he orchestrates a charade beyond the imagination of authors who took to heart the portrait of Tom, the devoted slave in *The Sword and the Distaff* (1852) dreamed up by Simms. Melville's character displays a brilliance possessed by Madison Washington, the African American protagonist in *The Heroic Slave* (1853) written by Frederick Douglass.

Benito Cereno indicates that Melville picked up the fact that slavery, sad to say, brought into being a "peculiar institution," which flew in the face of the founding principle that "all men" are born with equal rights. The author's novella suggests that he grasped how slavery pressed the enslaved to conceal their desire for freedom. *Benito Cereno* features a plot that advises whites against counting Blacks as fools. While the tales told by white writers akin to Simms, Kennedy, and Stowe make everything about Blacks seem uncommon, the story by Melville renders people of African descent as normal human beings who breathe and bleed, sweat and shiver, and hurt and heal with an innate mind for freedom and fulfillment. *Benito Cereno* removes grounds staked by contemporary white writers for whites to behave as if they were brighter than Blacks, or to suppose that Blacks are too dense or deranged to profit from their own designs. It illustrates that Melville realized treating skin color as a status symbol caused the nation to produce a Black persona distinguished by discreet conduct for which identification by complexion failed to account.

By the time he decided to write *Benito Cereno*, Melville no doubt had surmised that the mutiny on the *Tryal* was predictable. The writer had researched the details of the event. He had learned that a short Black slave with the mien of a shepherd's dog had harbored a secret disdain for the lot of the ship's enslaved captives. Melville had gathered that the little rebel had conceived and commanded the revolt aboard the vessel. Moreover, Melville had discovered that the leader of the revolt had taken the captain and crew of the *Tryal* by complete surprise. Melville sensed that the white sailors, blinded by belief in color as a sign of character, became easy marks for the Black mutineer to pull the wool over their eyes.

From a voyage at sea, Melville acquired a sense of identity based on achievement rather than association. The bulk of his contemporary white writers like the captain and crew of the *Tryal* clung to the notion that their color signified their character. Their worth in the eyes of the whites sprang from their affiliation with bodies of their shade. They held it to be a certain truth that their complexion testified that they were born brighter and better than Blacks. Most of Melville's peers took it for granted that a Black man would never pull a fast one on them. The unflattering impression of Blacks promoted smugness, which inclined white authors to suppose that the mastermind of the *Tryal* mutiny was an enigmatic evil.

Through contact with dark-skinned islanders in the South Seas, Melville grew detached from the identity ascribed to him by color prejudice. By way of his adventure abroad, he gained respect for people of color. The experience followed the death of his father, which caused his family to suffer bankruptcy and hardship. Finishing his teens, Melville turned to seafaring for a living as a common sailor. He made his maiden voyage on a merchant ship that sailed to Liverpool and returned to New York. Afterward, a transfer to a whaler run by a tyrannous captain raised an aversion to oppression in him. Sailing out of the Bahamas, Melville was riled by the despotism on the ship; he was infuriated by the captain as the vessel rounded Cape Horn, skirted the coast of Chile, and reached Polynesia. Melville jumped ship and swam ashore on an island near Tahiti. As the young renegade fell head over heels for the brown beauty of a native girl, he came to appreciate the humanity he shared with the dark islanders. This provides some explanation for why Melville produced a Black figure who contradicts the images of Blacks presented in the novels of Simms, Kennedy, and Stowe, who kept faith in color as a sign of character.

Well before Melville drafted *Billy Budd, Sailor* in 1888 at the age of sixty-nine, disdain for indignity visited on underdogs ran through his opus. The contempt lays low in *Typee* (1846) and *Omoo* (1847), offering a tantalizing glimpse of Polynesians and his adventures in the South Seas; the books thrilled his contemporaries. *Mardi* (1849), which issues harsh criticism of slights to the dark denizens of the South Seas by white interlopers, elicited serious questions about Melville's state of mind. His attribution of mindfulness to dark Queequeg and madness to white Ahab in *Moby-Dick; or, the Whaler* (1851) won him few fans. The novel *Pierre* (1852), whose hero favors brunette Isabel over blonde Lucy, drove a reviewer to declare him insane. Lampooning social hierarchy, "Bartleby, the Scrivener" (1853) excited increasing concern about the mental health of the author. *The Confidence-Man: His Masquerade* (1857), portraying identity as a fiction, which a con artist manipulates for his pleasure, left Melville in isolation from his fellow white writers.

Benito Cereno stars a small Black slave with a mind to turn the tables in his favor by improvised means. The hero is a dead ringer for the principal figure in *The Heroic Slave*. Both of the given characters contrast the predominant antebellum literary representation of Blacks in bondage. The stories of Melville and Douglass are novellas with a breadth that explodes the myth of the day about color as a sign of character. Each of the fictions pegs slave mutinies unsurprising. The works bear witness that slavery cultivated among African Americans a knack for swiftness and subtlety in the interest of their dignity. Together, *Benito Cereno* and *The Heroic Slave* illustrate that Black bondage was a terrible imposition that called for quick thinking by the enslaved to make the best of a bad situation.

Fifteen years after Douglass took flight from Black bondage, he had *The Heroic Slave* published in *Autographs for Freedom*, a volume of writings that was edited by Julia Griffiths. Douglass's novella was inspired by a real-life story involving a slave, slave ship, and court case concerning the right of a Black man to resist enslavement. As the legal dispute commenced in 1842, Douglass was celebrating fewer than sixty months of freedom. He identified with Madison Washington, the principal party in the lawsuit. If allowed, Douglass would have jumped at a chance to defend Washington's plea for liberty in an amicus brief. The court case, which won a favorable verdict for Washington, stayed on Douglass's mind as he rose to become a prominent advocate for the abolition of Black bondage. Following the passage of the 1850 Fugitive Slave Act, slamming the door tight on shelter from slavery in the North, Douglass wrote *The Heroic Slave* to remind the public of the Washington trial.

Washington was a Black man from Virginia who fled slavery by improvised means. The fugitive flew to Canada, where he found relief from enslavement. Yet he left his wife, whom he loved, down South. Therefore, he returned to the United States in secret with a plan to take his spouse out of the country with him. To his regret, his scheme failed. He was caught and transported from Richmond to a coastal port, where he was dumped in the belly of a brig christened the *Creole* with a cargo of Black bodies slated for sale at a New Orleans slave auction.

By the time he found himself stowed under the deck of the *Creole*, Washington was too familiar with liberty and contemptuous of slavery to take his captivity lying down. He hatched a plan to seize control of the brig. On the sly, he talked more than a tenth of the Blacks aboard the ship into giving him a hand. When he decided the time was right, Washington and his allies put his scheme into action; they caught the captain and crew off guard and commandeered the *Creole* in short order. Without a thirst for blood, the mastermind behind the uprising saw that fatalities were avoided other than the execution of a slave trader; few crewmen suffered injury. He sought lives and looked to bandage wounds. Learning from his partner, Ben Blacksmith, that the British had outlawed slavery in the West Indies, Washington set sail for the port of Nassau in the Bahamas, where the local court, following the law, set him and his fellow mutineers free.

In the man behind the *Creole* mutiny, Douglass recognized a kindred spirit. The two men knew in their heart that they were not cut out for bondage. Like Washington, and unlike any Black character concocted by Simms, Kennedy, or Stowe, Douglass harbored a compelling yet cerebral desire for liberty. The two real-life African Americans found that color said nothing about their natural ability. They perceived identification by complexion as fool's gold. Every shade, they sensed, reflects surrounding circumstances. As far as they could see, it was best to base social roles on acquired skills. Placing people by hue, they deduced, created awful confusion with dear costs in the country. Most of all, the fates of Douglass and Washington credited a common mode of clever conduct for enabling them to throw off the shackles of Black bondage.

Douglass in his own right amounted to a paragon of a smooth operator. He professed in his third autobiography, the *Life and Times of Frederick Douglass* (1881), "A man's character always takes its hue, more or less, from the form and color of things about him" (50). In the book, he gives the full details of the steps that he took to become a freeman. The narrative establishes that slavery prevailed on him to exercise ingenuity. First, the system challenged him to achieve literacy. Devising strategies to tackle the problem served to sharpen his wits. Through the discipline of teaching himself to read and write, he gathered ever more reasons to take flight from bondage and grew more and more convinced that the business was bankrupt of morality. Realizing the social order rested on the mistaken belief that Blacks think too little to chart on their own a profitable course to pursue, Douglass concluded the mindset made him seem to whites too shallow to envision fleeing bondage by donning a naval uniform and borrowing a sailor's pass; thus, he resorted to the ruse, and in doing so, he escaped slavery.

On top of his autobiographical writing—*Narrative of the Life of Frederick Douglass, My Bondage and My Freedom* (1855), and his last memoir mentioned above—Douglass hoped for his novella to disabuse the nation of the notion that Blacks lack the necessities to overcome oppression by discreet designs. Constituting an embellished remembrance of the real Madison Washington, the hero of *The Heroic Slave* works as an alter ego for Douglass. The character strives to open eyes to the reality that slavery is harmful to Blacks and whites alike. Bearing the name for the *Creole* mutiny's mastermind, the imaginary Washington as a result evokes James Madison, the "Father of the Constitution," and George Washington, the "Father of the Country." Alluding to the Founding Fathers, the protagonist's name underscores the irony that the national leaders enslaved African Americans while the revolutionaries accused King George III of trying to reduce them to his retainers against the laws of nature.

The hero in *The Heroic Slave* warns, "Where there is seeming contentment with slavery, there is certain treachery to freedom" (190). By implication, he counsels whites against supposing that Blacks harbor little interest in self-government. Conceived by his creator as a credit to his kind, the character declares, he is "*yes*, a man!—with thoughts and wishes, with powers and faculties" that fit him for freedom, "the inalienable birthright of every man, precious and priceless" (177). He airs a fierce desire for emancipation followed by a firm determination to fulfill his wish. The fictional Washington is an individual "who [carries a torch for] liberty as well as Patrick Henry did,—who [is entitled to] it as much as Thomas Jefferson" (175). Sounding like Henry in 1774 crying for freedom from the King George III, the Black Washington swears, "*Liberty* I will have, or die in the attempt to gain it" (178). He signifies it could be a fatal measure to bar a person of his hue from the pursuit of happiness.

The hero in Douglass's novella seems resigned to slavery and enjoys the full faith and trust of whites until one day his master accuses him of insolence. It is a false allegation arising from his delayed return to the slave quarters after working all day at the mill. His tardiness has been "no fault" of his own. In attempting to establish his innocence, he upsets his master, who pronounces the slave an "impudent rascal" (188) for neglecting to remain silent. Washington indicates, "Slave-holders are so imperious" (188) toward the enslaved that they are prone to "construe" any argument from a slave as a brazen act warranting harsh punishment. Hence, his master has the overseer give Washington a painful whipping, as if he were a steer cut from a herd of cattle by his master and beaten to break his spirit.

Washington suffers cruelty well beyond reason. He is "tied up to the limb of a tree." The Black man has his "feet chained together." Moreover, he has "a heavy iron bar placed between his ankles." He takes "on his naked back forty stripes." Afterward, he is left bound "in this distressing position three or four hours" (188). In the wake of the mistreatment, he starts to "devise ways and means" (189) to improve his lot.

The Heroic Slave, the only work of fiction written by Douglass, takes place between the spring of 1835 and the autumn of 1841. There is a moment that occurs at a home in Ohio. Locations around the capital of the Old Dominion—Richmond, Virginia—are the sites for every other scene. The settings are stuffed with significance. A model home by contemporary standards, from which custom bars Black slaves, provides the background for events in Ohio. The Virginia venues remind the reader that the state gave birth to legendary Henry, Madison, and Washington as well as Jefferson, each of whom was a slaveholder who felt "all men" are born with an equal right to freedom. None of the given white revolutionaries ever expected to know a Black man with the genius of Nat Turner, whom Virginia slaveholders took as a pious, peaceful, and pliant persona until Turner orchestrated the epic slave uprising that shook up Southampton County during the dog days of summer 1831.

By chance, the fictional Washington in *The Heroic Slave* catches the ear of Mr. Listwell, a compassionate white gentleman. The latter character handles his business without dependence on the labor of enslaved African Americans. Listwell's depiction gives cause to hope that a fair hearing of the trials and tribulations confronting Blacks in bondage could enlighten whites and spread support for abolitionism. From Ohio, Listwell, traveling through Virginia on a commercial venture, overhears Washington, alone in the woods, lamenting his misfortune. The slave's complaint is in steeped in anguish. It touches the heart of the white listener and turns him against the institution of Black bondage.

Listwell stays out of sight while the slave rails against the intolerable cruelty of slavery. Washington broods over whether to suffer the slave system any longer. He is pained by the thought of leaving his dear wife at the mercy of slaveholders. However much he grieves, he has no choice. Unknown to him, his words convert Listwell into an abolitionist. Though the white man has lived without slaves, he has never before equated a Black person as anybody on par with him. Even so, Listwell listens well; his soul overflows with regret about his prior lack of consideration for Blacks in bondage. He resembles a person born again after he discovers Washington pouring out his heart in secret. "From this hour," Listwell declares, "I am an abolitionist" (182).

Next, Listwell appears cozy at home with his dear spouse, relaxing by the fireside while their children sleep on a cold, dark night in Ohio. He ignores a harsh wind that bends trees and batters his property. But ferocious growls from his watchdog seize his attention. It leads him to spot Washington by his door. Invited into the house, the Black man shares a harrowing tale of a hasty attempt to escape bondage that went awry and stranded him in a forest, where he dwelled in a cave for five years until a raging fire consumed the woods. Deeply touched, Listwell gives the fugitive shelter for the night. The following evening, breaking the law prohibiting Ohioans from helping Blacks to escape bondage, Listwell provides Washington with fresh, warm clothing, conceals the runaway in his wagon, and transports him to Cleveland, where Listwell secures Washington safe passage on a steamer bound for Canada. Not too many days later, Listwell receives a letter of gratitude from Washington with a Canadian postmark. As the white man recognizes and respects the depth and dignity of Blacks, he becomes a steadfast opponent of their enslavement.

Listwell meets Washington once again on a second trip to Virginia. The Black man is back in chains and headed for sale at auction in New Orleans. The Ohioan is primed to act against white men profiting off the treatment of Blacks as merchandise. He arranges a clandestine meeting where he learns Washington was recaptured when he returned to Virginia with the intention to free his wife from slavery. Appreciating the Black man's sorrow and sure that Washington possesses "the head to conceive, and the hand to execute" a scheme to go free once more, Listwell buys three files and slips them to the slave before the African American boards the *Creole*. Listwell's development stands in stark contrast to the depiction of other white figures like Jack Williams, "a regular old salt" (226) habituated to an imperious attitude toward Blacks.

The last bit of *The Heroic Slave* cautions whites against misjudging the capacity for resourcefulness in Blacks. Once aboard the brig headed for New Orleans, Washington uses the files he had received from Listwell to break his chains and the manacles of several other captives as well. Under his direction, the unshackled take command of the ship. Washington persuades the first mate, Tom Grant, to steer the vessel into the port of Nassau, where authorities in accordance with British law set the rebels free. Washington makes a lasting impression on Grant. It spurs the white sailor to reject the imperious attitude toward Blacks held by whites like the noted old salt Williams. In the end, Grant understands the *Creole* mutiny as comparable to the American Revolution.

In a tavern after the uprising, recalling Washington, Grant remarks, to the surprise of his companions, "I forgot his blackness in the dignity of his manner, and the eloquence of his speech" (235). The first mate recounts the Black man's regret and reason for the mutiny. He quotes the insurrectionist verbatim:

> "You call me a *black murderer*. I am not a murderer. God is my witness that LIBERTY, not *malice*, is the motive for this night's work. I have done no more to those dead men yonder, than they would have done to me in like circumstances. We have struck for our freedom, and if a true man's heart be in you, you will honor us for the deed. We have done that which you applaud your fathers for doing, and if we are murderers, *so were they*." (234–35)

Grant says, "The leader of the mutiny in question was just as shrewd a fellow as ever I met in my life, and was as well fitted to lead in a dangerous enterprise as any one white man in ten thousand" (232). Intending to discredit the mistaken assumption that Blacks are too dimwitted to chart on their own a profitable course to follow and to disabuse the nation of the notion that Blacks lack the necessities to overcome oppression by discreet designs, the first mate confesses with regard to Washington:

> "I felt myself in the presence of a superior man; one who, had he been a white man, I would have followed willingly and gladly in any honorable enterprise. Our difference of color was the only ground for difference of action. It was not that his principles were wrong in the abstract; for they are the principles of 1776. But I could not bring myself to recognize their application to one whom I deemed my inferior." (237–38)

Through *The Heroic Slave*, Douglass aimed to open white eyes closed by custom to the humanity of Blacks. He wished to remove doubt that Black lives matter as much as any white one does. Douglass aspired to show that African Americans desire and deserve to exercise freedom of choice. His hero alludes to a historical figure to prove that his fictional character amounts to more than a figment of his imagination. Blacks no less than whites, the story of Washington demonstrates, come to life with a right and reason for liberty.

The Heroic Slave memorializes the development of a smooth operator. At first, Washington bolts from bondage, like a raging bull, breaking from the confines of a foul pen. Like a dumb animal, he ends up lost in the woods. He descends into the life of a solitary bear. The fugitive gathers food from the wild. For shelter, Washington dwells in a cave. The intense blaze that forces him out of the forest puts him on the road to securing the assistance of Listwell and the admiration of Grant. Learning from his mistakes, he grows cognizant and canny. Once he lands in chains on the *Creole*, he acts full of awe for the crew and gains the full faith and trust of the captain. He strikes the whole contingent of whites as the last figure aboard the brig prone to mastermind a mutiny.

As *The Heroic Slave* moves to its conclusion, the regular old salt Williams appears as a caricature of the imagination that justified Black bondage. The white sailor embodies a false consciousness that Douglass sought to discredit for the sake of Blacks in particular and the country in general. After the mutiny led by Washington, Williams's claims about Blacks ring hollow. The veteran seaman insists, "that whole affair on board of the *Creole* was miserably and disgracefully managed" (226). Upbraiding Grant,

Williams contends, "Those black rascals got the upper hand" because of the crew's "ignorance of the real character of *darkies*" (226), which according to Williams smacks of spinelessness and stupidity. He declares:

> "I cannot see how a dozen or two of ignorant negroes, not one of whom had ever been to sea before, and all of them were closely ironed between decks, should be able to get their fetters off, rush out of the hatchway in open daylight, kill two white men, the one the captain and the other their master, and then carry the ship into a British port, where every '*darkey*' of them was set free." (231–32)

The regular old salt epitomizes the type of thinker that *Benito Cereno* ridicules. Melville's tale credits Blacks with a knack for ingenuity. It delivers the assessment through its portrayal of Babo. The character pulls the wool over the eyes of white men who deny the capacity of Blacks for courage and craftiness. Again, like *The Heroic Slave*, *Benito Cereno* is a work of fiction based on an actual event. Being drawn from a real occurrence serves to ground Babo in reality. The figure is a Black slave who leads the rebellion around which the action in the narrative revolves. He performs a succession of swift strokes that poke holes in the picture of Blacks to which white chauvinists like the old salt in *The Heroic Slave* subscribe.

Melville gathered *Benito Cereno* from a memoir written by Captain Amasa Delano. The captain was a seaman and an ancestor of President Franklin Delano Roosevelt. In 1817, the naval officer published his book. The work is titled *A Narrative of Voyages and Travels, in the Northern and Southern Hemispheres: Comprising Three Voyages Round the World; Together with a Voyage of Survey and Discovery in the Pacific Ocean and Oriental Islands.* It records his passages around the world during his career as a mariner. A chapter recalls an 1805 voyage when the *Perseverance*, an American ship under his command, happened upon the *Tryal*, a Spanish slave ship adrift in an island bay scores of leagues off the coastline of Chile. Because the *Tryal* appeared to be in distress, Delano boarded the vessel to offer some assistance. It took him some time fraught with danger to realize that the slaves onboard were perpetrating a charade designed to mask their command of the ship in the wake of a revolt engineered by their organizer, named Babo, who at first sight struck the historical Delano as an obliging pet.

The setting for Melville's novella is located where the real insurgency transpired. A key character in the fictional tale is Captain Amasa Delano.

Benito Cereno starts to unfold when the captain notices a strange brig in the cove of Santa Maria off the Chilean shore. In the murky fog of a silent and still morning, he cannot make out the boat through his spyglass from the poop deck of his vessel. Mystery shrouds the strange craft, as it shows no colors, flies no flag, and draws too close to a sunken reef. For a second, to the imaginary Delano, the odd boat favors an abbey with Black Friars pacing behind bulwarks washed white by the fury of a storm.

One of three primary figures in *Benito Cereno*, Delano is the principal reporter on a majority of the scenes. Benito Cereno and Babo are the other characters central to the plot. From Delano's point of view, the identities of the other two figures are first framed. The captain is prone to judge people by their looks. A rowboat, the Rover, stocked with provisions and lowered from his ship, the *Bachelor's Delight*, carries him to the other boat, the *San Dominick*. Aboard the intriguing brig, he spots Cereno outfitted in a Spanish commander's uniform, leaning against the mainmast with, according to Delano, the anxious air of a fickle and feckless captain unable to manage a rowdy swarm of white sailors and Black slaves buzzing below him. Delano is comforted by the sight of Babo, a diminutive Black man in coarse baggy trousers stationed by the side of Cereno, evoking a hound eager to serve his master.

Delano observes:

> The Spanish captain, a gentlemanly, reserved-looking, and rather young man to a stranger's eye, dressed with singular richness, but bearing plain traces of recent sleepless cares and disquietudes, stood passively by, leaning against the main-mast, at one moment casting a dreary, spiritless look upon his excited people, at next unhappy glance toward his visitor. (Melville 120)

Then the American captain comments on Babo. Delano describes the third figure as "a black of small stature" with "a rude face." Intermittent squints at the Spanish captain by Babo has Delano compare the small Black man to "a shepherd's dog." Babo's looks at Cereno seem to meld "sorrow and affection" (120) in the view of Delano.

The American captain has fixed ideas about Blacks. They prevent him from catching hints that the slaves are in charge of the ship. His reasoning echoes the thoughts of the regular old salt in *The Heroic Slave*. Delano believes Blacks are by nature menial and musical. In his mind, they lack the ingenuity necessary to pull off and cover up an insurrection. With training from whites, he supposes, they make delightful servants and faithful companions. He imagines that Babo embodies the ideal sort of Black—handy and devoted to pleasing his master.

On the *San Dominick*, Delano reminds himself, "The whites . . . by nature, were the shrewder race" (180). He supposes that Blacks have "a certain easy cheerfulness, harmonious in every glance and gesture; as though God had set the whole negro to some pleasant tune" (200). They possess, he thinks, a "docility" that stems "from the unaspiring contentment of a limited mind." He adds, Blacks own a "susceptibility of bland attachment" that is every so often inherent in "indisputable inferiors." In the past, when the captain has "chanced to have a black sailor" on a ship with him, he has been "on chatty and half-gamesome terms with him." Delano takes "to negroes, not philanthropically, but genially, just as other men to Newfoundland dogs" (200–1).

Seeing color as a sign of character, Delano is predisposed to marvel at the attention that Babo gives Cereno. Watching the slave prepare to shave the Spanish captain, Delano drifts into a flight of fancy about Black qualities. He muses, "there is something in the negro which, in a peculiar way, fits him for avocations about one's person" (199). The American captain believes that "most negroes are natural valets and hair-dressers; taking to the comb and brush congenially as to the castinets." It also appears to Delano that Black barbers have "a smooth tact about them," involving "a marvelous, noiseless, gliding briskness, not ungraceful in this way, singularly pleasing to behold." He envisions white men taking to their heart's Black slaves, "almost to the exclusion of the entire white race," because Blacks are born with a wonderful potential to provide gratifying service (199–200). As Babo finishes sharpening the razor to give Cereno a close shave, Delano is beside himself with admiration for the little fellow. The American captain considers it an unfortunate accident when Babo nicks the Spaniard with the blade, drawing drops of blood.

Blinded by his beliefs, Delano misreads successive indications of trouble on the *San Dominick*. He pays little mind to the grizzled old Black men, crouched on the ship at the four different points of a compass, picking oakum, and eyeing the rowdy swarm like sentinels alert on guard. His observation of six other Blacks scouring hatchets and clashing them at intervals like cymbals assures him that Blacks have a talent for spicing up mindless labor with music. He observes a Black boy stabbing a white boy and he chalks up the incident to child's play stemming from a lack of discipline imposed by Cereno. The sight of Atufal, alone, a dark mass of brawn, paraded on deck in shackles, alarms Delano. The American captain's unrealistic association of color with character puts his life at risk.

In the eyes of Delano, people come in three shades. His outlook conforms to the worldview expressed by Benjamin Franklin in *Observations Concerning the Increase of Mankind*, in which the Founding Father divided people into white, black, or tawny bands. From Delano's perspective, intelligence and shrewdness are the chief endowments of the first type. Inanity and servility distinguish the second variety. The tawny kind is set apart by a proclivity for sentimentality and intrigue. Delano situates Cereno in the last group and Babo of course in the second collection.

Taking the tan Spanish captain as a perfect example, Delano holds, "These Spaniards are all an odd set; the very word Spaniard has a curious," conspiratorial, "twang to it" (188–89). The American captain ponders, "How unlike we are made" (145). He starts out by judging Cereno as inscrutable, as the Spaniard's stances seem to shift between "incivility" and "duplicity." In the beginning, when Cereno airs "a sort of sour and gloomy disdain," Delano "in charity" attributes the behavior to "mental distress" caused by the fury of the powerful storm, which Cereno blames for all the disorder aboard the *San Dominick* (124–26). The Spanish captain sports a frilly wardrobe that Delano rates as indicative of a man whose mettle is soft. As time wears on, the behavior of Cereno is ever more puzzling, and its strangeness is heightened by his unexpected excuse for a retreat to his quarters. "From something suddenly suggested by the man's air, the mad idea" enters "Captain Delano's mind, that Don Benito's plea of indisposition, in withdrawing below, was but a pretense" to conceal the development of a plot (179–80). Bewildered, Delano asks:

> Could then Don Benito be any way in complicity with the blacks? But they were too stupid. Besides, who ever heard of a white so far a renegade as to apostatize from his very species almost, by leaguing in against it with negroes? (180)

Delano ignores the evidence of his senses that tells him his judgments are skewed. Beyond reason, he clings to the notion that Blacks lack the intelligence to outwit whites. He maintains confidence that whites by birth are shrewd and Blacks are stupid. Meanwhile, tawny people he deems too fickle to trust. It is beyond his comprehension that Babo is the conductor of an orchestrated charade in which Cereno acts as the little Black man's puppet. *Benito Cereno* comes close to the end before Delano realizes Babo has been holding Cereno hostage. The American captain remains oblivious to the danger he faces until Babo flourishes a dagger with an eye to stab Cereno for getting out of hand.

Delano conveys the conventional white perspective in the era of Black bondage. Through him, Melville's novella ridicules the imperious attitude toward Blacks sustained by contemporary whites. In addition to the portrayal of the American captain, B*enito Cereno* is flush with allusions to ancient African culture that mocks the assumption that Blacks have forever lived in want of savvy. Delano, for instance, compares the four gray oakum pickers to the Sphinx. He regards the hatchet polishers as Ashanti wizards. At one point, he feels escorted by a Caffre honor guard. Also, Atufal seems to him like an imposing marble statue of a gatekeeper posted at the door of an Egyptian crypt. In truth, the narrative sprinkles hints that Africans in the past were clever, and so one should expect the same of their descendants.

Delano would grant that Blacks have great imaginations. The man would offer their supposed passion for making music as proof. However, he would miss that they are much brighter than dogs and in dire straits well able to outshine whites. He would expect Blacks to waste time on flights of fancy without guidance from whites. A description of Babo as a revolutionary on par with George Washington would make Delano laugh. The American captain would fail to count the slave uprising abroad the *San Dominick* as equal to the American Revolution. He would position Blacks a notch below tawny types of whom he would remain wary. *Benito Cereno* illustrates that Delano reflects a precarious grasp of different complexions.

The actual reason for the mutiny aboard the *San Dominick* hovers over the head of Delano. "With scales dropped from his eyes" (238), at the sight of Babo wielding a knife, his "long-benighted mind" has "a flash of revelation" (237) unmasking the little fellow's cunning. Delano, yet and still, does not scrap his disposition to look at other colors in a condescending manner. As his well-armed crew from the *Bachelor's Delight* assaults the *San Dominick* on his orders to suppress the rebellion, he regards his men as exemplars of a real trooper. But he describes the Blacks fighting for liberty and justice as "ferocious" bandits and "delirious black dervishes" (238). Following the capture and trial of Babo, the American captain grants area authorities the right to chop off the Black man's head and stick it on a stake.

It bothers Delano that Cereno remains melancholy in the aftermath of the mutiny. The American captain reminds the Spaniard, "You are saved." Flabbergasted by Cereno's continued depression, Delano implores, "What has cast such a shadow upon you?" Cereno replies, "The negro" (268). The

Spaniard suggests he has come to see that souls are not signified by the shade of their skin. Cereno strains to broaden Delano's understanding of different hues. The tan figure tries to share the lesson that he has learned, which has opened his eyes to the riskiness of tying character to color. He reflects, "So far may even the best man err, in judging the conduct of one with the recesses of whose condition he is not acquainted" (267).

Benito Cereno in unison with *The Heroic Slave* placed the best shot at justice for enslaved Blacks in lifting the scales from the eyes of whites, which blinded them to the humanity they shared with Blacks. Both stories strove to do the trick in their time. Each tale features a hero whose deeds assail the beliefs behind Black bondage. *The Heroic Slave* endorses judging people according to their objectives and obstacles, which in due course is how Listwell happens to appraise Washington. *Benito Cereno*, leaving Delano's eyes unopened by Babo's swift strokes, gives a warning that categorizing individuals on the basis of their appearance invites havoc. The American captain stands in consort with the regular old salt in *The Heroic Slave* as well as most white writers of the antebellum age who thought as Simms, Kennedy, and Stowe about Blacks. In the face of whites, flush with faith that they were born better than Blacks, Douglass and Melville realized, African Americans had resort to smooth operating for the sake of their dignity. In sum, the authors of *Benito Cereno* and *The Heroic Slave* saw that Blacks in the era of Black bondage sought to make the best of a bad situation by putting on shows staged to fool whites.

Game of Charades

Old salts tack to the winds as found.
Overblown sails run ships aground.

William Shakespeare understood human spheres as dramatic settings where people behave as actors in a play. The bard could have added that all of the players are expected to abide by a given script with an end in store for them. He might have observed that social orders set the stage, compose the score, and distribute the scripts. Shakespeare could have said that societies work as a masquerade with roles that people are trained to performed for a chance not to kick the bucket waiting in the wings. Samuel Clemens, behind the *nom de plume* of Mark Twain, in *The Adventures of Huckleberry Finn* (1884) vouched for the related perception, as the title character adopts the part of an underdog that was assigned to Blacks and adapted by them.

Twain's celebrated novel uncovers the way of acting that Blacks used to combat the ravages of slavery. Through undertones, the acerbic writer's work compares the unveiled behavior to a manner in which women have resisted the imposition of patriarchy. A century before Judith Butler, in "Performative Acts and Gender Constitution," defined sexual identities as social fabrications, Twain discerned that male domination induced women to promote their interests by putting on false fronts in the presence of imperious men. The picture of Judith Loftus presented in *The Adventures of Huckleberry Finn* renders her a model of a person with a developed talent for improvising ways to work around male chauvinists. Meanwhile, the portrayal of Jim on the run is an excellent illustration of a figure with a cultivated knack for playing tricks on white supremacists.

Patriarchal impressions have bothered woman since long before Aristotle found them in want of reason. Grating on their last nerves, such views have goaded woman to undertake acts of resistance. Margaret Fuller professed in *Woman in the 19th Century* (1845) that "there exist in the minds of men a tone of feeling toward women as toward slaves" (Schneir 65). It follows that Twain had cause to sense a connection between female behavior and Black conduct. During the historical period covered by *The Adventures of Huckleberry Finn*, the given groups were plagued by oppression. Both had to deal with exasperating restrictions that provoked them to think up ruses to abate the galling circumstances. They had something in common with the caged bird represented in the poem "Sympathy" (1899) by Dunbar:

> I know what the caged bird feels, alas!
> When the sun is bright on the upland slopes;
> When the wind stirs soft through the springing grass,
> And the river flows like a stream of glass;
> When the first bird sings and the first bud opes,
> And the faint perfume from its chalice steals—
> I know what the caged bird feels!
> (*Lyrics of the Hearthside* 40)

In *The Gender Knot*, Allan G. Johnson pinpointed the source of the traditional trouble confronted by women. He identified patriarchy as the root of the difficulty that females faced. The social system sustains a "*male-dominated, male-identified, and male-centered*" culture entailing "as one of its key aspects the oppression of women" (158). Johnson wrote, "At the heart of patriarchy is the oppression of women, which takes several forms" (162). He offered a reason for them to develop a subtle side under the sway of the system. "Many women, of course," he held, "do dare to see and speak the truth, but they are always in danger of being attacked and discredited in order to maintain the silence" (163).

Ruth Hubbard, in agreement with Judith Butler, encouraged regarding sexual identities as mere social roles. "There is no 'natural' human sexuality," submitted Hubbard in *The Politics of Women's Biology*. "This is not to say that our sexual feelings are 'unnatural,' she argued, "but that whatever feelings and activities our society interprets as sexual are channeled from birth into socially acceptable forms of expression" (65). She wrote that "each of us writes our own sexual script out of the range of our experiences." No "script is inborn or biologically given" (66). In sum, for her, human sexuality amounts to parts picked up and played under the direction of custom.

Jean Baker Miller asserted in *Toward a New Psychology of Women* that subjugated groups in general and dominated women in particular are pressed by their position in society to mask dissatisfaction with their predicament. "A subordinate group has to concentrate on basic survival," observed Miller. "Accordingly, direct, honest reaction to destructive treatment is avoided." Such parties are prompted by social standards to steer clear of blatant initiatives to improve their lot. "It is not surprising then," Miller supposed, "that a subordinate group resorts to disguised and indirect ways of acting and reacting." She noted, "Folktales, black jokes, and women stories are often based on how the wily peasant or sharecropper outwitted the rich landowner, boss, or husband." The related type of narratives, Miller concluded, revolve around the means by which an underdog fools an "overlord" without being caught in the act (113). Huck Finn's account of his adventures in the Old South lends considerable credence to this judgment.

Huck dwells on the margins of a society dominated by white males trained to think that their shade and sex mark them made to play leading roles in the social order. Custom calls for women to act in support of the white men. On the social ladder, white women sit a rung above Black men and stand two steps ahead of Black women. White males grow accustomed to rank Blacks a squat notch higher than livestock. Tradition demands that Blacks perform bit parts in the interest of white men. Stepping out of line leads to excoriation or exile, if not execution.

Huckleberry Finn is a motherless child whose father has deserted him. His orphan status has prevented the boy from picking up lessons that his community means for him to learn. As a result, he grapples with bewilderment over what he feels and what he is expected to feel. Custom directs him to act in the manner of Tom Sawyer, who conducts himself as a white boy entitled by a sublime imagination to treat white women and enslaved Blacks as simple toys created to please him. For Huck, taking the attitude to heart is hard. Over a fair stretch of his narrative, he favors an actor cast in a role that mismatches him. Huck is deeply lonesome at the start of his story. Frustration hounds him like the angst of an actor stuck waiting in the wings for a juicy part. The boy is conflicted time and again about his behavior until he comes out of a fog during his passage on the raft with Jim down the Mississippi River. Afterward, he takes his cue from Miss Watson's "nigger."

In the beginning, directions from whites around Huck leave him mystified. They strike him as ridiculous. Conduct prized by his community at length comes across as phony to him. Huck develops contempt for titles and types that are supposed to elicit awe. In time, Tom, a model white boy in the town, switches in Huck's view from a smart kid to a simple kook. An alleged fugitive on the run, in effect, captures the respect of Huck. The outlook of the boy, which shifts like a river current headed upstream, serves as a suitable vessel for a dry exploration of a social order that anchors people to parts based on shades and shapes.

The women in Huck's world, as a rule, stay at home and mind their manners. Their actions render it apparent that they are regimented to count the welfare of others as their utmost concern. The women's disposition is exemplified by the Widow Douglas, who takes Huck into her home with an aim to socialize the boy and keep him on the straight and narrow. Her sister, Miss Watson, who lives with her, backs up her sense of duty with stern measures. Around the sisters, the orphan stays ill at ease. For him, living in their home is close to being buried alive in a tomb. By implication, Huck proposes that the lives of the women would be better spent if they thought less of acting as caretakers for his sake.

Huck recalls, "The Widow Douglas she took me for her son, and allowed she would sivilize me." He regrets that "it was rough living in the house all the time, considering how dismal regular and decent the widow was in all her ways." She drives him up a wall with her efforts to convert him into a "respectable" (8) boy like Tom. Soon, Huck cannot tolerate the situation any longer and he starts to hit the road in search of freedom from the widow. Nevertheless, Tom tracks him down with news of a plan to start a gang of marauders that he welcomes the orphan to join if Huck forgets his plan to fly the coop.

The promise of adventure put forward by Tom leads Huck back to the custody of the widow, whose identity, besides serving as a surrogate mother, rest on her survival as a wife who has lost her husband. Be that as it may, by Huck's account, her dedication to decorum sticks her in a tight groove that turns her into a fake paragon of propriety. She presses him to wear tailored clothes to supper that make him fidget and sweat; she has to say grace before every meal; and, in addition, she expects Huck to be thankful for a plate of grub all "cooked by itself," despite his taste for "a barrel of odds and ends" where "things get mixed up, and the juice kind of swaps around," because, then, [he] feels, "the things go better" (9). The widow prays for Huck to emulate Moses, but the boy means to "take no stock in dead people" (9). She pitches morals in Black and white terms. While she enjoys a pinch of snuff, she frowns on Huck's wish to smoke a pipe. Huck figures that the widow is dead wrong about what should make someone tick.

Huck develops the same misgivings about Miss Watson. He depicts the sister as a pretty uptight person. She views the world as a sphere devoid of gray areas. He remembers her as a "tolerable slim old maid, with goggles on," who rides him about his posture and behavior:

> "Miss Watson would say, 'Don't put your feet up there, Huckleberry;' and 'Don't scrunch up like that, Huckleberry—set up straight;' and pretty soon she would say, 'Don't gap and stretch like that, Huckleberry—why don't you try to behave?' " (9–10)

Intolerant of dissent, Miss Watson warns Huck that he is not about to "go around all day long with a harp and sing" in "the good place," with her after he dies if he refuses to follow her rules while they live under the same roof. He is ready to go to "the bad place" to escape her "pecking," which "got tiresome" (10). He confides:

> "Well, I couldn't see no advantage in going where she was going, so I made up my mind I wouldn't try for it. But I never said so, because it would only make trouble, and wouldn't do no good." (10)

At night, after Miss Watson with her widowed sister, by rote, fetches "the niggers in and had prayers, and then everybody [is] off to bed" (10), Huck, by a window in his room, feels, the place is "as still as death" (11). A grave lonesomeness shrouds him. Rustling leaves mourn in his ears. Some owl hoots about some dead body. A whippoorwill and dog cry about a body soon to die. Huck imagines he hears a ghost in the woods unable to rest for want of understanding. The boy senses the two white sisters sustain in sum a deadening norm.

One person in Huck's story performs the role of a white woman devoted to being a helping hand, with her tongue in her cheek. She is too wise to let anyone pull the wool over her eyes. Her name is Judith Loftus. Huck meets the lady while he scouts for news about himself and Jim after the two of them have taken shelter together on Jackson Island. Starting to fall under the influence of the slave, Huck puts on a dress to hide his identity and assumes a name given to girls. Although Loftus peeks Huck's game, she plays dumb; the woman fills him in on a party of men forming a posse to hunt for Jim because the "nigger," against the law, has taken flight from slavery. Before she sends the disguised lad on his way, in observation of custom, she offers Huck fare prior to drifting into a reverie that relays more than it relates. The boy remembers that "the woman fell to talking about how hard times was, and how poor they had to live, and how the rats was as free as if they owned the place." A den of rats infests her home; Huck sees she is "right" (82) about the pervasion of a pack in the house. Still, her musing gathers a particular air of forewarning when she urges, "Keep your eye on the rats" (83). Eventually, she lets Huck know she is on to him, and then she allows him to leave with helpful tips on how to act like a girl so that he "might fool men" (85), betraying a furtive opposition to patriarchy.

A daughter of a proud white family stirred by tugs at her heartstrings makes a cavalier move. The girl elopes with a boy raised by kinfolk hostile to her own. Her deed inflames a feud, igniting a storm of fury that explodes into a terrible bloodbath from heavy gunfire. Named Sophia, the white girl is guilty in the surrounding community of breaking the peace by claiming a right not granted her. The reactions of the two clans involved, the Grangerfords and Shepherdsons, sicken Huck. He feels it is mad for men to shoot one another over the desire of a female to choose her own mate.

The average white female character in Huck's narrative never pursues a single end for her own sake. She looks to white men for guidance. Her inclinations allow her to become an easy mark for con artists who amount to dirty rats. Mary Jane Wilks epitomizes the type at issue. She showers men with kindness. Her dead uncle has left her a fortune to share with her two sisters, Susan and Joanna. She risks losing her inheritance as she buys the falsehoods peddled by the swindlers who bill themselves the duke and dauphin.

The royal impostors intend to fleece Mary Jane and her sisters. The rogues pretend to be two long-lost brothers of the deceased stricken with grief. In the presence of the phonies, Mary Jane retains a subservient posture and cajoles her siblings to do likewise. She welcomes the frauds to a chunk of her heritance. The teenager says, "Take this six thousand dollars, and invest for me and my sisters any way you want to, and don't give us no receipt for it" (219). Then Mary Jane serves the villains food and provides them with shelter, including giving "her own room" (220) to the Dauphin posing as Uncle Harvey. The impostors would have bilked the teenager and left her high and dry save the growing sense of morality in Huck that leads him to foil the plot of the crooks. His conduct suggests Mary Jane needs a pointer from Loftus to discover how to act slow on the uptake with an eye out for dirty rats.

Huck's narrative advances a theme shared a century later by Kurt Vonnegut in *Mother Night* (1962). The novelist wrote, "We are what we pretend to be, so we must be careful about what we pretend to be" (v). In other words, people become the parts that they play and pay a price for roles not taken with a grain of salt. Tom's Aunt Sally serves as a good example. Abiding by custom as the wife of a white male farmer who observes propriety, the woman acts pacified by letting her husband sort things out for her; still, she is plagued by butterflies in her stomach; her anxiety is evident when Tom goes missing. Huck says, "Aunt Sally was a good *deal* uneasy; but Uncle Silas he said there warn't no occasion to be"; hence, "she had to be satisfied." However, "she said she'd set up for [Tom] a while anyway and keep a light burning so he could see it" (258), proving her husband's advice has failed to ease her mind.

White men in Huck's story, trained to pretend they belong by birth at the top of the heap, swell with pride and dispense with compassion. On the whole, they possess a feeling of entitlement that inclines them to grow "awful cruel" (294). Tom borders on a budding shoot planted by a yeoman in muddy soil to replenish a staple crop. His upbringing has accustomed him to judge others by their skin and sex. Sandy-in-shade Spaniards and camel-in-color Arabs are jokes to Tom. Blacks are wonderful playthings. He believes women are easy to fool. His dearth of empathy is evident, as he never fails to trifle with Jim. It is significant that his wild wishes to pull the Black man's leg just about cost Tom a limb.

Tom enters the story out of the darkness blackening the yard outside Miss Watson's place. At the time, Huck is parked by his bedroom window hankering to take flight from the air of death around the house. The arriving kid is seen as the star of his peer group. He stands for a true hero by local standards. Tom seems ordained to save Huck from suffering gloom. It looks like he has a bright idea for Huck to enjoy a lively escapade out of the house in the dead of night. But all he means for them to do is toy with Jim.

Tom believes that Blacks are "niggers" bedded in the base of society as supports built by nature to work for whites. The instant he spots Jim, the kid sees a bullseye for a potshot. Nonetheless, in the picture painted by Huck of "Miss Watson's big nigger, named Jim," the Black man sits "in the kitchen door" with "a light behind him" (13), which in effect outlines the slave with a halo. The first impressions of the Black man held by Huck and Tom foreshadow the divide due to come between the boys that is radical in extent. Neither boy starts with a qualm about playing a trick on the "nigger." Huck though after a while develops scruples with respect to such conduct, as he determines that it is fiendish nonsense. The first time Huck crosses Jim's path in the company of Tom, he follows the lead of his mate and trifles with the slave; during their final moments shared with Jim in the story, Huck plays up to Tom for the sake of the "nigger."

Conceitedness fueling cruelty brands Tom. It escapes Huck's notice in the beginning. Tom's true colors surface when he brings together a secret circle of the boys in town with pledges and oaths. The gang's modus operandi is foolish pranks such as springing "out of the woods" and "charging down on hog-drivers and women in carts taking garden stuff to market." They make believe that they are a bunch of robbers for "about a month, and then" Huck and all of the other boys resign. The gang, Huck recalls, "hadn't robbed nobody, hadn't killed any people, but only just pretended." He surmises, he "couldn't see no profit in it" (22–23).

Tom looks to bring the gang back together with a report of a caravan involving "Spanish merchants and rich A-rabs" going "to camp in Cave Hollow with two hundred elephants, and six hundred camels, and over a thousand 'sumter' mules, all loaded down with di'monds." Standing certain his group can "lick such a crowd of Spaniards and A-rabs" and loot their rich convoy without a snag, despite "a guard of four hundred soldiers," Tom betrays that he feels a good shade better than the targets of his proposed ambush. Huck agrees to return to the fold, for he wants "to see the camels and elephants," and he is "on hand next day, Saturday, in the ambuscade; and when [he gets] the word [he rushes] out of the woods and down the hill" (23). He laments:

> But there warn't no Spaniards and A-rabs, and there warn't no camels nor no elephants. It warn't anything but a Sunday-school picnic, and only a primer-class at that. We busted it up, and chased the children up the hollow; but we never got anything but some doughnuts and jam, though Ben Rogers got a rag doll, and Jo Harper got a hymn-book and a tract; and then the teacher charged in, and made us drop everything and cut. I didn't see no di'monds, and I told Tom Sawyer so. (23)

Huck confides, "Tom Sawyer said I was a numskull" (24). In turn the orphan challenges the gang leader's stance, which, he implies, justifies mean and stupid acts. Huck distances himself from his playmate, and thus brings loneliness to haunt him once again, and even more so once a spooky sign materializes.

In a pile of snow on the Widow Douglass's front yard, Huck notices a trail of boot prints with a cross in the left heel. He realizes that the tracks belong to Pap, the person who happens to be his father. Although tradition commands children to honor their parents, there is no love lost between the boy and Pap. The combination of conceitedness and cruelty that lurks in Tom mushrooms in Huck's father. Pap is a deadbeat dad who feels that his shade and sex entitle him to his heart's desire. His character is reflected by an eerie cast that excites trepidation when the boy catches him sitting in his room. Huck notes that Pap has "no color in his face." The white man's mug is "white" beyond compare to a horrifying degree, "a white to make a body sick, a white to make a body's flesh crawl," a hideous "fish-belly white" (31).

Pap has a warped sense of paternity, twisted by conceitedness. He knows Huck has money in the bank. The father wants the funds for himself. Pap calls for his son to empty his account and hand him the cash. The boy has gotten funds as a reward for a kind turn. If Pap gets hold of it, he is sure to waste every penny because he is a tramp who lives for shots of whiskey. For safekeeping, Huck signs over the funds to Judge Thatcher. Anyway, the step stops Pap from getting the cash, but it leaves Huck stuck in a shack at the mercy of his father. After Pap fails to browbeat the money out of the judge and is rebuffed by the law, he returns to the cabin, drunk out of his head and swearing he has been denied his natural right to have his way.

The deadbeat breaks into a tirade against the government; the boozy bum claims he has a right to his son's bounty. Next, upholding the local bias counting Blacks as inferior beings belonging in slavery, Pap complains about the liberty of "a free nigger" in town from Ohio, a light kind of Black, "most as white as a white man," with "the whitest shirt on you ever see." The interloper is a professor "who could talk all kinds of languages, and knowed everything," and by law cannot be "put up at auction and sold" because he has not been in Missouri for six months, which to Pap is a travesty; what's worse is that the Black man can vote in Ohio. Seeing it is Election Day, Pap has had a mind to vote, if he "warn't too drunk to get there." Hearing that the professor enjoys the right at home, the drunk declares, "I'll never vote agin as long as I live" (41–42). His words of course drip with irony, since he stays too pickled ever to exercise the franchise or come up with the discipline to become as a professor of any subject other than the maddening effects of the whiskey.

In the dark of night, an evil spirit pours out of Pap. He guzzles whiskey until he succumbs to a bout of delirium tremens. The tramp trembles and hallucinates. Pap spooks Huck. He stalks the boy with a blade. Pap calls his son the "Angel of Death" (44) and threatens to stab him. Horror-struck by the malice, the boy ducks and dodges his dad until Pap peters out and slips into a deep sleep. It is a nightmare that spurs Huck to conjure up a plan to escape the custody of his vain and vicious parent; the boy fakes his own death and skips town in search of good company.

"Pap" in *The Adventures of Huckleberry Finn* signifies an individual unworthy of respect. His behavior prompts Huck to take no stock in titles. Ensuing events bring the boy to get that no name names a soul. Conduct discloses much more character than a designation. Huck soon gathers that even bearing the title of duke or king never warrants an automatic bow. The orphan boy also realizes, through contact with the Grangerford patriarch, that a man who bears a title for an army officer does not merit an unconditional salute. Most of all, he learns to brush aside the belief prevalent in his neck of the woods that the word "nigger" identifies a breed formed to serve as a tool or toy for the benefit of a master race.

Huck starts off seeing Colonel Grangerford as "a gentleman all over." With awe, the boy studies the colonel's dark pale complexion, "high nose," and "blackest kind of eyes" (140). He thinks the man has a charming family, even though the son "Buck and his ma" after meals "smoked cob pipes" (133). The boy figures he has never known anyone of more "quality," except for the Widow Douglass, maybe. From Huck's initial perspective, it seems that everything about the colonel smacks of nobility, especially the fact that he owns "a lot of farms, and over a hundred niggers" (142). Grangerford presents Huck with Jack a slave boy for the orphan's personal use, which signals, beneath a genteel veneer, that the gentleman conceals a substantial sum of madness prone to provoke the malice that skews Pap.

The feud that flares up between the Grangerfords and the Shepherdsons following the decision of the Grangerford lass Sophia to elope with the Shepherdson lad Harney alters Huck's opinion of the colonel and his family. Before the rival clans engage in senseless slaughter, they attend church together. With guns on hand, they listen to a "good sermon" about "brotherly love" in addition to "good works, and free grace" (145). The Sunday homily lacks the power to stem the tide of bloodshed that ensues. In honor of their heritage, the fathers and sons of the hostile clans, strapped with guns, shoot to kill as many members of the other side as possible. Up a tree, Huck witnesses the mayhem. It turns his stomach and leaves him dying to get away from the "quality" (142) folks.

Social satire packs *The Adventures of Huckleberry Finn*. Streams of irony course through the text. The material mocks strains of madness and malevolence that spread across the heartland around the Civil War. Since Huck's initial remarks about characters are contradicted nine times out of ten by their conduct, his first impressions bring on second thoughts about everyone. For instance, Huck showers Colonel Grangerford with praise until the colonel charges his clan into the gruesome gunfight with the Shepherdsons. Upon making the acquaintance of the gentlemen, Huck admires him; in the aftermath of the bloodshed, he abhors him. Eventually, Colonel Grangerford looks crazed by a conceitedness that stokes cruelty.

Titles in the tale are vital elements of the satire. Figures with noble designations turn out to be ignoble characters, while ignoble names, "nigger" in particular, designate noble souls. Again, by custom, the titles "duke" and "king" call for treating the bearers as noblemen. While, at first, Huck addresses the fake royals as "your Grace" and "your Majesty," once the boy knows them well, he forsakes the courtesy. The duke and dauphin introduce themselves as exiles from a foreign kingdom. In truth, they are dirty rats native to the land who drift from town to town in search of people on whom to prey. They serve to flag as sheer folly any tendency to take stock in titles. The white men are so lowdown they plan to steal a dead man's money from his next of kin; to boot, the duke and dauphin have no scruples about selling Jim down the river for a pile of cash. It is ironic what the villains allege about Black people as the crooks plot to steal the inheritance of the Wilks sisters from under their noses. The king declines to stash the loot in Mary Jane's room seeing as he supposes a Black servant will find the dough and swipe a bit:

> "You know the nigger that does up the rooms will get an order to box these duds up and put 'em away; and do you reckon a nigger can run across money and not borrow some of it?" (228)

Regardless, the conduct of the dirty rats earns them a ride out of town on a rail with tar and feathers.

Miss Watson's "nigger" Jim picks up the true colors of the duke and dauphin on sight. He tries to alert Huck. In reference to them, Jim says, "But, Huck, dese kings o' ourn is reglar rapscallions; dat's jist what dey is; dey's reglar rapscallions" (199). The boy has yet to see enough to catch the Black man's drift. Jim is a mature adult. With prudence, he has suffered bondage. The system has trained him to say what he says and do what he does in order to appease or amuse whites and in the process advance his own interests. He has honed a mode of survival where he sizes up others to present a front formed to win him their fancy. The logic behind the approach dawns on Huck fully in the middle of his tale.

Jim stomachs slavery until he hears that Miss Watson means to put him on the auction block for sale down the Mississippi to a slaveholder in the deep South where the master class works slaves to death for a fast buck. Besides threatening to separate Jim from his spouse and daughter, his sale portends he may end up a basket case in a tight spot at best. The prospects impel the grown man to get the lead out and hit the road as a last-ditch attempt to keep body and soul together. His spirit affects Huck. The orphan converts into an understudy to the Black man, able to lead others down the garden path with an eye out for his own good. It is a gradual process peaking when the boy makes up his mind to set Jim free by improvised means. In the run-up to the climax, Huck is a sucker for cruel, conceited posers including Tom and Colonel Grangerford as well as the duke and dauphin.

Huck only begins to follow Jim's example after the Black man delivers the hair-ball prophecy, which imparts Jim's conduct code on the sly. At the moment, the boy stands shaken at a crossroads over the eventual return of his father. He craves advice about how to handle the return of Pap from the wilderness. Jim charges the boy a coin for his counsel and then proceeds to take the edge off the child's worry. The adult intimates that decent and decadent drives propel people. Jim spouts common sense:

> "Yo' ole father doan' know yit what he's a-gwyne to do. Sometimes he spec he'll go 'way, en den agin he spec he'll stay. De bes' way is to res' easy en let de ole man take his own way. Dey's two angels hoverin' roun' 'bout him. One uv 'em is white en shiny, en t'other one is black. De white one gits him to go right a little while, den de black one sail in en bust it all up. A body can't tell yit which one gwyne to fetch him at de las'. But you is all right. You gwyne to have considable trouble in yo' life, en considable joy. Sometimes you gwyne to git hurt, en sometimes you gwyne to git sick; but every time you's gwyne to git well agin. Dey's two gals flyin' 'bout you in yo' life. One uv 'em's light en t'other one is dark. One is rich en t'other is po'. You's gwyne to marry de po' one fust en de rich one by en by. You wants to keep 'way fum de water as much as you kin, en don't run no resk, 'kase it's down in de bills dat you's gwyne to git hung." (29)

In essence, Jim directs the youth to "res' easy." Like a father, the Black man recommends Huck bear in mind that he is bound to confront rich and poor, light and dark, smooth and rough patches in life, but he is going to be "all right" so long as he stays on an even keel and finds a way around treacherous shoals.

Alone together on Jackson Island, Huck and the runaway slave form a bond. The boy is impressed when it rains after Jim forecasts the event from the flight of birds. Huck says, "Jim knowed all kinds of signs" (64). Because Huck has been expected to see Jim as a "nigger" without a natural right to liberty, it bothers him to learn that the Black man is seeking to escape slavery. His misgivings abate while he communes on the island with the fugitive. It becomes evident in the wake of his reconnaissance mission in town, where he meets Loftus, that Huck has come to identify with Jim. Returning from his scouting trip, aware that a posse is being formed to hunt for Jim, Huck tells the Black man, "They're after us" (86).

Loneliness flees Huck while he floats on the river alone with Jim. Early on, their bond is tested at moments when the boy's superego checks his ego and propels him to engage in tomfoolery at the expense of the adult. Atmospheric pressures putting the screws on Huck incline him in spurts to treat the grown Black man as a plaything made for his pleasure. His monkey business stops, though, as their separation at night in the fog ends. In the aftermath of the given affair, the slave dresses the boy down, and Huck never again toys with him.

In reality, Jim plays along with Huck for as long as he can stand to indulge the boy. As a fugitive in a region where his skin color functions as a status symbol branding him unfit for freedom and better off in bondage to whites, Jim has to maintain the child's favor to have any real shot at pulling off a successful escape. So he does whatever it takes to keep the kid on his side. Jim is a smooth operator improvising a flight to freedom. While his heart can take it, he keeps up a servile guise, cloaking a shrewd gamesmanship. In his best interest, he humors Huck until the orphan gets on his last nerve. Then he bares his soul.

Like a loving father, Jim is worried sick about Huck's welfare during their separation in the fog. Afterward, he cannot stomach that the boy has been chewing over how to dupe and disgrace him. Jim quits acting the part of a dumb toy. He scolds Huck with the air of a disgusted parent. Pointing to debris on the raft, Jim declares, "Dat truck dah is *trash*; en trash is what people is dat puts dirt on de head er dey fren's en makes 'em ashamed." The upbraiding makes Huck "feel so mean" he is tempted to kiss Jim's "foot" (116) to make amends for his hurtful conduct. It snuffs out the boy's desire to trick the man. Huck confesses:

It was fifteen minutes before I could work myself up to go and humble myself to a nigger; but I done it, and I warn't ever sorry for it afterwards, neither. I didn't do him no more mean tricks, and I wouldn't done that one if I'd a knowed it would make him feel that way. (116–17)

At a later date, being lured to the swamp from the Grangerford manor by the slave boy Jack whom the colonel has given Huck as a present, the orphan begins to acquire a deep appreciation for the servile guise with which Jim cloaks a shrewd gamesmanship. Jack's performance on the road heading to the marsh, where Jim gives a wide berth to the Grangerfords, demonstrates the young "nigger" practices a mode of role-playing observed by the older one. Near in age to Huck, the Black boy puts on a masterful show for the white boy. Knowing he faces awful abuse if he is caught acting outside the boundaries prescribed for "niggers" and well aware facilitating a reunion between the orphan and the fugitive slave is a business in which he is not supposed to be "mixed up" (149), Jack transgresses the rules for Blacks with an act that gives him cover from charges of flouting convention. The Black boy baits Huck, offering, "if you'll come down into de swamp I'll show you a whole stack o' water-moccasins" (147). Jack behaves as if he wants to amuse the white boy, while he beckons him without beckoning him to Jim's hideout. After Jack has completed his mission, the fugitive slave says, "Dat Jack's a good nigger, en pooty smart" (149). Huck agrees:

> "Yes, he is. He ain't ever told me you was here; told me to come, and he'd show me a lot of water-moccasins. If anything happens he ain't mixed up in it. He can say he never seen us together, and it'll be the truth." (149)

The slaves in general about the Grangerford estate are engaged in a charade designed to pull the wool over the eyes of their masters. They have acted to hide Jim from detection in a spot where they know that dogs cannot track him. After work in the field, they bring him food to eat. At night, they give him reports on Huck's fortunes around the Grangerford household. Meanwhile, they afford Jim chances to patch up the raft and stock the vessel with pots, pans, and provisions. Through improvised means, the enslaved avoid having any of the Grangerfords catch them in the act of breaking the law against giving aid and comfort to a slave on the run. Their exploits attest, akin to Jack, that they are pretty smart.

In the long run, Jim proves to be a quick thinker. At times he seems like a coward or dummy. The Black man cowers and shivers at the first sight of Huck on Jackson Island. He also shudders at the idea of going aboard the shipwrecked *Walter Scott*. By standard measures, his speech sounds stupid. He expresses an appalling ignorance of the world beyond the perimeters of Miss Watson's circle. Nonetheless, there are always good reasons for his manners.

The want of a formal education has limited Jim's knowledge. He has been denied schooling by tradition, which holds "niggers" just worth teaching to obey white men. Jim's learning is restricted to the experience of being a slave around the Mississippi Delta. He presumes everyone is born to speak a dialect of his tongue because it is the only language that he has ever heard spoken. His actions indicate he is neither foolish nor fainthearted. On Jackson Island, the Black man has cause to believe Huck is a ghost when he encounters him. And the last thing he needs while he is on the run is to get caught snooping around the *Walter Scott* with a white boy. Jim lacks information, but not logic; all of his deeds make sense in light of his narrow background.

Although the runaway slave dons, at the direction of the duke, a "King Lear's outfit" made of a "long curtain-calico gown" plus "a white horse-hair wig and whiskers" on top of "theater paint" smeared around his "face and hands and ears and neck all over a dead, dull, solid blue" (203), which leaves him reminiscent of a wallflower, the acceptance of the garb does not certify Jim as a thick sap ready to be sucked dry for the pleasure of white men. Wearing the costume is a smart move on Jim's part. He is trying to escape slavery without seeming to be trying to escape slavery. The Black man needs to act obliging and guileless. Jim's success depends on looking like a dummy in the eyes of the duke and king, who would lose their tongue from the discovery that Jim has freedom on his mind. It is smart in effect for him to act daft and craven in order to seek liberty.

An ironic exchange between Huck and Jim about language illustrates that the Black man has limited awareness, but unlimited logic. Through a cogent refutation of Huck's argument about why the French speak French, Jim displays a capacity to employ deductive reasoning. Huck holds that it is "natural and right for a cat and a cow to talk different from us" and "natural and right for a *Frenchman* to talk different from us" (108), too. Having heard people speak only English, Jim initiates the following dialogue:

"Is a cat a man, Huck?"
"No."
"Well, den, dey ain't no sense in a cat talkin' like a man. Is a cow a man?—er is a cow a cat?"

"No, she ain't either of them."
"Well, den, she ain't got no business to talk like either one er the yuther of 'em. Is a Frenchman a man?"
"Yes."
"Well, den! Dad blame it, why doan' he talk like a man? You answer me dat!" (108–9)

Choosing to drop the subject, Huck thinks "it warn't no use wasting words—you can't learn a nigger to argue" (109). The statement of course is satirical because Jim's reasoning is sound.

A readiness to blame violations of convention on witches, a habit Jim shares with his enslaved fellows, bears out the conclusion that the runaway along with his peers has grown adept at shuckin' and jivin' to deflect responsibility for neglect to toe the line. The practice tells that Jim reads the minds of people as well as he deciphers the expressions of fowl on Jackson Island. Whites present in Huck's narrative, including the boy, believe in witches. When Huck kills a spider, he considers it bad luck that could bring witches after him. So Huck gets "up and [turns] around in [his] tracks three times and [crosses his] breast every time; and then [he ties] up a little lock of [his] hair with a thread to keep witches away" (11). In the Royal Nonesuch shows staged by the dirty rats who pretend to be blue bloods, the duke entertains white audiences by acting as if he has a gift for "dissipating witch spells" (169). Fanciful yarns about witches spun by Jim delight Tom, not to mention Huck. Faith in witches sets up white people to accept witchcraft as an excuse for Blacks stepping out of line.

The slave on the Phelps farm named Nat is quick to place the blame for bad form on witchcraft. Nat denounces witches for every step taken by him that falls outside the parameters allotted for "niggers." He sneaks hefty piles of food and drink to the shed where Jim is held. When conventional Tom catches him in the middle of making a delivery, Nat vows with a broad grin that the provisions on the tin pan in his hand are intended for a cursed dog on the farm. He attributes his motivation to the "pestering" (300) of witches. Later, Nat uses an alleged desire for company to ward off witches at night as his reason for getting mixed up in Tom's ridiculous pretense to set Jim free from prison on the Phelps farm. As Nat talks Tom out of giving him a senseless assignment, he manifests a talent for shuckin' and jivin' like crazy to avoid trouble. Nat feigns genuine gratitude for the kid's pardon and swears he is bound to worship the ground beneath Tom's feet. Slipping out of Tom's control, he contends, "Dad fetch it, I jis' wisht

I could git my han's on one er dem witches jis' wunst—on'y jis' wunst—it's all I'd ast. But mos'ly I wisht dey'd lemme 'lone, I does" (318).

By the climax of the story, Huck has adopted the style of the slaves. It is a slow but sure conversion, starting after Jim relates the "hair-ball prophecy," urging Huck to "res' easy," stay on an even keel, and sidestep hazards. Prior to his receipt of the divination from the Black man, Huck tries to meet the standards established for a white boy. He endeavors to follow the rules dictated by Miss Watson and her sister, the Widow Douglass. Huck swears allegiance to Tom and his gang. All of his efforts at conformity to the code of conduct prescribed for his shade and sex cause him grief and drive him to engage in blatant acts of rebellion. He bickers with the "tolerable slim old maid" (9) and her widowed sister; he even runs away from them. He questions Tom's judgment and quits his gang after the bogus raid on the make-believe alien caravan. By the time Huck fakes his own death to escape the cruelty of his father, he is done with situations that cramp his style; then he is open to taking his cue from Jim.

His trial run at putting on a false front with the guile used by the enslaved, like Jack, Nat, and Jim, occurs when he confronts Loftus dressed in the clothes of a girl. From there, he uses false identities to introduce himself to white people. The orphan goes by an assumed name upon meeting Loftus and adopts a different one around the Grangerford estate. After the mess in the fog, he plays it straight just with Jim. His change is complete once he presents himself to Aunt Sally as Tom.

Huck's tale crests with the detestable duke and dauphin having put Jim on the auction block and sold him for a fast buck. Huck refuses to let the Black man perish in slavery. The boy resolves to emancipate the man from bondage. He rejects the widespread faith of the region that saving a slave from slavery will shut somebody out of "the good place" and condemn such a person to eternity in "the bad place." Huck decides that if liberating Jim is wrong, he does not want to be right. He resolves, "I'll go to hell" (274), and confesses, "I went right along, not fixing up any particular plan, but just trusting to Providence to put the right words in my mouth when the time come; for I'd noticed that Providence always did put the right words in my mouth if I left it alone" (280). His confidence captures the spirit embodied by Jim and his fellows. Huck elects to rest easy and allow matters to take their course; he trusts that a wise way to save Jim will strike him if he strives to keep his wits about him.

In the parlance of the period, Huck comes to act like the "niggers" do to advance their interests. He forgets about seeking the approval of "quality" folks. Instead, he looks to take them for a ride. At bottom, he commits to concealing a clever gamesmanship with a conformist guise. His conversion is detectable in the wake of his fabricated tale about the steamboat accident that he concocts to cover his tracks on the Phelps farm. Believing the fib, Aunt Sally cries, "Good gracious! anybody hurt?" Knowing she counts Blacks as lesser sorts, Huck eases her mind by saying, "No'm. Killed a nigger." Aunt Sally is very relieved. "Well, it's lucky," she says, "because sometimes people do get hurt" (282).

Critics have judged that the surprise reappearance of Tom, during the denouement, is a flaw in the plot of the novel. For instance, although Ernest Hemingway praised the novel, he felt the ending spoiled the story. The writer said:

> All modern American literature comes from one book by Mark Twain called Huckleberry Finn. If you read it you must stop where the Nigger Jim is stolen from the boys. That is the real end. The rest is just cheating. But it's the best book we've had. All American writing comes from that. There was nothing before. There has been nothing as good since. (29)

About the ending of *Huckleberry Finn*, Bernard DeVoto in *Mark Twain at Work* stated, "In the whole reach of the English novel, there is no more abrupt or more chilling descent" (92). Thinking Huck pledges allegiance to Tom again, Lionel Trilling said, "It is a rather mechanical development of an idea, and yet some device is needed to permit Huck to return to his anonymity, to give up the role of hero, to fall into the background which he prefers, for he is modest in all things and could not well endure the attention and glamour which attend a hero at a book's end" (xv-xvi). Introducing an edition of the novel, T. S. Eliot said, "Readers sometimes deplore the fact that this story descends to the level of *Tom Sawyer* from the moment that Tom himself re-appears." Wishing to justify the supposed flaw in the novel, Eliot insists, "It is right that the mood of the end of the book should bring us back to that of the beginning" (xiii). Leo Marx thought that the conclusion of the work denotes a "failure of nerve" on the part of Twain; "The unhappy truth about the ending of *Huckleberry Finn* is that the author, having revealed the tawdry nature of the culture of the great valley, yielded to its essential complacency" (319–40).

Such claims suggest Huck fails to grow and change because in the final bit he goes along with Tom's antics. They overlook the effect that slaves like Nat, Jack, and Jim have had on the orphan. The criticism overlooks

Huck's dumbfounded responses to Tom's inane plans to free Jim, derived from literature like Alexandre Dumas's *The Count of Monte Cristo* (1888). Huck obliges Tom, for he figures it is the only way to secure the "respectable" kid's aid in snatching a "nigger out of slavery" (298). In truth, Huck aches to "tell Tom how [they'd] overdone this thing, and what a thundering hornet's-nest [they'd] got [themselves] into, so [they] could stop fooling around straight off, and clear out with Jim" (346).

The story does not finish with Tom as a hero and Huck as his faithful sidekick. They maintain the same shade and sex, but their outlooks clash. Tom is bent on being amused by Jim; Huck is intent on doing right by the Black man. The two boys work at odds with one another, which Huck knows, but Tom does not. Their relationship is comparable to the connection between a conceited slaveholder and careful slave. Huck's adventures with Jim have washed away his respect for Tom. Above all, Huck sees his fellow white boy making a laughingstock of himself with his kooky shenanigans. Huck can no longer abide by the customs that condition white men to intern Blacks on the bottom rung of society a level below white women. Huck has grown loyal to Jim alone.

Twain built a moral compass into the frame of *Huckleberry Finn*. It points in a direction diametrical to the outlook owned by Tom. Its orientation is undeniable once Tom's monkey business gets him shot. His heartless disregard for Jim lands him where he takes a bullet in his leg. At that point, he amounts to the butt of a joke.

The direction furnished by Twain in *The Adventures of Huckleberry Finn* inclines readers to recognize the humanity of underdogs, as Huck does in due course. It is underscored by Jim's forgoing his flight to care for Tom. The description of Jim given by the physician who attends Tom's wound makes plain, in the book, that the title "nigger" designates a noble person who is worthy of respect:

> "I never see a nigger that was a better nuss or faithfuller, and yet he was risking his freedom to do it, and was all tired out, too, and I see plain enough he'd been worked main hard lately. I liked the nigger for that; I tell you, gentlemen, a nigger like that is worth a thousand dollars—and kind treatment, too . . . He ain't no bad nigger, gentlemen; that's what I think about him." (363)

The noted depiction of Jim contradicts the assessment of him submitted by Ralph Ellison in "Change the Joke and Slip the Yoke" (1958), which alleges that the Black character just "struck [Ellison] as a white man's inadequate portrait of a slave" (222). Stanley Hyman's impression of the archetypal Black literary figure, related in "The Folk Tradition" (1958), comes closer to the truth about Jim. The character is neither unmanly nor pathetic; he is courageous and clever in addition to being empathetic. Deep fellow feeling moves the fugitive to halt his flight and nurse Tom in the child's hour of need. Jim turns silent and submissive in the face of the conceited mob that apprehends him as he cares for Tom because the Black man knows that he needs to perform what Hyman called "the darky act" (Hyman 199).

Hyman sought to persuade Ellison that figures portrayed in *Invisible Man* (1952) constitute "the fullest development" to date of "the darky act." The critic professed in Ellison's novel that "every important character turns out to be engaged in some facet of the smart-man-playing-dumb routine." Hyman refers to the grandfather figure on his deathbed who directs the nameless narrator to put on a false front for whites, in essence "to overcome 'em with yesses, undermined 'em with grins, agreed 'em to death and destruction, let 'em swoller you till they vomit or bust wide open." Hyman also refers to Dr. Bledsoe, the conniving Black college president who "pretends to be a simple pious Negro for the school's white trustees." The college president informs the narrator, "Yes, I had to act the nigger" (Hyman 200–11). Jim plays the part right through *The Adventures of Huckleberry Finn*.

Rhinehart in *Invisible Man* lends considerable credence to the argument advanced by Hyman. The character amounts to an invisible presence in the novel. He is a Harlem legend who never makes an actual appearance in Ellison's work. His identity is based on impressions of him gathered by others. He favors an inkblot whose character conforms to the view of the viewer. Some refer to him as a pimp; he is also spoken of as a preacher or numbers runner. When the narrator wears sunglasses, people mistake him for Rinehart. The elusive figure amounts to a master of improvisation who forms a face to affect the faces that he meets in order to manipulate them for his own sake akin to the manner in which Jim acts throughout *Huckleberry Finn*.

Research has yielded ample proof indicating that Twain knew Blacks too well to draw Jim as a weak and witless stooge. The biographer Dixon Wecter reveals in *Sam Clemens of Hannibal* (1952) that Twain spent many boyhood summers on a farm in the company of a slave named Uncle Dan'l who taught the author to tell tall tales. Wecter recalls that Twain said, "It was on the farm that I got my strong liking for [Uncle Dan'l's] race and my appreciation of certain of its fine qualities." The biographer identifies enslaved Uncle Dan'l as the "acknowledged original of Huck Finn's friend

'Nigger Jim'" (100). Shelley Fisher Fishkin, in her study, *Was Huck Black?* (1994), concerning Black influences on Twain, laments that white scholars, "by limiting their field of inquiry to the periphery, have missed the ways in which African-American voices shaped Twain's creative imagination at its core" (4). She presents substantial proof that Huck is based on a Black boy who became a friend to young Twain. Given the information, it is not surprising that Twain late in life paid for an African American student to attend Yale University.

In all likelihood, African Americans took Twain into their confidence during his youth and acquainted him with "the darky act," which permitted them without notice to flip the script on conceited and cruel leaders of the social order. They doubtless inspired the author to produce a tale that aims to have Blacks seen as noble figures. A sign of his intention exists in the last scene of his work. Huck abandons Tom and seeks "to light out for the Territory" (372). The boy is feed up with his old neck of the woods. He is done with white folks who want to "sivlize" (372) him. Huck is set to find a place where people are unaffected by titles and appearances. No matter what he faces, the boy looks certain to rest easy and allow events to take their course with an eye out for a chance to turn things in his favor. In other words, he appears destined to go on acting like Jim. Huck's final stance puts him at a fair distance from Tom, but real close to the Black man. Overall, Huck finishes his story on a note that allows that he has adopted the attitude of slaves similar to Jim as well as women like Loftus who learned to put on shows so that they might fool vain and vicious men.

Old Black Magic

A calm air marks a deep river.
A shallow stream makes a clamor.

Enslaved Black survivors of the Middle Passage—the voyage across the Atlantic to America—carried from Africa a passion for fables. In their native land, they had been delighted and directed by moral tales with supernatural elements involving animals as characters. The transplants instilled their arbor for magical stories containing parables in the hearts of their American descendants. The legacy left by the displaced Africans set the stage for African Americans to captivate white audiences with fantastic yarns. An enslaved Black storyteller charmed Joel Chandler Harris when the white writer was a boy and inspired him to think up Uncle Remus, the fictional raconteur of fanciful anecdotes whom Harris felt captured the essence of an "old timey Negro," ever eager to oblige others. However, given the exposure to African American folklore that Charles Chesnutt received, his novel *The Conjure Woman* (1899) signifies that Harris misunderstood and therefore misused the storytelling tradition transported from Africa.

In the sunshine beneath shade trees and the moonlit around campfires, early Africans told stories with sly sides. The storytellers of West Africa—home to the bulk of the enslaved Blacks who survived the Middle Passage—were called griots. They were poets who recited their work with music; at heart ancient hip-hop artist, they perpetuated a tradition observed by peers across the African continent. Entertainment was a key aspect of their mission. But they also endeavored to shed light on current events or environmental conditions to sustain an ethos that steered their culture. Before troubadours arrived in any European villages, griots spread over the western kingdoms of Africa, including Ghana, Mali, and Songhay. With music, in actuality, they rapped tall tales that ascribed human traits to animals. They placed emphasis on brains in lieu of brawn as the strength with which to tackle life.

A children's book written by Verna Aardema was adapted from an old African tale. The borrowed narrative is titled *Rabbit Makes a Monkey of Lion* (1989). It serves as an excellent example of the tradition out of which the given literary work was derived. The story is a fable that pits a rabbit against a lion. It was relayed by oral transmission in Swahili, the tongue of the Bantu people whose lines extend across the breadth of central Africa. In the tale, the rabbit wants honey from a tree that the lion claims to own. Seeking to nibble at the nectar, the bunny is caught by the big cat; the rabbit looks destined to become a dinner dish until he talks the lion into believing his skin will be too chewy to consume unless he is tenderized through being spun by the tail. Hence, the big cat twirls around the little fellow and ends up holding a wad of fuzz after the bunny shakes loose and skips off; stopped in his tracks, the lion remarks, "That little rascal made a monkey out of me" (17).

Of course, the moral of *Rabbit Makes a Monkey of Lion* places emphasis on brains in lieu of brawn as the might with which to meet danger. The stated ethos inspired sculptors in the kingdom of Benin to cast bronze bodies with huge heads, stressing the use of minds more than muscle. In light of the cited folktale's technique coupled with its theme in tune with the spirit behind the Benin sculptures, speculation that ties the fables of Aesop to Africa stands to reason. The true identity of the famed fabulist is unknown. Ancient Greeks wrote down the tales attributed to Aesop; the writers alleged that the celebrated storyteller was a slave who came from somewhere in Macedonia and won his freedom by impressing his master with his wit. On the other hand, modern scholars hypothesize that "Aesop" is a derivation of *Aethiops*, the term that Greeks employed to describe dark-skinned people from Africa; if so, then a logical English translation of *Aesop's Fables* would be *Ethiopian Parables*. Along with the Swahili story that led to *Rabbit Makes a Monkey of Lion*, the tales credited to Aesop feature beasts indigenous to Africa with human personalities. Perhaps the fact that most connects the fables of Aesop to Africa pertains to the conduct that the material commends.

"The Lion and the Mouse," a moral tale ascribed to Aesop, bears the typical form and function of ancient African folktales. A field mouse stumbles on a sleeping lion. Taking flight in a panic, the rodent scurries across the nose of the big cat. The lion awakens seething and traps the mouse under his heavy paw. Some quick thinking saves the little fellow from annihilation.

The mouse assures the lion no glory lies in slaying somebody much weaker than the king of the jungle. In exchange for sparing his life, the little fellow promises to do the big cat a favor someday; the lion mulls over the deal and decides to let the mouse go free. Later, the net of a hunter snares the big cat, causing the lion to issue a loud roar that catches the ear of the mouse, who responds by racing to gnaw on the netting until the little fellow manages to liberate the lion. The story illustrates that mercy sown yields fruit.

Another fable associated with Aesop is "The Dog and the Wolf." The creatures in the title meet in the woods. Hunger plagues the wolf; the dog meanwhile has a full belly. The hound invites the lupine home to work with him for his master and to share his steady diet. Interested, the wolf follows along with the dog up to the point of noticing that the hair around the scruff of the dog's neck has worn away and then learning the damage comes from wearing a collar fastened to a chain at night after the hound chows down on scraps off his master's table. Then the wolf hightails it back into the woods thinking life is better spent in the wild. It allows that independence is more valuable than slavery at any price.

The style and substance of the recited stories provide cause to assume that the fables attributed to Aesop were derived from a storytelling convention rooted deep in Africa. Before the Golden Age of Athens, the Dark Continent buzzed with tales of wildlife like lions and monkeys whose behavior brought to mind human beings. Therefore, even if ancient Greeks did not gather such yarns from an African store and name them *Aesop's Fables*, the famous material bears a striking resemblance to the African convention at issue, which enslaved blacks from Africa transported on slave ships to the New World. Folklorists like Lawrence Levine, author of *Black Culture and Black Consciousness* (1978), hold that slaves in the United States adapted the African storytelling custom to local conditions. The substance of the fables that blacks recounted in America differed from African models only in that they often swapped lions and monkeys for bears, foxes, or rabbits.

There is ample evidence that Africans in America entrusted their storytelling custom to their African American offspring. Few occurrences offer better proof than the origins of a hit jazz tune that Nat King Cole sang in 1943. The number is called "Straighten Up and Fly Right." A story shared in a sermon—delivered from an Alabama pulpit by the singer's father—inspired the song. It concerns a buzzard and a monkey. The bird of prey marauding lures weaker animals to their doom by inviting them to take a ride on his back high into the sky, where the buzzard flings the defenseless creatures to their death on the ground; afterward, the predator swoops down on his prey to chomp on their remains. A perceptive monkey figures out the vulture's game; when the little ape accepts a ride on the big bird's back, he strangles the neck of the buzzard with his arms and forces the predator to "straighten up and fly right." With all the earmarks of a classic African fable, the story of the buzzard and the monkey is a moral tale. It discourages judging the strength of others by outward appearances, while it promotes swift conduct.

A story known as "Tar-Baby" owns the distinction of being the most famous African American folktale. It has the properties of an Ashanti legend about a spider named Anansi who uses wit and wiles to prevail over the dangers posed by bigger beings. Given the tale's qualities, "Tar-Baby" corresponds to a conventional fable by Aesop. The renowned African American folktale recounts how Br'er Rabbit, caught in the clutches of Br'er Fox, keeps his head about him and uses reverse psychology to liberate himself from the prospect of becoming a meal for his captor. The story urges the use of wit as a shield to fend off ill treatment.

It figures that African Americans told their offspring the "Tar-Baby" tale to teach them to rely on their brains more than their brawn as the natural resource with which to handle Black bondage. The history of slaves in the system started with shock from the transport of their bodies out of Africa, packed like livestock in the belly of a brig, through a voyage across the Atlantic Ocean that lasted from two to three months. After the Middle Passage, the enslaved faced a dire need to think on their feet. A ceaseless white tendency to treat Blacks as if they were chattel met the Africans in America. The captives were expected to live like docile beasts at the beck and call of slaveholders. Daily, the survival of the slaves hung in the balance. They lacked arms to resist their misuse by the enslavers; blatant opposition to the system subjected the enslaved to floggings, mutilation, and lynching; their best chances for preserving their dignity lied in staying all eyes with an ear to the ground.

Scholars have labeled Br'er Rabbit a trickster emblematic of an African American folk hero. Research informed John Roberts that wily figures are prominent in African American folklore. In his study *From Trickster to Bad Man* (1990), Roberts reports, the most popular hero in tales told by enslaved Blacks featured little animals like a rabbit at a disadvantage in a rivalry with a larger creature like a fox. These tricksters were quick to mask their goals. They lived by their wits to best their opponents. Henry Louis Gates in *The Signifying Monkey* (1988) asserts that enslaved Blacks made use of trickster figures in stories to convey snide criticism of the slave system.

In other words, Gates infers that wily characters couched in fanciful tales afforded Blacks in bondage a means by which to express opposition to the slave system yet leave slaveholders in the dark about their true feelings. The scholarship on the subject supports the hypothesis that Blacks in slavery shared stories equivalent to fables by Aesop as instructive and inspirational lessons for coping with Black bondage.

To be sure, besides telling tales adapted from an African tradition to teach morals and manners, Black slaves used such stories to amuse white citizens who stood over them in the social order. The practice helped the enslaved cultivate benevolence among slaveholders. African Americans understood that their welfare depended on keeping white folks pleased with them. Nothing breeds goodwill like entertainment. In essence, the national underdogs thought up a sort of show business designed to secure the favor of their overlords. The career of Joel Chandler Harris verifies the fact of the matter. It likewise conveys proof that underlying themes relayed by subjugated Black storytellers went over the head of white audiences.

Born out of wedlock, thirteen years prior to the outbreak of the Civil War, Harris grew up an outcast from humble roots in a small Georgia village. On the social ladder, his rank sat a rung above the enslaved population. While his mother encouraged pride and ambition in her son, Harris developed an incurable shyness around other whites. In the company of Blacks, he came to feel at home. He was most animated when he was marveling at Blacks, or else mimicking them.

Harris felt he got to know the souls of Black folk after he became a teen. He went to work nine miles from his home at the Turnwold estate, a manor with a printing shop sustained by slave labor. The proprietor of the property was Joseph Addison Turner. His neighbors regarded Turner as a compassionate slaveholder who treated his slaves with humanity. He was a staunch advocate of Black bondage. On his property, he published a newspaper titled *The Countryman.* The editorial slant of his paper's issues condoned counting Black people as beings in nature a bit above beasts of burden with charming sides. He hired Harris to serve him as an apprentice printer. Turner taught Harris to consider Blacks inferior to whites. With this perspective, the future inventor of Uncle Remus left Turnwold to begin a long, celebrated stint as a feature writer for *The Atlanta Constitution.*

Through the Civil War, Harris worked at the Turnwold plantation and relished tales told by Uncle George, a senior slave at the estate. No doubt, Harris departed Turnwold for work at *The Atlanta Constitution* with a host of tales told by the old Black slave. From his eventual Uncle Remus stories, it is obvious that Harris presumed that Uncle George sought to amuse him without a wish for personal gain. Moreover, it appears the white journalist took his leave of Turnwold with an impression of the old slave that gave rise to Uncle Remus.

The invention of Uncle Remus, a faithful Black servant who regales a white child with magical tales, brought Harris fame following the passing of Black bondage. In the aftermath of the slave system, the Confederate states were in a shambles. Slaveholders lamented that gone with the wind was an idyllic world graced by lush plantations that had prospered from the care of gracious gentlemen, who enjoyed the affection of beautiful belles along with the aid of smiling slaves. Through the Reconstruction era, public posts and privileges hung in the balance. Favored and flattered by the past slave system, whites wished to see it rise again, while emancipated Blacks prayed the business was shut down forever. With the portrait of Uncle Remus, Harris raised hope among Southerners that their freed slaves longed for a return to the banned social order where Blacks were expected to spend their lives in service to whites.

In 1876, Harris introduced Uncle Remus as a comical commentator on current events in columns published by *The Atlanta Constitution*. The writer represented the character as a gray ex-slave who remains loyal to the home of his former slaveholders in the wake of the Civil War. His original depiction of Uncle Remus was a skeletal version of the final form. Harris fleshed out the figure in his book *Uncle Remus: His Songs and His Sayings*, published in 1881. The cited volume portrays the title character as an enchanting storyteller who lives to delight his boss, Miss Sally, and her child John. One evening after another, Uncle Remus fascinates the boy with accounts of a rabbit who outwits a bear or fox. The servant seems to possess a wild imagination. Given to self-depreciation, he speaks in the supposed dialect of the "old timey Negro" (13). His stories captivate John with intrigue and suspense; to the boy, Uncle Remus is a marvelous entertainer; at the end of every tale, John is speechless. The boy, however, never draws a moral from any of the Black man's fictions.

The story of "Tar-Baby" is the jewel of Harris's *Uncle Remus*. It stars Br'er Rabbit as a trickster who outwits the stronger Br'er Fox. The tale unfolds in two parts. Uncle Remus tells it to John after an anecdote through which the storyteller introduces the boy to Br'er Rabbit and teases the white child by leaving the creature's fate up in the air and sending John home for the night. John is left dying to know whether Br'er Fox has the bunny for dinner. In a day, when the white boy returns hungry for more of the rabbit tale, Uncle Remus tells him about the fox conjuring up Tar Baby to lay a trap for Br'er Rabbit.

In effect, Tar Baby is the equivalent of a scarecrow with a straw hat on his head and black tar smeared on his body. Hopping up to the effigy, Br'er Rabbit mistakes it for a person. He greets the dummy; then, when it fails to reply, the rabbit takes offense and whacks at it until he finds himself stuck to the tar and therefore at the mercy of Br'er Fox. At this point, Uncle Remus stops the story again and sends John home to Miss Sally. The boy has to wait for a seeming eternity to have his curiosity satisfied.

When Uncle Remus resumes the tale, Br'er Fox is licking his chops in anticipation of barbecuing Br'er Rabbit, who is still glued to the body of Tar Baby. The storyteller cautions the child not to fret about the fate of the rabbit. He represents the creature as an uppity rascal with an inveterate habit of making a racket and getting caught in a sticky situation. While Br'er Fox weighs how to make mincemeat of his prey, Uncle Remus reports, a bright idea hits Br'er Rabbit. The smaller animal starts pleading with the bigger creature to dispose of him by any means, except for one possible route. The rabbit begs the fox to roast him, hang him, or drown him, if not chop him up, but to please not toss him in the thorny briar patch. In reaction, wishing to injure the bunny, Br'er Fox flings him in the thicket, the birthplace and breeding ground of Br'er Rabbit, from which the rascal escapes without a hitch. "Bred en bawn in a brier-patch, Brer Fox—bred en bawn in a brier-patch" (Harris 64), the little animal quips as he takes flight. The outcome results from a marvelous exercise of ingenuity that passes over John's head.

A reason for slaves to handle the "Tar-Baby" story as an abstract tool with which to advise their offspring and amuse their oppressors appears never to have crossed the mind of Harris. It looks as if the white writer in conjunction with his imaginary white child John lacked the vision to suspect that the Tar Baby figure represented Black bondage to the people enslaved by the system. Harris's text is empty of signs linking the plight of Br'er Rabbit to the trials of a slave. The white writer's work never suggests the enslaved could have compared the ravenous fox to a white slaveholder. Harris seems to have just wanted to amuse readers.

A later tale in *Uncle Remus*, "Mr. Rabbit Grossly Deceives Mr. Fox," suggests that John functions as a proxy for Harris, who regards the old Black man's stories as flights of fancy with neither a moral for youth nor a benefit for the storyteller. The title gives away the plot. In total, the rabbit again outwits the fox. This time, Br'er Rabbit figuratively makes a monkey out of the fox as the bunny literally tricks the bigger beast into being saddled, bridled, ridden, spurred, and hitched to a post like a horse in front of several "ladies." The ending dissatisfies John; he asks, "Is that all, Uncle Remus" (70)? The storyteller replies that it is a small bit of the whole load, but too much of a belly filler for the white boy to have yet another morsel without bursting at the seams, which to John makes Uncle Remus seem pompous.

In writing, Harris stated that his aim in his accounts of Uncle Remus was to record verbatim tales that Blacks told him for the most part during the years that he spent around the slaves at Turnwold. On the whole, the white writer sought to mimic Blacks whose stories had subtle touches and secret themes to which Harris was not privy. Blacks bound by bondage for the pleasure of whites, who found slavery suitable for the enslaved, cloaked their conduct and shrouded their schemes. In all likelihood, enslaved storytellers aimed to arrest Harris's attention with outward shows and sensational optics. Aping old Black slaves, like Uncle George, the inventor of Uncle Remus captured a practice without its purpose. The "old timey Negro" portrayed by Harris acts as thoughtful as an actual parrot. Uncle Remus is in need of complexity to approximate a real person once stuck in slavery; the character is devoid of breadth and depth. The figure constitutes a kind of wish fulfillment for a white audience comforted by the image of a clown with a black face who is happy to offer amusement at the drop of a hat.

Frederick Douglass, in his first autobiography, *Narrative of the Life of Frederick Douglass* (1845), observed that Black slaves aired their anguish and aspirations over a grapevine (i.e., secret communication network) with shadings that kept whites on hand out of the loop. To and from their master's big house, for their allotment of provisions, Douglass wrote, the enslaved "would sing, as a chorus, to words which to many would seem unmeaning jargon, but which, nevertheless," were meaningful to the slaves. Such songs, Douglas surmised, related "the horrible character of slavery." The tunes "breathed the prayer and complaint of souls boiling over" with awful sorrow and stirred by a deep desire "for deliverance from chains." He confessed, "I have often been utterly astonished, since I came to the north, to find persons who could speak of the singing, among slaves, as evidence of their contentment and happiness." Nothing, he said, could be further from the truth. "The singing of a man castaway upon a desolate island might be as appropriately considered as evidence of contentment and happiness as the singing of a slave; the songs of the one and of the other are prompted by the same emotion" (47), Douglass professed.

Now, it is implausible that a former slave was the original source for "The Story of the War" recounted in Harris's *Uncle Remus*. The story betrays the shallow dimensions of the title character. Set in the aftermath of the Civil War, from the beginning to the end of the yarn, Uncle Remus declines to pursue any private benefit. He puts down his fellow former slaves. Furthermore, he declares them too lazy to work and also misguided enough to expect honest folks to support them. Uncle Remus charges other Blacks with bumming his tobacco, borrowing his tools, and bilking him out of his food. Meanwhile, he insinuates that Blacks are lost without direction from whites. He claims to be so tired of the former slaves that he is ready to seek work elsewhere, but he stays on the plantation where he has spent his entire life. To the delight of white readers nostalgic for the days when Blacks were enslaved and expected to be accommodating, the old Black character always makes it his business to oblige former slaveholders.

In "The Story of the War," Uncle Remus is flattered to make the acquaintance of Miss Sally's sister-in-law, Miss Theodosia from Vermont, whom he greets at the train depot in Atlanta, while the city suffers as a casualty of the hardship inflicted on the state of Georgia during the dying days of the Civil War by order of the Union General William Tecumseh Sherman. Back home on the plantation, Miss Sally's husband prevails on Uncle Remus to share with their guest the story of his participation in the fight over Black bondage. Prompt in response, Uncle Remus recalls his old master, Mars Jeems, joining the Confederate army and leaving the whole plantation in his hands; the old former slave harks back to how he dedicated himself to staying on the backs of his fellow slaves to keep them on their toes. When Union soldiers swarmed the estate, he recalls, he committed himself to protecting Miss Sally and her mother. All the while, he says, he was guided by his gut feelings. While surveying the grounds with a rifle in hand, he spied a Yankee sniper up a tree with his sights set on Mars Jeems, coming home fatigued from battle; never mind that the Union soldier was fighting to end Black bondage, Uncle Remus shut his eyes tight and blasted the blue coat. As it turns out, the Yankee sniper was wounded and nursed back to health by the faithful servant and Miss Sally, who afterward married the Union soldier, prompting the following dialogue:

> "But you cost him an arm," exclaimed Miss Theodosia.
> "I gin 'im dem," said Uncle Remus, pointing to [Miss Sally], "en I gin 'im deze"—holding up his own brawny arms. "En ef dem ain't nuff fer enny man den I done los' de way." (Harris 185)

Harris's sketch of Uncle Remus at best traces the prevailing Southern white picture of an "old timey Negro." The heart and soul of a true person who bleeds when pricked is absent from the portrait of Uncle Remus present in "The Story of the War," ending with a blue coat attached to a Confederate lady in the company of a servile former slave, implying that the abolition of Black bondage was a mistake. It stands to reason that the slaves seemed excited to give the children of slaveholders pats on the back and offer the kids piggyback rides, and it is likely that slaves appeared eager to thrill the offspring of their masters with baked goods and animal tales. Indeed, slaves must have positioned themselves at the beck and call of slaveholders. Slavery called for exhibitions of deference by slaves. The fates of the enslaved were tied to the impressions that slaveholders had of them. It is logical to assume that Harris around Turnwold never glimpsed Uncle George's honest self. In all probability, the "old timey Negro" never did more than put on a false front for Harris.

The Conjure Woman offers a figure with a slight resemblance to Uncle Remus that happens to expose the superficiality of Harris's invention. It is an innovative novel written by Charles Chesnutt. In it, Uncle Julius is the name of the figure who favors Uncle Remus. Chesnutt's imaginary persona is an old former slave who stays on the plantation of his birth in the wake of the Civil War. Uncle Julius is disposed to tell a white couple fantastic tales about Blacks in bondage. However, unlike Uncle Remus, Chesnutt's invention is motivated by self-interest. In spirit, Uncle Julius is akin to Br'er Rabbit.

Born on the brink of the Civil War in 1858, the creator of *The Conjure Woman* lived by his wits from his early teens until the day that he passed in 1932. Chesnutt was born in Cleveland. His parents were free Black people from the South. In 1866, they moved to Fayetteville, where Chesnutt came of age. At fourteen years old, he was working as a teacher at a Charlotte school for ex-slaves. The rigid color bar erected by Jim Crow laws in North Carolina aggravated him. So, early in his twenties, he resettled by Lake Erie in Ohio. He earned a law degree and afterward set up a successful court-reporting business along the lines of the shop run by the narrator of Herman Melville's "Bartleby, the Scrivener" (1853).

Chesnutt managed a legal service instead of a law practice because color prejudice bred by Black bondage restricted African American attorneys from serving in the fashion of accessories to white outfits. The embedded bias incurred public and private costs disclosed by the fortunes of Chesnutt. While beginning to write fiction in 1887, the author took the Ohio state bar exam and passed the test with flying colors, scoring the highest grade of all that year. He showed he was bright enough to do a good bit for the Ohio legal system as a lawyer, given a fair chance. Instead, he was confined to conducting a stenography shop for the convenience of select white counselors. In consequence of the color line, dug deep in the heart of the country, his bank account amounted to less than those belonging to members of the Ohio bar who scored grades on the entrance exam that were far lower than what he achieved. No less unfortunate, because of the limits placed on the Black man, Ohio got in practice less than all of the best and brightest possible legal minds around the state.

Prior to becoming a member of the Ohio bar, Chesnutt was a schoolteacher for close to a decade in North Carolina. He developed intimacy with a host of former slaves. They opened their hearts and homes to him. He listened to their stories and songs, and, like a folklorist, he studied the culture of the past slaves. He sensed Black bondage had seared the souls of African Americans who lived under the system. Chesnutt gathered though that slavery induced the enslaved to grow creative to survive the treatment of chattel. The circumstances yielded maestros of improvisation, he felt. Heroic former slaves, he determined, behaved in an intelligent and inventive manner for the sake of their dignity.

Living in the postwar South allowed Chesnutt to learn that life for Blacks in bondage was far from a pastoral paradise constructed by benevolent masters. He came to understand that slavery rendered the wits of the enslaved their best defense against the indignities imposed by the system. The social order permitted a white slaveholder to trade a slave for a horse and in the process break up a Black family without guilt. It propagated a lust among whites for profit from the exploitation of Black bodies. The past slave society was plagued by misery and mourning among its captives. It tested the mettle of African American minds. Stuck in bondage, slaves had to conjure up myriad schemes to charm their oppressors like an obligatory clown, hiding tears under a black mask with a broad grin of red lips, flaunting a strand of pearly whites.

Chesnutt very much appreciated a particular trick to which certain slaves turned for relief from indignity. The ruse is known as "passing." It is the ploy recalled in *Running a Thousand Miles for Freedom*, where Ellen Craft uses the trick to be mistaken for a free white person when she is fleeing Black bondage. Besides Craft, Chesnutt descended from parents with Black and white ancestors. He inherited a skin tone and hair texture that qualified him to be taken as white, given the prevailing custom of identification by complexion. Chesnutt took it for granted that countless Blacks with looks and locks similar to his own chose to assume a white identity to escape injustice; the writer appreciated why individuals decided to engage in the subterfuge. In any event, Chesnutt declined to portray himself as anything other than a Black man; therefore, at a cost to himself and Ohio, although he achieved the highest score on the state bar examination in 1887, he was ruled out of an actual private law practice by Jim Crow ethics that prohibited Black lawyers from competing with white attorneys. Chesnutt forsook the practice of "passing," but he realized that it was part of Black culture. The novelist planted proof of the reality in *The Conjure Woman*.

From his literary work, Chesnutt gained a brief bit of fame. Between 1887 and 1905, he published several works of fiction. The material includes a volume of short stories titled *The Wife of His Youth and Other Stories of the Color-Line* (1899), plus three novels: *The House Behind the Cedars* (1900), *The Marrow of Tradition* (1901), and *The Colonel's Dream* (1905). An apparent collection of short stories, *The Conjure Woman* contains the coherence of a novel; likewise, the work conveys the character of a culture through an approach followed by Sherwood Anderson when he composed the novel *Winesburg, Ohio* (1919). Chesnutt's first novel evolved from "The Goophered Grapevine," a short story that received rave reviews in 1887, when it appeared in *The Atlantic Monthly*. In the hearts of African Americans, his oeuvre struck the right chord. It prompted the National Association for the Advancement of Colored People in 1928 to award Chesnutt the Springarn Medal in honor of "his pioneer work as a literary artist, depicting the life and struggle of Americans of Negro descent."

When "The Goophered Grapevine" appeared in *The Atlantic Monthly*, it garnered rave reviews due in large part to the fact that the short story appealed to a contemporary taste for tales that fed an appetite, whetted by the Reconstruction, for signs that Blacks belonged back in bondage where being of service to whites fulfilled them. Stories that recalled past plantation life became the vogue that satisfied the wish to turn the clock back to a fanciful time before the Civil War. The novel *The Grandissimes* (1880) served the desired purpose and brought George Washington Cable fame. Thomas Nelson Page made a splash with his volume of short stories *In Ole Virginia, or Marse Chan and Other Stories* (1887). *Two Runaways and Other Stories* (1889) won Harry Stillwell Edwards distinction. The typical plantation tale featured a white man who keeps a paternal eye on his Black servants, the best of whom care for him with pleasure. Black figures typical of the plantation genre speak in supposed genuine "Negro dialect," and they display a talent for tickling whites pink with quaint stunts and quirky stories. Such elements put Harris's *Uncle Remus* on library shelves right next to the work of Cable, Page, and Edwards; the form of *The Conjure Woman* warrants cataloguing the book with the aforementioned plantation tales, but its plot has twists and turns that render its content at odds with the related texts.

The Conjure Woman includes seven short stories starting with a revision of "The Goophered Grapevine." Uncle Julius occupies every portion of the book and furnishes the work with the unity and cohesion of a novel. A white man named John, who has come down to North Carolina from Ohio for business reasons and the health of his wife, opens and closes the different segments of the text. Uncle Julius is an old and gray ex-slave like Uncle Remus. Likewise, he is rather quick to tell a fantastic tale. The fictions of the two Black characters differ when it comes to the types of figures who populate them. Uncle Remus rivets a white boy with stories of animals disposed to behave like people; Uncle Julius regales a white man with accounts of people demanded to act like animals. At the end of the fictions told by Uncle Julius, John suspects the presence of a secret motive behind their telling. Yet, like the boy engrossed by Uncle Remus, the man entertained by Uncle Julius fails to tease out any morals.

In "The Goophered Grapevine," John is a white gentleman. Looking to buy the past slave plantation where Uncle Julius has spent his life, he arrives on the scene with Miss Annie, his wife, in tow. A vineyard languishes on the land; it has been ignored by whites since the Civil War. John has confidence that an investment in the old property will yield him a handsome profit. The white man believes that the climate is ideal for grape cultivation. Also, he supposes that the warm weather will do wonders for his spouse, whom he feels has been debilitated by the cold winds that blow in Ohio off Lake Erie. At the outset, the town by the plantation gives the white man pause; to him, it seems like a run-of-the-mill sleepy Southern village. However, as he gains more knowledge of the area, he finds the vicinity full of energy and all of the passions and problems that reside elsewhere. His initial view of the locality hints that his judgment is affected by preconceived notions. The habit of mind is further implied when he meets Uncle Julius and thinks to his surprise that the "colored man" has a glint of "shrewdness in his eyes" (10).

A few minutes into meeting Uncle Julius, John's initial impression of him is tested. He arrives at the plantation expecting to encounter frail and forlorn Black freedmen floundering around the property. At first sight, the image seems to fit the figure Uncle Julius cuts. The Black man seems to be spending his day loafing on a log in the shade of "a spreading elm." Uncle Julius has "on his knees a hat full of grapes, over which he [is] smacking his lips with great gusto, and a pile of grapeskins" at his feet suggests to the narrator "that the performance [is] no new thing." John is ready for Uncle Julius to be "slightly bowed by the weight of years." But the white man notices that the old fellow is "tall" and "quite vigorous" (8–10). Therefore, the latter persona becomes a curiosity to the former character.

After the Black man hears that John intends to buy the plantation, he conjures up a fantastic tale about an unfortunate slave. With a drawl in the "Negro dialect" of a typical plantation tale, Uncle Julius begins telling John that the vineyard has been "goophered (11)," that is, cursed, by a Black witch at the bidding of a tightfisted slaveholder who wanted to keep his slaves from eating the produce. Uncle Julius avows that a new slave on the grounds named Henry, ignorant of the spell, once consumed a batch of the grapes, and it caused him to wax and wane, sprout and shrivel with the seasons, until, like a weathered elm, he withered away. The Black man says that fresh vines, which are not jinxed, are mixed among the old, cursed plants. Uncle Julius contends that because he can tell the stalks apart, he knows which grapes are safe to eat. Wrapping up his tale, he explains that John should not bother to invest in the vineyard because a stranger will not be able to sort out the good fruit from the bad crop and risks being "goophered."

Though entertained, John rejects the Black man's counsel. The white man buys the farm, and his "income from grapes packed and shipped to the Northern markets [becomes] quite considerable" (34). He discovers that Uncle Julius "had occupied a cabin on the place for many years, and derived a respectable revenue from the product of the neglected grapevines." The business that the Black man has operated on the land, John figures, "accounted for his advice to me not to buy the vineyard." With respect to Uncle Julius's attempt to talk him out of buying the plantation, the white man is unable to tell "whether it inspired the goopher story." Still, John dispossesses Uncle Julius of the land on which the ex-slave has built a private enterprise. Missing how he deprives the Black man of the means to enjoy an independent life, John says, "I believe, however, that the wages I paid him for his services as a coachman, for I gave him employment in that capacity, were more than an equivalent for anything he lost by the sale of the vineyard" (34–35). He never imagines that Uncle Julius has possessed a conscious wish to protect his private enterprise by using the "goopher story" to change the white man's mind; and too, a kernel of truth in the fantastic tale, obscured by supernatural elements customary in African folktales, which issues a denunciation of Black bondage as well as the disruption of Uncle Julius's business, is undetected by John.

Time after time in *The Conjure Woman*, the white man, who narrates the novel, patronizes the Black fabulist, while Uncle Julius stuffs the meat of his material with details as far-fetched as the animal tales of Uncle Remus. John pegs Uncle Julius as a shallow thinker suited by nature for servility, and John feels his opinion of the Black man is wise beyond words. In the meantime, committed to personal gain, Uncle Julius aspires to exploit the white man's psychology. The old man makes up incredible stories to turn the tables on John. Uncle Julius's fables divulge that slavery spurred slaves to live by their wits. Led by the lessons of yesteryear, the Black figure engages in a mind game designed to enhance his standing. Uncle Julius in sum epitomizes a heroic Black type, a clever character, who dodges disempowerment by improvised means, a smooth operator, who serves himself while seeming to serve a white man. On a few occasions, he makes a monkey out of John without the gentleman realizing it.

The former slave has gone to work as a coachman for the new owner of his home when he tells the story of "Po' Sandy." As in "The Goophered Grapevine" and every other tale told by Uncle Julius, the second story he recounts comes in response to a situation that causes him some concern. This time he acts to dissuade John from a plan "to save expense" for a new kitchen by demolishing "the old schoolhouse" on the plantation and using "the lumber, which [is] in a good state of preservation" (38) to build the new facility for his wife's pleasure. Uncle Julius tells a story of an enslaved Black woman, named Tenie, whose master sold her first two husbands and rented out her third spouse, Sandy, on so regular a basis that she shared rare moments with him. As a consequence, she sought out the local Black witch and begged the conjurer to cast a spell that would permit her and Sandy to put down permanent roots; thus, the witch turned Sandy into a tree, to which Tenie clung, until her master sawed the tree embodying her husband into lumber for a new kitchen. Tenie cried herself to death; wails from Sandy haunt the boards, Uncle Julius sighs; and after the war, he relates, whites relinquished the troubled dwelling to Blacks for use as a schoolhouse.

When Uncle Julius is done with the tale "Po' Sandy," Miss Annie cries out, "What a system it was under which such things were possible" (60). However, her husband scoffs at her. John wonders if his wife believes a slave could have been turned into a tree. Her reply stuns him:

> "What things?" [the white man] asked, in amazement. "Are you seriously considering the possibility of a man's being turned into a tree?"

"Oh, no," she replied quickly, "not that"; and then she murmured absently, and with a dim look in her fine eyes, "Poor Tenie!" (60–61)

The exchange suggests that the wife has learned a lesson about the routine breakup of Black marriages by the slave system. John misses the reality behind the impossible parts of Uncle Julius's tale. In the end, John chalks up "Po' Sandy" to the old man's desire to use the old schoolhouse on the plantation for gatherings by members of the Sandy Run Colored Baptist Church, who have seceded from the rest of their congregation over the issue of temperance. Annie grasps that the purpose of the tale has been to gain Uncle Julius an advantage as a form of reparations for past deprivations.

En route to "Mars Jeems's Nightmare," John admits he has "found old Julius very useful" around his "new residence." About the old man, the white gentleman says, "He had a thorough knowledge of the neighborhood, was familiar with the roads and the watercourses, knew the qualities of the various soils and what they would produce, and where the best hunting and fishing were to be had." Also, John concedes that the Black man is "a marvelous hand in the management" of mares and mongrels "with whose mental processes he manifest[s] a greater familiarity than mere use would seem to account for." The white man ascribes Uncle Julius's valuable traits "to the simplicity of a life that [has] kept him close to nature" along with the lifelong habit of looking "upon himself as the property of another." In other words, Uncle Julius is worthwhile to John because the Black man is helpful and humble. For that reason, John takes "quite a fancy to him" (64–65).

Through "Mars Jeems's Nightmare," Uncle Julius in effect bids John to put himself in the shoes of a so-called "nigger" after the boss dismisses the servant's grandson Tom from the farm staff. Uncle Julius recounts the fortunes of a cruel slaveholder with a vicious overseer who abuses his slaves without a break. Mars Jeems enrages his slave Solomon when the master separates the bondsman from his sweetheart by selling her to a slaveholder in a county at a good distance. Bent on payback, the heartbroken slave appeals to Aun' Peggy, the witch who haunts the surroundings. By an incantation, the sorceress traps Mars Jeems in a living nightmare of being a Black man enslaved on his own plantation and brutalized by his cruel overseer; the transformed master undergoes great suffering before the spell wears off. Afterward, he is a changed man; he is filled with compassion for his slaves. "Sententiously," according to John, Uncle Julius attributes a moral to "Mars Jeems's Nightmare"; the Black man maintains, "Dis yer tale goes ter show dat w'ite folks w'at is so ha'd en stric,' en doan make no 'lowance for po' ign'ant niggers w'at ain' had no chanst ter l'arn, is li'ble to hab bad dreams, ter say de leas', en dat dem w'at is kin' en good ter po' people is sho' ter prosper en git 'long in de worl' " (100). Then, patronizing the Black man, John remarks, "I am glad, too, that you told us the moral of the story"; next, proving he deemed Uncle Julius shallow, he asks, "Did you make that up all by yourself?" (101). Anyway, moved by the tale, Miss Annie goes behind her husband's back and rehires Tom.

The Conjure Woman illustrates Black bondage fostered a social psychology, which stayed anchored with fast ties in the national development through the Reconstruction era. The mindset disposed white gentlemen to assume, in a room of white women and Black people, that they stood analogous to a beacon invented to shed light on sound conduct for the others. John embodies the stated bias. The prejudice blinds the white figure to the reality that Uncle Julius is a deep thinker who applies his wits and wiles to promote his general welfare. Furthermore, the bias leaves John unable to see that his spouse, Annie, is pretty quick and employs guile to go her own way; in effect, she too is an underdog who pursues her interests through smooth operating. The "mental habits of a lifetime" (65) incline John to rate the others by their shape and shade. His disposition blurs his view of his spouse and servant. It exposes him to having the wool pulled over his eyes.

As effective underdogs against a common opponent, Annie and Julius form a bond. The white woman recognizes that the Black man's tales have a magical power to unearth "the deeper currents of life" (4), which flow "not less steadily" in either of them. Miss Annie realizes that Uncle Julius piles his tales as tools with which to amuse and affect others. His stories delight her when they appeal for compassion. Still, she labels one "nonsense" (127), as it helps Julius play a cruel joke on John; titled "The Conjurer's Revenge," it involves a man turned into a cross between a donkey and a horse. It wields the power to trick John—hot for a fast buck—into buying a blind mule from Uncle Julius's buddy. Miss Annie wants justice for everyone. Because "The Conjurer's Revenge" boosts a bad deal, it displeases her. Hence, in this instance, the white woman feels Julius misuses his storytelling skill.

From then on, recognizing that Annie is not so much sentimental as sensible on top of shrewd, Julius acts to keep her on his side. When she is filled with melancholy and her health declines, he lifts her spirits with the story of "Sis Becky's Pickaninny," about an enslaved Black woman who lacks a lucky charm to fend off sorrow and her mean master snatches her spouse and son and sells them down the river, leaving her lost in mourning until a resident witch returns the slave's beloved by way of Black magic. Miss Annie's reaction to "Sis Becky's Pickaninny" uncovers her connection with Uncle Julius. It bares her realization that the story conveys a history lesson in addition to a note of cheer. Yet John treats it as a pile of rubbish.

> "That is a very ingenious fairy tale, Julius," I said, "and we are much obliged to you."
> "Why, John!" said my wife severely, "the story bears the stamp of truth, if ever a story did."
> "Yes," I replied, "especially the humming-bird episode, and the mocking-bird digression, to say nothing of the doings of the hornet and the sparrow."
> "Oh, well, I don't care," she rejoined, with delightful animation; "those are mere ornamental details and not at all essential. The story is true to nature, and might have happened half a hundred times, and no doubt did happen, in those horrid days before the war." (159)

Miss Annie never has another bad word to say about the fanciful tales of Uncle Julius. She clamors to hear "The Gray Wolf's Ha'nt." His relation of how a Black slave put a hex on a married couple, who had offended him, absorbs her. The slave turned the spouses into a gray wolf and a black cat unable to get along. The story leaves Miss Annie not saying anything even after her husband guesses that Uncle Julius has told the tale to dissuade him from clearing a wooded patch where the old man runs an underground honeybee business. Later, the Black character brings tears to Annie's eyes with "Hot Foot Hannibal," about the ghost of a woman who cried herself to death over lost love. Hearing the tale inspires Miss Annie's niece to put a quarrel with a beau behind her.

Julius's purposeful use of stories with supernatural parts and subtle points renders him an excellent example of a person who practices an art involving African strokes applied with local color. Given Chesnutt's intimacy with real-life former slaves, he must have had in mind someone akin to Uncle George when he conceived his Black storyteller, Uncle Julius. It stands to reason that the Black man, who regaled Harris with stories at the Turnwold estate, told stories to secure the favor of whites and was a far deeper thinker than his audience ever imagined. Harris's Black storyteller makes idle use of the craft with which Uncle Julius amuses and affects others in pursuit of his own interests. Unlike the behavior of Uncle Remus, the manners of Uncle Julius place a premium on freedom in lieu of servitude at any price. Next to Chesnutt's Black character, it is fair to conclude, Uncle Remus stands as a pale imitation of an "old timey Negro." The portrait of Uncle Julius, in contrast, amounts to a vivid painting of a beaming star brightened by dark surroundings.

Lost in Translation

A swift old lemming stands stock-still
While fellows go over the hill.

In diverse world cultures, the oak tree symbolizes endurance as well as enlightenment. Greek mythology treats it as an emblem of the strength and wisdom associated with the sovereign god Zeus. Credited with similar importance, it represents the state tree in Connecticut, Iowa, and Maryland. At the heart of Hampton University, one stands as a monument to African American passages from slavery to freedom, enabled by fortitude and skill. The type of tree captured the imagination of Ernest Gaines and inspired the main motif in his novel *The Autobiography of Miss Jane Pittman* (1971).

Without a doubt, the customary qualities ascribed to an oak tree designate the attributes that distinguish Pittman in the account of her rendered by Gaines. Her story starts with a slog through slavery and runs to a sojourn on the margins of society under conditions prone to make a person lose her grip. In the beginning, she favors a sapling whose limbs a ferocious storm is set to throw out of joint. Growing strong and wise, however, lets her stay grounded and live to a ripe old age. Most of all, Pittman's development of mental prowess empowers her to avoid being undone by adverse circumstances that confront her time and again.

The CBS network presented a made-for-television film adaptation of Gaines's book in 1974. Starring Cicely Tyson as the title character, it won rave reviews. The movie garnered nine Emmy awards, including Best Lead Actress in a Drama, Best Directing in Drama, and Best Writing in Drama. Generally, critics felt that the picture complemented the book. Nikki Giovanni adored the TV production and railed against Stephanie Harrington, a *New York Times* reviewer, who found the film unexciting.

In a piece published by the newspaper, Giovanni confided that the movie version of *The Autobiography of Miss Jane Pittman* "fulfilled [her] deepest expectations." She added that "it was a triumph of and for the enduring strength of black people" (115).

Giovanni offered a truthful assessment of the film. Through its portrayal of Pittman, the TV production credits Blacks with a talent for endurance. Still, unlike the novel on which the film is based, the movie fails to tie the fortunes of the principal figure to learning to use her head. *The Autobiography of Miss Jane Pittman* written by Gaines embodies a literary form engendered by the Black experience in the national development. The novel sustains a point of view that pins African-American prospects on a commitment to knowledge. By contrast, the film adaptation stakes Black hopes on an ability to endure hardship with slight if any intelligence. The difference makes the picture less praiseworthy than the book because the movie upholds the hackneyed idea that pitches Blacks as strong bodies begging for sense.

Stereotypes save people the trouble of sorting out individuals one by one for just treatment. Because no two people have the exact same personality, not even identical twins, a fair sense of a person's character demands a willingness to suspend judgment until after a meeting of the minds, which requires some daring because strangers arouse wariness. It is far less worrisome to prejudge an unfamiliar person based on a visible trait taken as an outward sign of a disposition borne by a group. From the moment that Black bondage took effect in the national development, skin color has functioned as a marker of character. The system taught people with light complexions to regard individuals with dark hues as an inferior lot, crying for subjection or salvation, according to the separate angles of their superiors. White men came to feel born to act as a master or messiah of Blacks. In the main, they agreed that the dusky sorts were short on sense, but hardy at heart. The TV production of *The Autobiography of Miss Jane Pittman* reinforces the cited stereotypes.

Doubtless, it took plenty of strength for the enslaved to survive the burdens of Black bondage. They faced measures designed to make them fear taking steps to spend their lives doing more than laboring for the good of someone else. It was a heavy load to bear. The system distorted the humanity of Blacks in white eyes. In *Scenes of Subjection*, Saidiya Hartman offered a mound of evidence that terror and torture sustained Black bondage and constructed a frame of mind that condemned the enslaved to find no relief from brutality. Hartman finds the outlook so fixed in the culture that "declarations of slave humanity intensified the brutal exercise of power upon the captive body rather than ameliorating the chattel condition (5). In substance, she leaves a capacity for endurance as the saving grace of the enslaved. Hartman conceded that "the everyday practices of the enslaved encompassed an array of tactics such as work slowdowns, feigned illness, unlicensed travel, the destruction of property, theft, self-mutilation, dissimulation," with an aim to improve their situation. Still, she maintains that the "acts of redress are undertaken with the acknowledgment that conditions will most likely remain the same" (51).

The film version of *The Autobiography of Miss Jane Pittman* strikes a similar note to the argument in *Scenes of Subjection*. It is reasonable to infer that the producers of the picture were white men who occupied a social position that prompted them to assume a paternal attitude toward African Americans. Tracy Keenan Wynn, who wrote the screenplay, descended from Hollywood royalty, and John Korty, who directed the movie, came from a middle-class corner of Indiana where African Americans were rare sights. The orientation of their project indicates that they were operating under the influence of the outlook derived from Black bondage that counted hardiness as a distinctive Black trait. Their backgrounds blocked them from recognizing African Americans as complicated individuals endowed with reason. As a result, they portrayed Miss Jane Pittman as a hardy figure with a shallow mind deserving of sympathy from white folks.

Wynn and Korty detached their portrait of Miss Jane Pittman from its roots. The story was drawn from the Gaines novel intended to replicate the form and content of a slave narrative. The related genre, of course, involves enslavement. As a rule, the storyteller is a slave who endures terrible treatment. In the end, however, the narrator devises a means of escape from the burdens of Black bondage. Credit for the getaway goes to what Patricia Hill Collins labeled "intellectual activism" (3) in *Black Feminist Thought*. Fundamentally, a typical slave narrative records fortunes that turn on a calculated campaign for freedom from oppression, which proves successful. As written by Gaines, *The Autobiography of Miss Jane Pittman* stands in tune with a slave narrative trumpeting a triumph over tyranny achieved through thoughtful measures.

Though upon publication the novel was mistaken for a true story, it is a narrative about an imaginary person born a slave on a Louisiana plantation. Raised like livestock as a girl in bondage, the protagonist knows little more of the world than a calf. Over a span of a 110 years, running from the outbreak of the Civil War to the high point of the Civil Rights movement, she learns that the wages of ignorance are desolation. The understanding situates *The Autobiography of Miss Jane Pittman* in the company of numerous narratives that recall the lives of historical Black figures such as Frederick Douglass, Harriet Jacobs, Elizabeth Keckley, Booker T. Washington, and Maya Angelou. The cited African American identities recorded personal histories that chalk up their fortunes to ingenuity on top of durability. Their content is not peculiar to Black letters, but it is characteristic of African American autobiographies, especially slave narratives.

In substance and style, the Gaines novel bears a striking resemblance to a classic slave narrative. Take for instance *The Narrative of the Life of Frederick Douglass* (1845), where Mr. Auld orders Mrs. Auld to cease and desist her endeavor to help Douglass grow literate, leading the Black boy to associate liberty with learning, and the understanding prepares him to take flight from slavery. *Incidents in the Life of a Slave Girl* (1861) by Harriet Jacobs contends that literacy endows an individual with the power to overcome straits as dire as captivity in a snaky swamp; the work achieves the effect through its passage where the author recalls writing a letter that fools her master about her whereabouts and saves her from his sexual advances. *Twelve Years a Slave* (1853) by Solomon Northup brings to light the story of a historical Black person who learned to use his head in the clutches of slavery; intent on a fuller life, he pursues the goal with all of the resourcefulness that he can muster, including the dispatch of a letter that secures his release from captivity. As a type of autobiography, the slave narrative descends from *The Confessions of St. Augustine* (c. 400 AD), produced in North Africa by the Bishop of Hippo. Like the seminal work, a classic slave narrative relates a sort of conversion from a lower to a higher level of existence made possible by the use of knowledge.

In reality, *The Autobiography of Miss Jane Pittman* conveys themes prevalent in a genre of fiction that began with William Wells Brown's novel *Clotel* (1853), followed by Harriet Wilson's *Our Nig* (1859). The average work counts ignorance as a source of misfortune. A classic example of the tradition, *Iola Leroy* (1892) by Frances Harper, draws the given conclusion. Zora Neale Hurston's *Their Eyes Were Watching God* (1937) features a protagonist who grows in wisdom. A lack of education subjects Bigger Thomas to fear and anger and total devastation in Richard Wright's *Native Son* (1940). Furthermore, the narrator in Ralph Ellison's *Invisible Man* (1952) finds knowledge central to the pursuit of happiness. In fact, an archetypal narrative in this genre of fiction, including *The Street* (1946) by Ann Petry along with *The Color Purple* (1982) by Alice Walker, presents learning as key to fulfillment for African Americans.

In any event, *The Autobiography of Miss Jane Pittman* is fiction with an epic character that puts it on par with diverse novels from different parts of the world. It has the narrative thrust belonging to *The Tale of the Genji*, the oldest acknowledged novel written in the eleventh century by a Japanese woman named Lady Murasaki Shikibu, centering on character development. It also shares an episodic format with *The Adventures of Don Quixote* created by Miguel de Cervantes in seventeenth-century Spain. In addition, akin to Voltaire's *Candide* (1759), the novel by Gaines contains social criticism. *The Autobiography of Miss Jane Pittman* likewise is a mock autobiography at home in the company of Charlotte Bronte's *Jane Eyre* (1847), Charles Dickens's *Great Expectations* (1861), and Mark Twain's *Huckleberry Finn* (1884), in addition to Gertrude Stein's *The Autobiography of Alice B. Toklas* (1933). Along with the protagonists of the related texts, the hero in Gaines's book grows in wisdom over the course of her story. As Alice Walker noted in the *New York Times*, Gaines's accomplished work is a "grand, robust, most valuable novel that is impossible to dismiss or to put down" (6). There is no good reason for it to take a back seat to any novel in history.

Regardless, *The Autobiography of Miss Jane Pittman* is most consequential because of its emphasis on knowledge as power. The novel implies that elevations in life result from advances in learning. Classic slave narratives rest on the theme. The premise marks distinctive Black letters. Works of fact and fiction strike the same note. African American literature shares a consensus that a want of knowledge breeds misfortune in human affairs. Through the portrayal of Pittman, Gaines implied, as a tree is bent, so it is inclined; as a person is taught, so she is disposed to conduct herself. The author's suggestion conveyed by his depiction of the hero in his novel seats him in the class of major African American authors whose work pins Black hopes on devotion to learning for proficiency in the exercise of prudence in order to avoid the fate of a leaf blown through the air by wind gusts.

The institution of Black bondage first enacted in 1661 pressed Africans in America to choose between deference and defiance for the system. The challenges that confront Pittman before and after the Civil War, her ordeals in Black bondage, and her trials in the face of Jim Crow laws demonstrate that the options of Blacks changed little throughout the span of history covering her life; it is clear Blacks were pushed to oblige or oppose expectations for them to live under the weight of whites. Even so, notable African American writers offered a third course of action. The alternative way involves living by one's wits. An excellent example in the form of fiction is exhibited by

Uncle Julius when he tells stories to turn adverse situations to his advantage in *The Conjure Woman* (1899) by Charles Chesnutt.

In "The Ethics of Living Jim Crow," Wright commends the third way to Blacks. The story is a semi-autobiographical sketch included with five tales in *Uncle Tom's Children* (1940). It tells how the hero comes to exercise discretion. In the beginning, he is very eager to defy whites. The approach proves disadvantageous. In a scuffle with a gang of white boys, he gets his head gashed by a shard of a broken bottle. Employed at an optical company, he aspires to break through a glass ceiling and rise in the business until his white peers suspend him on the horns of a dilemma that gives him a choice between deference and defiance. He chooses deference to no avail because the white workers run him out of the business anyway and kill his dream of success. He realizes, "I had to exercise a great deal of ingenuity to keep out of trouble" (14). The alternatives strike him as "distasteful" or "dangerous." He happens "upon an acceptable course of action" that falls "safely" between the other two possibilities. In sum, the hero resolves to act with discretion to turn "adverse circumstances" to his advantage (14–15).

Gaines has Pittman's adopted son, Ned, make a strong pitch for cultivated smarts in his Sunday sermon at the river. Beforehand, when Ned plays in the water with the children to teach them how to swim, he emphasizes schooling with the exclamation "Swimming is good to learn" (120). In his sermon, Ned blames inequality between whites and Blacks on a lack of knowledge. He says, "it was ignorance that put us here in the first place." In fact, he insists that their position in society stems from "ignorance on the part of the black man and the white man" (114). A student of history, Ned has determined that few people alive at the moment are aware that Black bondage evolved from trade deals between European and African kingdoms. He regrets that African "people fought each other, and the white man bought the captives for a barrel of rum and a string of beads" (114). Because of the old slave system, he indicates, whites look to confine Blacks to a poor cranny of society, and the success of the white aim depends on the control of black minds. He proclaims that he means to build a school for Black youth so they will "have a chance to get out of that corner" (116).

At ten years of age, the protagonist in the Gaines novel is ignorant of clocks and calendars. She marks time by events and seasons. Like a cow, she answers to the name Ticey and thinks of freedom as sleep until Union soldiers march on the plantation where she suffers bondage. A corporal named Brown who feels called to act as a messiah for her imparts to her a sense of the right to define herself. Then she adopts the name Jane. Afterward, the hero refuses to answer to Ticey, for which her white mistress beats her to a pulp, dismisses her from the post of chambermaid, and condemns her to pick cotton in the fields. She remembers:

> My mistress face got red, her eyes got wide, and for about a minute she just stood there gaping at me. Then she gathered up her dress and started running for the house. That night when the master and the rest of them came in from the swamps she told my master I had sassed her in front of the Yankees. My master told two of the other slaves to hold me down. One took my arms, the other one took my legs. My master jecked up my dress and gived my mistress the whip and told her to teach me a lesson. Every time she hit me she asked me what I said my name was. I said Jane Brown. She hit me again: what I said my name was. I said Jane Brown. (9)

The right to name herself is new knowledge that Pittman does not yet know how to apply without negative repercussions. It is evident later in her life that she has grown in awareness of how to deal with a white person who has a master complex, for she knows by the election of Woodrow Wilson to the White House that she needs to temper her response to the evil done by the witless butcher Albert Cluveau.

Early on, *The Autobiography of Miss Jane Pittman* testifies that the wages of ignorance are unhappiness. The point is made by the outcome that follows the decision of adolescent Pittman to go with the band of emancipated slaves, led by Big Laura, who heads North on a trek in search of better fortunes than the plight of farm animals, which has marked their past.

> We didn't know a thing. We didn't know where we was go'n, we didn't know what we was go'n to eat when the apples and potatoes ran out, we didn't know where we was go'n to sleep that night. If we reach the north, we didn't know if we was go'n to stay together or separate. We had never thought about nothing like that, because we had never thought we was go'n to be free. (16)

Unfamiliar with the territory beyond the fields of their old plantation home, the band is soon lost in the woods. None of them can tell how to survive in the wilderness. They face hunger and strife until a gang of white marauders attacks them under the cover of darkness and slaughters everyone, except for teenage Pittman and preteen Ned, both of whom hide themselves from the brutal mob. Then the two survivors set out on a mission to reach Ohio and track down Corporal Brown. For days, they walk many miles, and after a while, they cross a river on a ferry to find themselves still stuck in their home state. Left dumbfounded, Pittman supposes that Louisiana "must be the whole world" (35), exposing the breadth of her ignorance.

The Autobiography of Miss Jane Pittman provides a few grounds to envision the title character as a rugged rather than a reasonable creature. For one thing, a person other than Pittman writes her story. The fact leaves the Black woman open to being taken as a natural illiterate. She seems at best a lowbrow intellect when she wishes for Jimmy to read her "nothing in the papers side the sports and the funnies" (213). And, too, she is subject to seem as impervious to heartache as a cow, given that the three loves of her life die a tragic death and she carries on never stricken with visible grief in the wake of a single passing. The related matters render it conceivable that Pittman constitutes a model of resilience akin to the Black maid Dilsey in *The Sound and the Fury* (1929) by William Faulkner.

Despite the grounds for imagining the title character as a rugged as opposed to a reasonable individual, in effect an emblem of endurance, the Gaines novel is loaded with other features designed to sustain the discrete social perspective peculiar to Black literature, which negates the notion that Pittman symbolizes strength sans smarts. For instance, although an amanuensis gets Pittman to tell him the story of her life, the ghostwriter of the tale does not imply an inability on the part of Black people to write because he is not depicted as a white person, the usual identity of the standard amanuensis who wrote a slave narrative from the dictation of a historical Black person. The figure credited with composing *The Autobiography of Miss Jane Pittman* appears at home in the Black community. He teaches history at a local school; he feels confident that Pittman's story "can help [him] explain things to [his] students" (vii). With respect to the historian's composition of the pretend autobiography, he confides, "What I have tried to do here was not to write everything, but in essence everything that was said" (ix). The historian acts in the manner of a West African griot trained to relate a tribal tale through the story of a representative member. Concluding his introductory remarks, he says:

> In closing I wish to thank all the wonderful people who were at Miss Jane's house through those long months of interview-

ing her, because this is not only Miss Jane's autobiography it is theirs as well. This is what both Mary and Miss Jane meant when they said you could not tie all the ends together in one neat direction. Miss Jane's stories are all of their stories, and their stories are Miss Jane's. (x)

From the end of the eighteenth century to the beginning of the twentieth, scores of slave narratives were published. They were intended to be taken as personal histories that captured Black lives in general, and the works are divisible into two categories. One set consists of volumes about the lives of historical Black people written by them. Stories about historical Black people dictated by them comprise the other group of slave narratives. The full titles of publications like *A Narrative of the Life of Frederick Douglass, an American Slave, Written by Himself* and *Incidents in the Life of a Slave Girl, Written by Herself* reveal that they belong to the first category of memoirs from former survivors of slavery. The second type of works includes manuscripts like *The Confessions of Nat Turner* (1831) and *The Narrative of Sojourner Truth* (1850), which were produced by a white amanuensis, a writer to whom a historical Black person dictated the story.

The authors of *A Narrative of the Life of Frederick Douglass* and *Incidents in the Life of a Slave Girl* along with their peers wanted the title of their slave narratives to affirm that they wrote their own book to refute a persistent bias, which held that Blacks lacked the ability to write books. Because the institution of Black bondage prohibited teaching the enslaved how to read and write, the system disposed Blacks to look like natural illiterates. The publication of a slave narrative produced by an amanuensis supported the belief that Blacks did not possess the mental capacity to write their own life story. Thomas Jefferson expressed the prejudice in his *Notes on the State of Virginia* (1785) where he imagined that Black lives involve more feeling than thought. Jefferson compared the poetry of Phillis Wheatley to the echoes of a parrot. The third president could picture Blacks as a resilient breed, but not a reasoning band. As the historian in Gaines's novel converts Pittman's reminiscences into an autobiography very close to her heart, he proves that a Black person afforded a suitable education can serve as an effective amanuensis, particularly because in actuality the historian functions as the alter ego of Gaines, who earned a degree in literature from San Francisco State University in 1957.

Note too, unlike a heifer, Jane grieves the passing of her three loves; in each case, her grief is measured and mindful of how the tragedy might not have happened. She remembers, "When Joe Pittman was killed a part of me went with him to his grave" (103). She suspects he would be alive if he had exercised discretion and not bothered to try breaking the wild Black stallion. She never ceases to miss the man:

> No man would ever take his place, and that's why I carry his name to this day. I am knowed two or three other men, but none took the place of Joe Pittman. I let them know that from the start. (103)

Following the assassination of her adopted son, the fact that "the white people told Cluveau to make Ned crawl before killing him" (122), plus the remaining "trail of blood all the way from where Ned was shot clear up to his house" sticks in her mind for a spell, as she lives with the thought that "his talk at the river that day definitely hurried him to his grave" (122). She says:

> Even the rain couldn't wash the blood away. For years and years, even after they graveled the road, you could still see little spots where the blood dripped. (122)

Through the death of Jimmy, Pittman ties fortunes to a readiness to face the era. Anger, she figures, blinded Jimmy and caused him to misread the moment. She guesses he thought the period was ripe for open rebellion against the color bar, but he was mistaken because there was "nothing out there now but white hate and nigger fear" (240). She recalls warning him:

> The people here ain't ready for nothing yet, Jimmy," I said. "Something got get in the air first. Something got to start floating out there and they got to feel it. It got to seep all through their flesh, and all through their bones. But it's not out there yet. (241)

Throughout her days, Jane can use a good laugh to keep up her spirits in a society put together to treat her as if she "wasn't much better than the mule" (250). And so her desire to have Jimmy read her comic strips makes good sense. Likewise, her interest in sports columns is a reasonable reaction to adverse circumstances. It is a pastime that fills her with pride and hope because it lets her know about the exploits of the prizefighter Joe Louis and the baseball player Jackie Robinson. She admires the Black athletes for using their heads to get the better of their opponents. Jackie, as well as Joe, she maintains, "showed them a trick or two" (214).

Through her days with her man Joe Pittman and her boys Ned and Jimmy, and in the wake of their passing, Pittman like an oak tree unfazed by stiff winds keeps her wits about her. She grows well-grounded in her native land. The woman never discovers how to put her life story on paper by her own hand, but she develops a mind sharp enough to talk about it with grace and humor. Time after time, her heart is broken; she feels great grief. At points, a "black curtain hang over [her] window" and a "veil cover [her] face" (250), but she gathers wisdom and becomes disposed to meet every moment with her eyes wide open, her ear to the ground, and the teeth to wing it.

Kirkus magazine published a book review of *The Autobiography of Miss Jane Pittman* that noted, "Gaines's Miss Jane is an invented character roughly in the standard mammy mold, but with such strong personal presence that readers may still have to remind themselves this is fiction." It described the novel as the story "of the southern Negro, particularly the southern Negro woman." The review held that Pittman "seems strangely to have the upper hand with circumstances beyond her control" (Kirkus). It hit the nail on the head. Gaines's novel is the story of an African American woman from the Old South who represents African American people in general and African American women in particular. The portrayal of the hero shows that Black bondage gave birth to a culture that put a premium on strength and smarts. Indiscretion causes the death of Joe Pittman, Ned, and Jimmy. Discretion keeps Pittman alive for more than a century.

The heroic figure in *The Autobiography of Miss Jane Pittman* exhibits an undeniable identification with an old oak tree. She cherishes the "old oak tree up the quarters where Aunt Bolin . . . used to stay" (155). The Black woman attributes strength and knowledge to it. "The tree has been here, I am sure," she says, "since this place been here, and it has seen much much, and it knows much much." She confides, "I'm not ashamed to say I have talked to it. . . . but when you talk to an oak tree that's been here all these years, and knows more than you'll ever know, it's not craziness; it's just the nobility you respect" (155).

Indeed, Pittman converses with the old oak tree and calls it "Sis Oak." An exchange with a friend Yoko is most telling:

> Yoko said: "One of these days that tree go'n answer you back and you go'n break your neck running down them quarters." I

told Yoko, I said: "I got news for you, Yoko, she talks back to me all the time." (231)

The dialogue illustrates that Pittman identifies with the old oak tree. Meanwhile, it nudges readers to ascribe the tree's stated properties to Pittman herself. It reveals that Gaines intended for the character to be associated with more than a capacity for endurance.

The Autobiography of Miss Jane Pittman ends with the hero taking a stand against the Jim Crow law that prohibits Blacks from drinking water out of the fountain in front of the Bayonne courthouse. Although her action follows the assassination of her dear Jimmy, she is not driven by blind rage. Experience has taught her that the time is right. Prior to taking the subversive step, she told Jimmy, "Something got to get in the air first" (240). As she resolves to protest the racial injustice persistent in the Louisiana town, she professes, "I felt something funny in the air" (255). She deduces the presence of a wind blowing against the unfair treatment of African Americans. Her wisdom evinced at the moment goes unadmitted in the film adaptation of the novel. So, scripted by Tracy Keenan Wynn and directed by John Korty, the movie version of the book makes Pittman's "intellectual activism" seem like a mere knee-jerk reaction to a kick in the teeth.

Something is always lost in translation, which is what occurs when a book becomes a movie. In *Novels into Film* (1957), George Bluestone testifies that the conversion of a novel into a film is a "mutational process" (5). He grants that "changes are inevitable the moment one abandons the linguistic for the visual medium" (5). André Bazin, in "Adaptation, or the Cinema as Digest," describes movie adaptations as abridgements of novels. Because "faithfulness to a form, literary or otherwise, is illusory," Bazin says, "what matters is the *equivalence in meaning of the forms*" (33). Indeed, the film version of *The Autobiography of Miss Jane Pittman* is an amended and condensed form of the written text. Unfortunately, the film strays from the focal point of the book. Hence, the picture and novel lack equivalence in meaning.

Several scenes in the book are left out of the picture. Most of the deleted incidents reflect the tendency of a film derived from a novel to function as a digest of a literary form. There is a difference in the manner in which Pittman comes to settle on her name. It is noteworthy too that the speech of Ned at the river fails to take whites to task for their ignorance. Still, the bulk of the material cut out of the movie leads the picture to deviate little from the basic plot of the Gaines work.

At any rate, the movie adds new elements to the story that shift its focus from an exposition of an African American concern for education to an exhibition of a Black capacity for endurance. The film opens with Pittman surrounded by friends gathered to celebrate her birthday. More than a hundred years old, she struggles to blow out the candles on her cake. She appears to be a woman whose strength is on the wane. Beginning to recollect her life, she bears the air of someone at the end of a long struggle.

In the adapted film, a white journalist instead of a Black historian records Pittman's memory. Unlike the historian in the book who introduces the story and then disappears from the text, the white writer has a recurring role in the film. The reporter works for a magazine interested in Pittman as material for a fascinating human interest story about an old Black woman who has survived Black bondage. As he coaxes Pittman to tell him all about her, she picks up two rocks from a shelf of knickknacks, and thereafter the movie treats Pittman as a figure marked by a capacity for endurance. The benefits of learning stressed by her depiction in the novel is muted in the movie as it relates what the white writer records on tape of impromptu reminiscences by her. One night in the middle of the film, the reporter sits alone at a desk in a motel room, listens to a tape of Pittman's memories, and wonders how to document her recollections on paper. By implication, he fosters the bias that literacy is natural for whites only.

A scene late in the picture likens Pittman to an old oak tree that has weathered countless seasons of harsh winds with amazing resilience. It occurs during the penultimate sequence in the movie. Pittman sits in a chair by an oak and rambles on about her faith and favorite things while the reporter, seated cross-legged at her feet, makes mental notes of her prattle. She admits that she feels close enough to the tree to talk to it. In her eyes, the business is no dumber than having Bible verses, sports columns, and comic strips read to her. Pittman contends her life has always been in the hands of the Almighty. It seems she and the tree have seen much without understanding much. She creates an impression of a figure able to exert as much power over her lot as an ancient tree toppled by a violent wind.

In the book, Pittman walks with a growing crowd of her Black neighbors to Bayonne. A pickup truck transports the woman with a handful of her fellows to the courthouse in the film. By having her delivered to the site of the water fountain by way of a motor vehicle, the movie implies that she has reached the end of the road over which she has traveled with the aid of mere brute strength dwindling away. It withholds signs that the old woman has grown in wisdom, and the development has brought her to the final moment in her story. The movie suggests she is lucky to have survived under harsh conditions for as long as she has.

The novel concludes with a different image of Pittman. She stands as someone who has dwelled along the banks of the Mississippi River and has gotten wind of her world. It is evident in the text that she has found it wise to bide her time. She recognizes that the air can be a funny thing to tell. All the same, in the end, she seems prepared to rise above ill winds and "lift the colored people's heart" (214). Pittman's demeanor assures the downtrodden that they can beat their foes by showing "them a trick or two" (214) in the way that Joe Louis and Jackie Robinson managed to get the better of their competition. She picks up a mode of behavior that empowers her to transcend her times and free herself from serving a master as well as from soliciting a messiah.

Learning the Ropes

Snakes and weasels more lands destroy
Than any flak loons might deploy.

A habit of mind inculcated by Black bondage attributed a knack for smarts to white men. It reserved freedom, the right to choose, simply for their kind. The way of thinking rested on the assumption that other people wanted the ability to deliberate and therefore lacked any use for choice because they were bound to disgrace themselves when allowed to live by their own designs. White men were disposed to assume that they were too smart to act stupid and other people were too stupid to act smart. The given mentality sanctioned the darkest deeds of Black bondage involving sexual abuse. *Kindred* (1979) by Octavia Butler testifies that the reasoning caused smooth operating to become a particular strength of enslaved Black woman.

The Butler book expresses Black feminist thought through an imaginative rendering of the social situation that brought about the discernment. Identifying the thinking as a discrete brand of reasoning, Patricia Hill Collins attributes it to "intersecting oppressions" (*Black Feminist Thought* 48), approved by false ideas of race, gender, and class, faced by African American women subjected to black bondage, arousing "intellectual activism" (3) devoted to self-definition and self-determination. *Kindred* features a twentieth-century Black woman, transported to the time of slavery in Maryland, who means to have a hand in her fate and stand on her dignity. The novel backs a claim by Collins, holding African-American women are due to apply a special sort of feminism so long as their "subordination within intersecting oppressions . . . persists" (22). During the 1980s, the term "womanism" came to signify Black feminist consciousness drawn from the image of a "womanist" as depicted by Alice Walker in her powerful short story "Coming

Apart" (1981). At heart, *Kindred* functions as a meditation on the social positioning of Black women occasioned by Black bondage and responsible for their womanist mind.

Although Butler's book features supernatural elements, it characterizes people in a way that is true to life. Dana Franklin is the protagonist in the novel. Her story opens in 1976 when the country is engaged in the year-long celebration marking the bicentennial of independence from the British Crown. Unpacking boxes in her new Los Angeles apartment that she shares with her spouse, a white man named Kevin, she is suddenly transported through time and space to a Maryland plantation at a date prior to the founding of the first railroad in the land, which occurred in 1827. As her story unfolds, Dana shifts back and forth between the past and the present. In the antebellum era, she confronts a world of lust and brutality where enslaved women must learn how to deal with a reckless disregard for them on the part of white men. Again and again, by magical means, she returns from the past relieved to escape horrors faced by female slaves, but she realizes that vestiges of the earlier period, the epoch of Black bondage, persist in the collective unconscious of the nation. In any event, while her shifts in time are unearthly, Dana's account of characters are down to earth, based on solid research by Butler, leaving the impression that the slave system amounted to a bad school that twisted white male minds.

By starting the narrative during the national celebration honoring the bicentennial of freedom from monarchy, *Kindred* serves to underscore the former paradox of slavery in a land sold on liberty. In 1976, through the publication of *Roots*, about an African American family descended from an African kidnapped from Africa and sold into American slavery, where he suffered outrageous brutality while whites declared that "all men" are made alike with a right to liberty and justice, Alex Haley brought public attention to the awful irony surrounding the birth of the nation with the preexisting condition of Black bondage. The matter was on lots of lips a year later when a television adaptation of Haley's novel premiered and made broadcast history as the first American miniseries. The bulk of the nation's primetime viewing audience for a week stayed tuned to a major network's airings of *Roots* episodes. Viewers marveled at the picture of African civilization that appeared in the beginning; viewers expected to see a culture akin to the existence of monkeys in a *Tarzan* film rather than a society of thoughtful villagers. Every color in the land tuned into every presentation of the miniseries. Scenes of Blacks surviving the scourge of slavery and the subsequent strain of segregation left whites nonplussed and added dignity to blacks. *Roots* inspired conversations around watercoolers about the "peculiar institution" of Black bondage in the "land of the free"; however, while the television program raised awareness about the contradictory nature of slavery in the social order, it sidelined the most shocking and disgusting aspect of the unjust system.

The irony uncovered by *Roots* was still a topic of conversation when *Kindred* arrived on the scene set to tackle the darkest deeds of Black bondage. With a nonlinear plot and supernatural elements, Butler's novel made critics count it as science fiction. The stated classification discounts its realism. *Kindred* approximates real-life stories related in slave narratives as wells as interviews of former slaves commissioned by the Works Progress Administration (WPA) in the 1930s. Familiarity with the narratives and interviews of once-enslaved African Americans, such as Frederick Douglass, Harriet Jacobs, and Elizabeth Keckley, afforded Butler ample cause to depict the old slave states as sexual cesspools. For instance, in a WPA interview, W. L. Bost, a past North Carolina slave, remembered:

> Plenty of the colored women have children by the white men. She know better than to not do what he say. Didn't have much of that until the men from South Carolina come up here [North Carolina] and settle and bring slaves. Then they take them very same children what have they own blood and make slaves out of them. If the Missus find out she raise revolution. But she hardly find out. The white men not going to tell and the nigger women were always afraid to. So they jes go on hopin' that thing[s] won't be that way always. (National Humanities Center [NHC] 1)

Another interviewee, Richard Macks, enslaved in Maryland, said:

> Let me explain to you very plain without prejudice one way or the other, I have had many opportunities, a chance to watch white men and women in my long career, colored women have many hard battles to fight to protect themselves from assault by employers, white male servants or by white men, many times not being able to protect [themselves], in fear of losing their positions. Then on the other hand they were subjected to many impositions by the women of the household through woman's jealousy. (NHC 1)

Sylvia Watkins, who suffered slavery in Tennessee, told an investigator:

> Durin' slavery if one marster had a big boy en 'nuther had a big gal de marsters made dem libe tergedder. Ef'n de 'oman didn't hab any chilluns, she wuz put on de block en sold en 'nuther 'oman bought. You see dey raised de chilluns ter mek money on jes lak we raise pigs ter sell. (NHC 2)

The canon of slave narratives is loaded with accounts of sexual abuse. The *Life and Narrative of William J. Anderson* (1857) identifies "concubinage and illegitimate connections" as a "curse of Slavery." William Anderson calls the American South of his day "undoubtedly the worst place of incest and bigamy in the world" (NHC 4). Henry Bibb regretted, in *Narratives of the Life and Adventures of Henry Bibb* (1849), that "Licentious white men can and do enter at night or day the lodging places of slaves, break up the bonds of affection in families, destroy all their domestic and social union for life; and the laws of the country afford them no protection" (NHC 5). Moreover, in *My Bondage and My Freedom* (1855), Douglass wrote:

> There was a whisper that my master was my father; yet it was only a whisper, and I cannot say that I ever gave it credence. Indeed, I now have reason to think he was not. Nevertheless the fact remains, in all its glaring odiousness, that, by the laws of slavery, children in all cases are reduced to the condition of their mothers. This arrangement admits of the greatest license to brutal slaveholders and their profligate sons, brothers, relations, and friends, and gives to the pleasure of sin the additional attraction of profit. A whole volume might be written on this single feature of slavery, as I have observed it. (NHC 5)

Keckley knew sexual abuse too well. In her memoir *Behind the Scenes: Or, Thirty Years a Slave, and Four Years in the White House* (1868), she confessed:

> I was regarded as fair-looking for one of my race, and for four years a white man—I spare the world his name—had base designs upon me. I do not care to dwell upon this subject, for it is one that is fraught with pain. Suffice it to say that he persecuted me for four years, and I—I—became a mother. The child of which he was the father was the only child that I ever brought

into the world. If my poor boy ever suffered any humiliating pangs on account of birth, he could not blame his mother, for God knows that she did not wish to give him life. He must blame the edicts of that society which deemed it no crime to undermine the virtue of girls in my then position. (NHC 6)

Jacobs lament in *Incidents in the Life of a Slave Girl* (1861):

No pen can give an adequate description of the all-pervading corruption produced by slavery. The slave girl is reared in an atmosphere of licentiousness and fear. The lash and the foul talk of her master and his sons are her teachers. When she is fourteen or fifteen, her owner, or his sons, or the overseer, or perhaps all of them, begin to bribe her with presents. If these fail to accomplish their purpose, she is whipped or starved into submission to their will. She may have had religious principles inculcated by some pious mother or grandmother or some good mistress; she may have a lover whose good opinion and peace of mind are dear to her heart; or the profligate men who have power over her may be exceedingly odious to her. But resistance is hopeless. (NHC 7)

Angela Davis, in *Women, Race, & Class*, pointed out, "One of racism's salient historical features has always been the assumption that white men—especially those who wield economic power—possess an incontestable right of access to [African-American] women's bodies" (175). She wrote, "Slavery relied as much on routine sexual abuse as it relied on the whip and the lash." Furthermore, "Excessive sex urges, whether they existed among individual white men or not, had nothing to do with this virtual institutionalization of rape." Davis explained, "Social coercion was, rather, an essential dimension of the social relations between slavemaster and slave." She went on, "In other words, the right claimed by slaveowners and their agents over the bodies of female slaves was a direct expression of their presumed property rights over [African Americans] as a whole" (175).

The findings of Davis coupled with the above related memories about sexual abuse authenticate the picture of the Old South rendered in *Kindred*. Thus, despite its nonlinear plot and supernatural elements, the novel is not mere speculative literature without a stitch of realism. The novel is fiction founded on facts complied from careful research. Wondering how her ancestors fared in Black bondage during the nineteenth century led Butler to collect from family and public records information about her early kin. She also delved into slave narratives. The writer got a firm grasp of her roots from *Incidents in the Life of a Slave Girl* and *Narrative of the Life of Frederick Douglass*. Butler's first-person narration shows that true stories authored by historical African Americans who suffered slavery affected the composition of her novel. *Kindred* is rightly classified as a "neo-slave narrative" in line with fictional approximations of life stories about past enslaved Blacks, such as *Jubilee* (1966), *The Chaneysville Incident* (1982), *Dessa Rose* (1986), *Beloved* (1987), and *Middle Passage* (1990).

Even so, before Butler passed in 2006, she received recognition and rewards for being an admirable author of science fiction. *Kindred* is Butler's fourth published novel. Her initial books, that is, *Patternmaster* (1976), *Mind of my Mind* (1977), and *Survivor* (1978), display the general substance and sum of her works. *Kindred* is distinguished from its antecedents in the corpus of Butler by the presence of a historical setting. Her other books take place in imaginary lands. In any case, a concern with compulsion and its costs surfaces in all of Butler's publications. Plus, a conviction that people reflect their backgrounds runs through her material. In sync with *Up from Slavery* (1903) by Booker T. Washington, *Kindred* by implication portrays Black bondage as a bad school that trains individual to behave in an impractical and immoral manner. Washington lamented that millions of Black people "went through the school of American slavery" (16); he confessed, "I condemn it as an institution, as we all know that in America it was established for selfish and financial reasons" (17).

Kindred is a novel in which the hero realizes a need for a reeducation of the nation with regard to race and sex because of perverse ideas imparted by Black bondage. Dana, the protagonist in the book, is a Black woman with a didactic bent. Her conjugal relationship challenges notions of decency that slavery spread. Under a decade after the Supreme Court ruling in *Loving v. Virginia*, which approved miscegenation to the dismay of bigots, Dana has married a white man. Her marital union functions as a lesson that demonstrates the possibility of a respectful interracial bond between a woman and man. It upsets her uncle, who has acted with her aunt as her guardian since her parents passed. The legacy of Black bondage, it seems, leaves the uncle feeling that Kevin will never see his niece as more than a concubine, which is the way in which the husband's sister thinks of Dana.

The hero hopes to become a successful writer. A blue-collar job in a factory gives her just enough pay to get by without a hand from her folks.

She works, writes, and waits to affect minds in a constructive fashion with her words until the specter of a distant ancestor drags her back in time to the era of Black bondage. Out of the blue, Dana feels dizzy and faint; in an instant, she finds herself at the edge of woods by a river where a white boy with red hair is drowning. She rushes to save the child; the woman drags him to shore. To restore his breathing, she applies her knowledge of artificial respiration. Her good deed almost gets her shot. Under the threat of death, she feels dizzy and faint once more and finds herself with her mate again in their new apartment.

The shifts in time that occur in the opening scenes of *Kindred* recur throughout the novel. Again and again, Dana grows woozy in the present and lands in the past faced with the need to save the life of the same white character, Rufus Weylin, who is her distant ancestor. The hero returns to the present whenever her own life is threatened. The mother of the white child, Margaret, better known as Mrs. Weylin, is inclined to let the hero get shot when the parent catches Dana nursing her son. Thus, having the barrel of a rifle stuck in her face sickens the protagonist; she falls into a swoon and recovers to find herself home again. By then, the magical thrust of the narrative is established: Dana is yanked into the past for the sake of Rufus and pulled into the present for her own sake.

In the Maryland world of Rufus, where Black bondage is in full effect, Dana stands at the mercy of white men with a reckless disregard for life and limb in relation to her and other Black women. She represents an affront to conventional wisdom. It is deemed outrageous for a woman to wear pants. Mixed-race marriages are forbidden. Custom trains white boys to assume authority over Black men, on top of all women, and to view the others as intellectual inferiors, mental midgets well short on sense. White men are credited with the smarts to read and write. Dana, a Black woman who has a white mate, aspires to write, and chooses to wear pants, arrives on the Southern scene bound to upset the ruling white patriarchy because her mind and mien fail to meet the expectations of the men. Her disposition is more disturbing than their egos can handle. To them, she has the unmitigated gall to dress and act like a white man; early on, her demeanor provokes a white man with a master complex to grab her and slap her and tell her, "'You got no manners, nigger, I'll teach you some'" (41).

The hero of *Kindred* faces a need to keep Rufus alive long enough for him to father Hagar, the matriarch of her maternal line. Unless he impregnates Alice, whom he enslaves, Dana will not descend from Hagar. Hence, the protagonist has to muster all of her intelligence to succeed. First, at the river, her use of artificial respiration to breathe life back into Rufus allows her to form a fragile bond with him. As her returns to the past stretch from mere minutes to many months, her knowledge fascinates Rufus more and more. Her possession of literacy and awareness of the future procures his admiration. When he breaks a leg and runs a high fever, she gives him aspirin and uses every other trick that she knows to reduce his temperature; upon recovery, Rufus, developing a master complex, cries out loud to keep Dana yoked to him as his caregiver.

Given her didactic bent, the protagonist imagines that she has the power to straighten out Rufus's mind and turn him into a humane figure, unlike his father, Tom Weylin, who slaps his spouse, smacks his son, and straps his slaves. *Kindred* places blame for Mr. Weylin's conduct on social conditioning. She offers assurance that the culture programs white men to see Black men as tools, white women as trophies, and Black women as trollops. It gets under Mr. Weylin's skin to see Dana in pants because it strikes him as a usurpation of his privilege. His discovery that she can read and write rattles his cage, since he is not much of a reader himself; fit to be tied, he dresses her down and means to tan her hide. Displays of her mental prowess enrages Mr. Weylin beyond words because they make him feel stupid, which she is not smart enough to do according to his sense of himself in relation to her kind. He acts on logic learned from his father that he intends to pass onto his son. In effect, Mr. Weylin expects his boy to become a chip off the old block and sexually exploit Dana besides other Black women.

The odds are against Dana's efforts to sow humanity in Rufus. She would love to render him a chivalrous gentleman who courts Alice to win her hand in marriage and in due course bring Hagar to life. However, the steady pull of his milieu affects him more than Dana's fleeting contacts with him. She has to accept that Black bondage inculcates a sort of stupidity in white men, a want of common sense, a lack of fellow feeling, which grants them license to treat others with callousness. A particular exhibition of the irrationality occurs during the scene where Dana watches a white male mob brutalize an enslaved Black man for the crime of sleeping with his free Black wife without the permission of his master. Dana draws some kindness out of Rufus; in the process, she stymies some of the idiocy he picks up from his surroundings. Yet she is unable to keep him from becoming a maniac who trusts he has a right to have a Black woman against her will and have his way with her for as long as he pleases.

Before a bittersweet ending, *Kindred* tells that the past slave system taught the enslaved to stake their fortunes on staying a step ahead of their enslavers. The novel is constituted to have the reader find the prospects of an antebellum "slave girl" close to the circumstances of someone stuck in a snaky swamp. It is a situation that asks women to keep their wits about them with an eye out for an exit. Scenes of slaves disposed to stay on their toes cover the better part of *Kindred*. They illustrate that it took intelligence applied with ingenuity to keep a shred of dignity in the bog of Black bondage. Dana recalls learning the ropes, discovering how to survive slavery from instruction conveyed to Nigel by his father, Luke, and gathered from Nigel's eventual mother-in-law, Sarah, who serves as the cook for the Weylins:

> I took some cookhouse advice I'd once heard Luke give to Nigel. "Don't argue with white folks," he said. "Don't tell them 'no.' Don't let them see you mad. Just say, 'yes, sir.' Then go 'head and do what you want to do. Might have to take a whippin' for it later on, but if you want it bad enough, the whippin' won't matter much." (96)

Dana confesses, "I decided to develop a similar attitude." In essence, she commits to becoming a smooth operator, a proponent of intellectual activism, entailing swift dissembling.

Proof that the slave system compelled the enslaved to become clever at dissembling is evident in their responses to the harm with which the social order threatens them. They are expected to obey the command of a white man without a hint of resistance no matter how cruel or corrupt the order might be. Luke is a Black slave who serves Mr. Weylin as a capable overseer until a whiff of defiance slips out of him, and his master, enraged, punishes Luke by selling the slave down the Mississippi River. *Kindred* offers attempted flights from Black bondage as fool's gold. There is no exit from the swamp of slavery. Luke's son Nigel tries to escape, but fails; also, Isaac, the loving Black husband of Alice, seeks to run away with her to free her from the hands of Rufus, but he fails too and pays a heavy price for his daring. Dana likewise at one point in the narrative makes a run for freedom to no avail. The novel shows that the best bet for the preservation of pride and person among the slaves lies in putting on a false front.

Nigel learns from the fate of his father, as well as his own failed escape, to mask indignation he bears from pressure to act as a flunky for his boyhood playmate Rufus. Sarah, the cook, who heads the household staff in the Weylin home, shows her master great deference while she harbors fierce disdain for him because of his callous sale of her children to places beyond her reach. She teaches Dana the score. Sarah helps her realize the need for ingenuity to overcome the indignities of Black bondage. The cook is happy that her last child, Carrie, whom she still has to hold, cannot say a word; the disability keeps Carrie from ever needing to bite her tongue and causes her to strike Mr. Weylin as an undesirable article. Sarah reflects:

> "First my man died—a tree he was cutting fell on him. Then Marse Tom took my children, all but Carrie. And, bless God, Carrie ain't worth much as others 'cause she can't talk. People think she ain't got good sense." (76)

The cook has learned to prepare a face for the white faces she meets with an eye toward fending off as much harm and hardship as possible.

The enslaved men in *Kindred* never dare make a pass at Mrs. Weylin, the white mistress of the manor, whose first name is Margaret. Black men who labor around the estate approach Mrs. Weylin as if she were a sacred figure too delicate and dignified for any sort of intimacy with any of them. On the other hand, the Black men are supposed step aside for Mr. Weylin to handle their mothers, sisters, and wives as articles for his pleasure. Black bondage, *Kindred* attests, established a code of conduct that handed white men all the chips in the mating game. The objections to the marriage of Dana and Kevin, raised by their relatives in 1976, emanate from the sexual mores of the antebellum age. For instance, Kevin's sister is disposed to live with her brother marrying a demure white woman and having an extramarital affair with a Black woman, but she is indisposed to take in stride her brother tying the knot with a Black woman; Dana's uncle feels Kevin as a white man can forever lust after his niece, but never love her. The attitudes of the sister and uncle betray the collective unconscious raised by the slave system.

Mrs. Weylin suffers a bizarre form of idolatry. She shows the predicament of white women during the era of Black bondage. In *My Bondage and My Freedom*, Douglass wrote, "Women—white women, I mean—are IDOLS at the south" (NHC 5). Mrs. Weylin, standing for her real peers subject to Victorian values, is expected to be prudish. Her husband, like his historical counterparts, believes that sex is a dirty business to be conducted with Black women, whom he imagines are wanton in nature. As a result, paroxysms of jealousy and rage plague Mrs. Weylin because enslaved children with looks that remind her of her husband surround her. She lashes out at the Black women who cook and clean for her even when she "couldn't find anything to complain about." In fact, one day without any good reason, she throws "scolding hot coffee" (81) at Dana.

Against the laws of nature, Kevin is hurled backward through space and time and finds himself living in the Weylin house along with Dana. His experience attests that people are products of a place, environments shape minds, and societies function as a school. In the nineteenth century, the social order accustoms Kevin to enjoy an unquestioned right to sexual freedom. He becomes "a part of the household, familiar, accepted, accepting" (97). Dana is disturbed by the ease which he comes to "acclimatize" to the Weylin world. Everyone sees Dana as Kevin's concubine, and as such the community, save Mrs. Weylin, takes their sleeping together in stride. Sarah smiles and offers Dana some advice on how to handle Kevin, in effect, how to act as a smooth operator:

> "Girl . . ." She smiled a little. "I see you and him together sometimes when you think nobody's looking. You can make him do just about anything you want him to do."
> Her smile surprised me. I would have expected her to be disgusted with me—or with Kevin.
> "Fact," she continued, "if you got any sense, you'll try to get him to free you now while you still young and pretty enough for him to listen." (96)

Mr. Weylin is amused by the thought that Kevin uses Dana as his concubine. Dana reports:

> Tom Weylin was up early one morning and he caught me stumbling, still half asleep, out of Kevin's room. I froze, then made myself relax.
> "Morning, Mr. Weylin."
> He almost smiled—came as near to smiling as I've ever seen. And he winked.
> That was all. I knew then that if Margaret got me kicked out, it wouldn't be for doing a thing as normal as sleeping with my master. And somehow, that disturbed me. I felt almost as though I was really doing something shameful, happily playing whore for my supposed owner [Kevin]. I went away feeling uncomfortable, vaguely ashamed. (97)

The relationship between Rufus and Alice suggests what the fortunes for Kevin and Dana would have been had they spent their youth under the social conditions of the Old South. Rufus and Alice were born free; the two of them have grown up together; they were playmates until they arrived at their teenage years. Rufus has always had some affection for Alice. Still, babied by his mother and bullied by his father while his parents in concert belittle their slaves, Rufus comes to lack compassion. He develops the callousness and stupidity that the system produces in slaveholders, which prevent him from winning Alice's heart. The Black woman is touched by the solicitude that Isaac shows her. Rufus reaches manhood primed to deny her the right to choose the person with whom she is going to mate. He enslaves her for daring to escape with Isaac. It follows that she has three possible ways to go: try to run away again, take her own life, or play the part of a paramour. Alice goes with the latter option for a while, but the situation brings her so much sorrow and shame that she resorts to suicide.

It takes Kevin a spell to recognize the awful horror of the antebellum age. At first, he supposes that the enslaved population is not treated badly. While Dana realizes that it is the worst of times for a Black woman, Kevin finds the period fascinating. His status as a white man blinds him to reality until he is separated from Dana for five years and witnesses on his own the true extent to which the system degrades and disgraces African Americans. He is transformed into an abolitionist (essentially a white man with a messianic complex) by the exposure of his twentieth-century sensibility to the extreme cruelty inflicted upon Blacks by nineteenth-century whites, leading him to seek the liberation of the enslaved.

Again, Butler's consideration of how her actual ancestors bound by Black bondage processed the stress and strain of slavery prompted her to write *Kindred*. Her work supports the conclusion that African Americans caught in the slave system had little chance for escape from the social order that subjected them to depravity. *Kindred* signifies that Butler's ancestors had to make some tough decisions like the resolve of Dana to coax Alice into serving as a concubine for Rufus so that Hagar can be born and Dana can descend from her. Through its accounts of the enslaved, *Kindred* suggests that the forebears of the author most often staked their well-being on skill at dissembling, and the failure of Alice to become adept at the practice leads to her downfall. The novel implies that Butler's ancestors in slavery became maestros of improvisation who put on shows for their masters to alleviate the dehumanization posed by the blindness of whites to their common humanity.

In the final bit of the novel, through research, Dana discovers a nineteenth-century Baltimore newspaper article that recounts the destruction of the Weylin estate by fire. The piece found in the paper leaves out any mention of the fact that Rufus has died from knife wounds inflicted by Dana in her fight to keep him from raping her after Alice in despair has taken her own life. Dana remembers that Nigel knows the truth about her stabbing the slaveholder to death, because he has caught her with the murder weapon in her hand. Thus, Nigel has not said a word to authorities in relation to the homicide. Dana figures that Nigel covered up the crime by setting the fire in a clever exercise of ingenuity:

> Nigel had probably set it to cover what I had done—and he had covered. Rufus was assumed to have burned to death. I could find nothing in the incomplete newspaper records to suggest that he had been murdered, or even that the fire had been arson. Nigel must have done a good job. (263)

It seems he learned to act as mute as Carrie, that is, he has kept silent about the cause of Rufus's death. Given that the newspaper article accounts for every Weylin slave but Nigel and Carrie, who have become mates, it stands to reason that they have taken advantage of the distraction created by the fire to slip away from slavery.

Kindred discloses scant possible profit for anyone affected by Black bondage. While peace of mind eludes the Black slaves, anxiety plagues the white members of the Weylin estate. Margaret, browbeaten time and again by Tom, shrouds her body in a black gown before she is a widow. She lives with jealousy of enslaved women who catch her husband's eye; to calm her nerves, she uses opium. Tom is a thorn in the side of everyone about the Weylin estate; he pushes them to want to kill him. It is evident that following in his father's footsteps leads Rufus to grow merciless and maniacal about controlling Blacks. He confides to Dana, "When you sent Alice to me that first time, and I saw how much she hated me, I thought, I'll fall asleep beside her and she'll kill me" (257). In substance, *Kindred* submits a cost-benefit analysis of the slave system that counts it as a tax on society because it twisted minds and corrupted behavior. The single redeeming value of the business, according to the novel, was its ingrained penchant for pushing the enslaved to sharpen their wits to stay on their toes and keep two steps ahead of their masters.

Blind Man's Bluff

*Eyes wide open are as good as blind
In a hard head with a closed mind.*

Nothing is beautiful from every point of view. What the mind thinks, the eyes perceive. The way in which a matter is considered depends on the disposition of the observer in relation to the observed. Believing becomes seeing. Three perspectives in *Dessa Rose* (1986) tell that pictures of others, which people see in their mind's eye, reflect acquired tastes.

Experiences frame minds, indicated John Locke in *An Essay on Human Understanding* (1689). *Dessa Rose* concurs with the conviction, as it ties perspectives to backgrounds. The novel fosters faith that American society has trained its members to judge their fellows by their looks. It lends credence to assertions by Judith Lorber in *Paradoxes of Gender* (1994) as well as claims by Michael Omi and Howard Winant in *Racial Formation in the United States* (1986). Lorber stamped definitions of gender as invented identities that characterize men as strong and smart and women at most as weak yet winsome. Omi and Winant labeled racial classifications as fanciful fabrications that ascribed brains and beauty to whites; moreover, their study implicated that the type of character imputed to Black women, at best, was sensuous and submissive. Together, the cited scholarship assures that the land has schooled folks to pick up specious notions of gender and race. The chief female figures in *Dessa Rose* uncover the truth of the matter.

One viewpoint in the cited novel written by Sherley Anne Williams belongs to a white male figure named Adam who feels superior to Blacks and women by virtue of an assumed genius deemed peculiar to his shade and sex. A white female character, Ruth, raised to regard herself as delicate and dependent on men for her welfare, conveys a telling outlook in the narrative at issue. And, last but not least, *Dessa Rose* presents the perspective of a Black female character, christened Odessa, who fumes with indignation from oppression and exploitation at the hands of imperious white men accustomed to the enslavement of her kind. The narrative renders the separate views in an order indicative of each persona's prescribed stratum on the social pyramid of the antebellum age that placed Adam at the pinnacle, Ruth in the middle, and Odessa on the bottom. Each of the three figures provides a provisional account of the title character.

The development of the three figures illustrates that their social positions have shaped their sense of themselves in relation to others. Their initial identities constitute cultural assignments. They have lived their lives in a social order that situates them on rungs according to their shade and sex. Adam, Ruth, and Dessa have learned to play parts fixed by custom. Their behavior confirms the thesis of Judith Butler stated in "Performative Acts and Gender Constitution" (1988), where she argued that "gender is in no way a stable identity or locus of agency from which various acts proceed; rather, it is an identity tenuously constituted in time—an identity instituted through a *stylized repetition of acts*" (519). The three *Dessa Rose* figures at issue attest through their turn of mind spotlighted by poetic flares that Butler's description of gender applies to race as well.

All of the given identities have a name that alludes to a legendary figure. Adam of course refers to the first man in the Bible. Ruth denotes the biblical woman who forsakes her tribe and its traditions yet finds happiness through divine intervention. In Greek mythology, Odessa represents the female version of Odysseus and is associated with wrath and wandering.

The allusions serve to fix the images of the characters with the evocative effect of poetry.

Throughout the text, *Dessa Rose* features poetic touches. It stands to reason, since the author was a successful poet. Her collection verses of *Peacock Poems* gained a nomination for the National Book Award in 1976. Reviewing *Dessa Rose* for the *New York Times*, David Bradley wrote in 1986:

> TWO things can happen when poets venture into fiction. They can approach the business with the arrogant (or naive) assumption that they already understand the purposes and problems of fiction, and end up producing books which, while sometimes pyrotechnic in terms of poetry, are duds in terms of prose. This, alas, is the usual case. Sometimes, however, a gifted poet comes to the novel with a humble determination to do what

fiction has to do: tell a story worth telling. The product in this case is not only good fiction, but fiction enlivened by symbolic connections and daring imagery—elements that those who write only prose often neglect. (7)

Bradley concluded that Williams produced a literary work that is "an absorbing fusion that is both elegant poetry and powerful fiction." Moreover, he adds, "while Ms. Williams shows that she can write a novel better than a lot of novelists, nowhere does she cut herself off from her poetic roots: the language of 'Dessa Rose' is everywhere infused with rhythm and image" (7).

Postmodern in style, *Dessa Rose* features a nonlinear plot. Mimicking classic slave narratives, such as *Incidents in the Life of a Slave Girl*, it is a historical novel on par with Octavia Butler's *Kindred*. *Dessa Rose* fits well in the genre of the neo-slave narrative, re-creating the form and content of true-life stories shared by historical individuals like Harriet Jacobs who suffered the scourge of Black bondage. The work of Williams unfolds in three parts. It starts with "The Darky," where the title character rots in prison for leading an insurrection and committing murder. "The Wench" is the next section of the novel. "The Negress," the final part of *Dessa Rose*, relates the development of the partnership that forms between Dessa and Ruth.

The first section of the narrative, containing Adam's point of view, is titled "The Darky." Odessa, an enslaved eighteen-year-old Black girl, who is surnamed Rose and nicknamed Dessa, dwells in the dark, foul basement of a sheriff on an Alabama farm, where she waits in shackles to be put to death for inciting a revolt by a coffle of slaves that has left five white guards dead and a slave trader without an arm. Because she is pregnant, her execution has been postponed until she gives birth to her infant. Adam, whose last name, Nehemiah, alludes to the biblical builder of walls in Jerusalem, meets Dessa in the cellar. He has come intending to interview her for material to include in a book on which he is working concerning slave rebellions, titled *The Roots of Rebellion in the Slave Population and Some Means of Eradicating Them*. Adam is reputed to be an authority on resigning Blacks to bondage.

The man finds Dessa taciturn, reluctant to share her personal history, unwilling to confide in a white person after the hardship and heartache his kind has caused her. She has suffered an awful time on a plantation where enslaved Blacks are pressed to work their fingers to the bone. Her former master, Terrell Vaughan, has stolen from her the love of her life. Dessa is unable to forget about a slave named Kaine of whom she was enamored. It is the sole part of her life that she is willing to share with the white interrogator. She remembers that her lover and the father of her infant had a "voice high and clear as running water over a settled stream bed" and a way of walking "the lane between the indifferently rowed cabins like he owned them, striding from shade into half-light as if he could halt the setting sun" (11). Her master, in a fit of jealousy and spite, has smashed Kaine's prized banjo and killed him.

Adam first finds "the darky," Dessa, "barely visible" (17), chained in the shadows of her prison, a root cellar owned by a slaveholder, who also happens to be the town sheriff. The speech of the slave girl is faltered, and her expression is fainthearted. It is hard for Adam to picture Dessa as the leader of a revolt by a coffle of slaves that left some white men dead. The white man gets lost in her backstory of her love for Kaine, butchered by her white master, as Cain killed Abel in the Bible; the slaughter provokes Dessa to smite Terrell. Adam cannot imagine how or why an expectant slave girl could have committed the cold-blooded deed. To acclaim, the white interrogator has published his book on slave uprisings. Dessa, yet a mere teenager, brings to light a thoughtful side that surpasses the white man's grasp. Letting an ability to act on a hidden agenda slip out of her account, Dessa throws Adam for a loop; in time, she blows his mind by vanishing from the basement without a single trace, demonstrating that his view of her in particular and Blacks in general is erroneous and absurd.

The second section of the novel, "The Wench," covers Dessa's life following her escape from the cellar, which renders Adam piqued and perplexed, leading him to pledge to track her down. Some escaped slaves have helped Dessa to take shelter from captivity. By means of an underground network organized by Mammy, agents of the operation, runaway slaves, arrange for Dessa to meet Ruth, a white Southern belle from the crème de la crème of Charleston, who is stranded in the sticks and disillusioned by the desertion of her spouse, a riverboat gambler. "They had come for her at night," Dessa recounts. "Nathan, Cully, and Harker, whom she hadn't known" (86). Ruth harbors the runaways and other fugitive slaves on her farm under the guise of owning them.

"The Wench" features Ruth's point of view. She muses on the problems she has faced. Her husband, Bertie, has disappeared. The loss of her dear handmaid Mammy, whom illness has taken, troubles Ruth the most because the older Black woman has guided her like a mother since before and ever after her rotten husband brought her to live in the half-built mansion on the Sutton Glen plantation in the backwoods of North Carolina. Dubbed Rufel by the Blacks surrounding her, the Southern belle from the elite of

Charleston broods over the passing of Mammy, who masterminded the faux slave operation for the benefit of Ruth:

> A cold had settled into Mammy's chest at the tail end of spring. It had seemed nothing serious at first and Rufel, roused at last from lethargy and anticipating Bertie's return any day, had enjoyed pampering Mammy, playfully bullying her into drinking Ada's noxious brews. The cough worsened and with frightening suddenness, Mammy died. Rufel could not get used to that fact. Nothing in the days and weeks since Mammy's death had filled the silence where her voice used to live . . . Who would scold her or laugh away her fears? (112)

Mammy has seasoned the three Black men who have facilitated the escape of Dessa from prison and given her shelter at the Sutton Glen plantation. The slave girl never has an opportunity to converse with Mammy, because the lady's maid has suffered her sudden death prior to the pregnant teenager's arrival at Ruth's door. In any event, Mammy has left behind her a legacy that guides the operation of the Sutton Glen plantation. Mammy has mothered Ruth; she has castigated and has cheered the Charleston belle when either action has been necessary. The older Black woman has set the regimen for planting and harvesting cotton to sell at market. She has put together the workforce from fugitive slaves and offered them refuge and an equal share of the profits in exchange for their labor in the field along with their agreement to help other Blacks escape bondage. In sum, Mammy has furnished the means by which Dessa, on top of Ruth, is able to improve her lot.

Prior to the unexpected passing of Mammy, Ruth has turned a blind eye to the subterfuge of the hands on the Sutton Glen plantation. Her upbringing has indisposed her to face harsh realities. She has endeavored to hold onto a dream of being swept off her feet by a gallant white gentleman who carries her to an ornate mansion on a lush estate, where she enjoys a life of leisure, attended by a bunch of happy servants. The loss of Mammy compels the Southern belle to accept that her husband is gone for good, and her welfare depends on collaboration with a band of runaways. While Ruth mistrusts Dessa because of the teenager's history of violence, the white woman nevertheless nurses the fugitive's baby, relaying hope that she can work in partnership with the Black girl. She suspects that there is something wrong with Dessa because the teenager courted trouble so close to her due date. Betraying a bias of her class, Ruth refers to Dessa as the "wench."

For Dessa, full of wrath for whites, it is beyond belief that Mammy, a slave, could have loved Ruth, a slaveholder. It disturbs Dessa to know that "the white woman nursed her baby." The deed goes "against everything she has been taught to think about white women" (117). Motivated by spite, the slave girl calls into question the sincerity of Ruth's bond with Mammy. So Dessa forces Ruth to concede that she has never bothered to learn the older Black woman's real name. Then, the female characters have a heated exchange:

> The white woman's baby started to cry and the white woman made as if to rise and go to get it. Dessa's voice overrode the tearful wail, seeming to pin the white woman in the chair. "See! See! You don't even know 'mammy's' name. Mammy have a name, have children."
> "She didn't." The white woman, finger stabbing toward her own heart, finally rose. "She just had me! I was like her child."
> "What was her name then?" Dessa taunted. "Child don't even know its own mammy's name. What was mammy's name? What—"
> "Mammy," the white woman yelled. "That was her name."
> "Her name was Rose," Dessa shouted back, struggling to sit up . . .
> "You are lying," the white woman said coldly; she was shaking with fury. "Liar," she hissed.
> Dessa heaved herself to her knees, flinging her words in the white woman's face. "Mammy gave birth to ten chi'ren that come in the world living." (119)

Dessa lists all of Mammy's ten children and she ends saying, "Dessa, Dessa Rose, the baby girl" (120). It is then apparent that Dessa is a slave girl who has been sold from her mother, Mammy.

To the fugitive Blacks, who maintain the guise of slaves on the Sutton Glen plantation, Mammy is Dorcas. In truth, Mammy is Dorcas Rose. She is the birth mother of Dessa. The reality shatters Ruth. The white woman struggles with the revelation:

> *Mammy have children.* What had the colored girl called her Mammy? *Rose. Dorcas. Rose—smooth black.* She remembered the phrase, the fresh airish smell that seemed to follow Mammy—

Dorcas. Rose? Would the wench call the coffee-dark skin "smooth black"? Rufel herself had seen Mammy's eyes in the wench's face. (130)

It proves that the white woman's view of the "wench" and other Blacks is off the mark. Hence, needing consolation, Ruth turns to Nathan. And she becomes intimate with the Black man.

Ruth's intimacy with Nathan steams up Dessa. The teenager figures, in the absence of her husband, that "Miz Lady"—insanely stressed out—is suffering a bad case of jungle fever, a sick yearning to have sex with a Black stud. Dessa feels that the white woman must have thrown herself at Nathan and pressed him to ravish her. The teenager takes to calling Ruth "Miz Ruint" behind her back because she thinks the Southern belle, not right upstairs, has stripped Nathan of his dignity as her crazy last master has done to her. Dessa locates true romance between Blacks and whites beyond the realm of the possible, for her experience has taught her that whites lack the humanity to hold Blacks dear.

The narrator holds, Nathan's "company came, in large measure, to replace the companionship Rufel had shared with Mammy." The text implies that the Black man, mentored by the older Black woman, is a smooth operator. He has learned how to put white people at ease and win their trust. Interacting with Ruth, "He treated her with a semblance of deference and indulgence that had characterized Mammy's attitude toward her." After a little while, Ruth pays heed to the fugitive slave. "Through talking with Nathan, Rufel came to know something of the people who lived in her Quarters." Tying Nathan to Mammy, Ruth thinks, "Even if Mammy herself had been spiteful, bitter, secretly rebellious, Mammy, through caring and concern, had made Rufel hers, had laid claim to her affections" (146–47). In effect, regardless of whether it is all a performance staged for their personal benefit, the way in which the Black people treat Ruth benefits them.

The third section of the novel, "The Negress," conveys Dessa's point of view. She stays furious about Nathan's involvement with Ruth until Harker appeals to her reason. Afterward, relating the view of the slave girl, *Dessa Rose* begins to relate the development of a partnership between Dessa and Ruth, involving the staging of a colossal masquerade meant to dupe slaveholders out of cash in the interest of amassing ample funds to finance going to the territories for a fair chance to live free and easy. The entire community of the Sutton plantation commits to the scheme. It entails having Ruth sell the men back into slavery and helping them escape so that she can resell them to other slaveholders. The group pulls off the scam several times and collects a fair amount of money. Every one of them puts on a swift performance that takes in white men. "Miz Lady," recounts Dessa, "would tell some story about her husband being laid up with the fever or a busted leg" (194) to explain why she instead of her spouse has gone on the road to sell slaves. The Black plotters, aware that they are doomed if caught by white men, act "dumb and scared" while "Miz Lady" behaves "high-handed and helpless" (194).

Through their shared adventure, Dessa and Ruth grow closer to one another. As they travel from county to county, Dessa poses as Ruth's personal maid. Their scheme is very successful, though they have a close call or two that threatens their prospects. In any case, at every turn, they come to one another's aid and avoid disaster. For example, one night, when the two of them are looking to pull the wool over the eyes of white men in the market for slaves, they run into trouble. With a smooth air, they ease into an unknown town prepared to stage an elaborate masquerade, aiming to sell some of their male crew and steal them back afterward. Quick thinking by Dessa saves Ruth from sexual assault.

On the stated occasion, Dessa plays a polite lady's maid and Ruth portrays a proper lady with some human merchandise for sale. They attract a mark named Mr. Oscar, who to all appearances, is a chivalrous Southern gentleman invested in Black bondage. He invites Ruth, along with Dessa, to accept his hospitality, call it a day in his home, and finish their business in the morning. In response, Ruth acts "all giggly and fly, like she didn't have two thoughts to rub together in her head" (200); the white woman intends to exploit a white male gaze conditioned to find a Southern belle weak yet winsome. Upholding custom, Dessa, the pretend lady's maid, goes to sleep on the floor beneath the bed of the putative white lady like a household pet resting on parquet below the mattress of her keeper until she is aroused by shrieks from Ruth, which Dessa mistakes offhand for outcries of passionate consensual sex, but, in reality, Mr. Oscar is attempting to rape Ruth. Once Dessa determines the truth, she partners with Ruth to bring the white man to his knees and kick him out of the bedroom; the experience establishes a bond between Dessa and Ruth, because the slave girl realizes that "Miz Lady" is just as susceptible, as she has been, to being dishonored by a shining example of a disgusting creep:

> I laid awake a long time that night while she snored quiet on the other side the baby. The white woman was subject to the

same ravishment as me; this the thought that kept me awake. I hadn't knowed white mens could use a white woman like that, just take her by force same as they could with us. (201)

The attempted rape gives Dessa a brand-new perspective about Ruth and herself. The young lady comments, "My thoughts on her had changed some since that night at Mr. Oscar's." She observes, "You can't do something like that with someone and not develop some closeness, some trust." Dessa begins to talk a lot with Ruth. She admits, "We even laughed about that bad Oscar one night" (206).

Grasping their mutual subjection to oppression founded on groundless impression of their gender, Dessa joined forces with Ruth just as Black female abolitionists locked arms with white suffragists against patriarchy in the nineteenth century. In *Women, Race, and Class,* Davis recalled how African American women like Sojourner Truth and Harriet Tubman won the support of white women like Sarah and Angelina Grimke, who recognized that the enslavement of Black women "bore a certain resemblance to their own" (19) domination by men. They reached a common understanding that "unless they defended themselves as women—and the rights of women in general—they would be forever" doomed side by side to the "destiny of passivity and dependence which society had imposed upon them" (42–43). The realization led to the appearance of Sojourner Truth (aka Isabella Baumfree) in 1851 at a Women's Rights Convention where she delivered her celebrated "Ain't I a Woman" speech. Women, the Black abolitionist contended, possess might and a mind as men do.

On the road, Ruth aka "Miz Lady" has a swift response to an ambush by two white highwaymen, which exhibits strength and smarts. Her reaction to the surprise attack fortifies her bond with Dessa. Miz Lady addresses the crooks as if they were "some rude boys" who have "tracked dirt across her clean floors." Then she flings her "big, floppy, drawstring bag" (209) stuffed with crocheting and things in the face of the horse carrying the robber with a gun; it causes the horse to rear up and makes the gunman lose his firearm. She releases her band of impostors to pounce on the bandits. Her young female partner reports:

Honey, they wasn't no match for us, smooth as we moved together. When she flung that bag, Nathan shoved them reins on me, went flying at the one held the mules; I ducked down with the baby between the seat and the front of the wagon and pulled Miz Lady down on top of us. By the time I looked up, Harker had the gun on one and Nathan had a choke hold on the other. Miz Lady was brushing herself off and fussing about scoundrels picking on defenseless peoples. That's the way it was: bam, bam, bam, just like that, just like we'd done this a hundred times before. (209)

The slick team of con artists leaves the robbers on the side of the road tied to a tree in a daze. It demonstrates that the group has melded into a crack team of smooth operators.

The final test of the partnership between the leading female characters comes as they are close to their end goal of swindling slaveholders out of enough bucks to bankroll a flight to freedom on the frontier. Doing their last job, Dessa is spotted on the street by Adam, the white reporter famous for writing about slave management. He has been obsessed with finding the slave girl since his discovery of her escape from being kept under lock and key. The white man hauls the teenager to see the local sheriff; Adam charges the girl with being a menace to society sentenced to capital punishment. Dessa plays it cool; she denies ever knowing the reporter and acts baffled by his accusations. Reminiscent of Huck Finn aiming to free Jim from prison on the Phelps farm, Ruth comes to help her partner out of the jam. In concert, Dessa and Ruth think on their feet, ad lib in sync, and make up tales as they go along, winging it, until they convince the law officer that Adam must be delusional. Through their performance, Dessa and Ruth capture the heroic ideal in Black culture; they become smooth operators who turn the tables on a subjugator. Strolling out of the sheriff's office, Dessa and Ruth corroborate the certainty that oppression produces among the oppressed improvising aces.

With their whole team of con artists, the female heroes pay their way to a happy ending. Their story warns that believing becomes seeing; it tells that bad beliefs tender shocking sights. In *Dessa Rose*, the leads discredit accounts of their gender, owing to conventional wisdom, which restrict their pursuit of happiness. Images of them propagated in the minds of men are rendered dopey impressions by the development of Dessa and Ruth. The evolution of the female figures exposes a shared flair for sizing up a situation and turning it favorable. It reveals a profound potential, borne from birth, to switch tragedy into triumph. The growth of the daring partners makes them fit leaders no matter the lot.

Besides their births, the band of men in the novel *Dessa Rose* owe a lot to the women of the book. The fortunes of the male figures spring from the exercise of ingenuity by their female partners. There is plenty of evidence that oppression produces among oppressed females of every shade improvising aces. The text signifies that Black bondage impelled women caught in the slave system to grow into smooth operators quicker than their white fellows. The work whispers through its body that a species of stupidity bred in slaveholders, which blinded the oppressors to the human nature of women, pressed the enslaved females to advance their private interests and those of their fellows by staying on their toes, two steps ahead of their masters.

Dessa Rose illustrates that women possess the capacity to be leaders. The story demonstrates that they can chart a prosperous course in life without men to guide or guard them. Females in the book grow ever more understanding of the world around them. Three women in particular are heroic. They prove to be endowed with a mind for a substantial amount beyond cooking, cleaning, and caring for children. Trial and error school the intrepid trio; passion tempered by reason moves them. Their identities are Mammy, Ruth, and Dessa; their maneuvers bring a dream of independence to fruition for a ring of men in addition to themselves.

The author of *Dessa Rose* was an extraordinary individual. She was born in California, a year before the end of World War II, to parents who picked cotton in the San Joaquin Valley. Williams earned a master of arts degree from Brown University during the tricky times of Richard Nixon in the White House; in due course she became a professor in the English Department at UC San Diego, where she was a member of the faculty until her untimely death on the downside of President Bill Clinton's "Bridge to the 21st Century." In 1975, she published her book of poetry *The Peacock Poems*. The publication was nominated for the Pulitzer Prize in addition to the National Book Award. She converted one of her verses, "Some One Sweet Angel Chile," into a phonograph record. *Dessa Rose* was the first of three novels from the author. Her many achievements affirm that she had a head for far more than picking cotton.

Williams was a leader of the Women's Liberation movement, peaking across the nation at the moment *Dessa Rose* was born. It made a decisive case for the dismissal of ancient terms and conditions that limited the pursuit of happiness by women. The author of the novel would be classified as a "womanist" partner in a feminist enterprise, meaning that, in alliance with Alice Walker—author of *The Color Purple* (1982)—she sensed a shade of difference between entrenched boundaries confronting Black and white women. Nevertheless, at heart, Williams championed a campaign to afford complete humans rights to persons of her gender irrespective of their color. With Women's Liberation icon Gloria Steinem, who wrote *Outrageous Acts and Everyday Rebellions* (1983), Williams backed freedom for females to seek fulfillment in every social arena that caught their fancy, including the fields of sports and science.

Through *Dessa Rose*, Williams placed leadership in all walks of life within the power of women. Basing her key female figures on real people, she shielded the characters from charges of being mere figments of her imagination. In 1829, an enslaved Black female, pregnant in Kentucky, was convicted of inciting a coffle of slaves, headed for sale at auction, to revolt against their captors. The expectant mother was sentenced to death; there was a stay of her execution pending the birth of her child. From the rebel leader, Williams drew the title character of *Dessa Rose*. The author gathered the figure of Ruth from the reported story of a single white female who owned an out-of-the-way North Carolina plantation in 1830. It was published that the white woman handled her business in collaboration with a colony of fugitive slaves who found safe haven on her property.

Bradley in his *New York Times* review of *Dessa Rose* characterized the book as an "artistically brilliant, emotionally affecting, and totally unforgettable" tale of two women who go "on the lam from race and gender" (7). As a matter of fact, Dessa and Ruth come to shatter stereotypes. The former serves to contradict fantasies of Black women, which count them born to serve male masters as caretakers or concubines. Ruth forsakes the conduct prescribed by the "cult of true womanhood" demanding that her class of females maintain the pose of a shrinking violet longing with all her heart to win the favor of a white knight. The Southern belle forgets her egotistical and errant husband and enters into an affair of the heart with Nathan. Clear-eyed, Ruth throws in her lot all the way with the collection of fugitive slaves situated on her grounds. Akin to Ruth in the Bible, her basic desertion of her tribe and its traditions brings her happiness. When Ruth and Dessa reach Council Bluffs with their booty, they look bright and beautiful in their eyes, and their success leaves them sure of their view.

Dress for Success

Our course is set not by a gale;
But how well we handle our sail.

Black bondage assured African Americans that discretion is the better part of valor. The system was stacked against their resistance so that open defiance on their part begged reason. Around every corner, white men with whips and arms waited to mortify, maim, or murder them if they opposed their enslavement. Challenged to make the best of a bad situation, they devised schemes to turn times with whites to their advantage. James McBride captured the reality through his depiction of enslaved Henry Shackleford in *The Good Lord Bird* (2013).

McBride's book is a novel that belongs to the genre of the neo-slave narrative. In *Neo-Slave Narratives* (1999), Ashraf Rushdy put forth an authoritative definition of the literary form. The type of writing, Rushdy held, emerged in the twentieth century, involving a fictional Black slave who recounts a life story that establishes Black bondage as a former convention with lasting cultural effects. Moreover, he maintained, the genre uncovers evidence that the slave system influenced enslaved African Americans to conceive an ethos by which they resisted succumbing to stupefaction and subservience. *The Good Lord Bird* represents an excellent example of the literary form as defined by Rushdy. It features an imaginary Black narrator who has suffered slavery in the land during the antebellum age. The accounts of the storyteller indicate that the system prompted African Americans to produce a culture that put a premium on canny conduct to save the enslaved population from sinking to the level of witless livestock. As a rule, circumspection marks the Black slaves portrayed in *The Good Lord Bird*.

Making its debut during the first year of Barack Obama's second term in the White House, the McBride novel in most cases received positive reviews. Baz Dreisinger, writing for the *New York Times*, credited the book's author with being "like a modern-day Mark Twain: evoking sheer glee with every page" (1). The following year, an unflattering critique from Justin Cartwright appeared in *The Spectator*, contending, "The book appears to be very random" and strewn with "language" that "is a kind of sub-Mark Twain, ludicrously overcooked" (Cartwright). At any rate, Marie Arana in *The Washington Post* asserted, "There is something deeply humane in this, something akin to the work of Homer or Mark Twain" (Arana). Several critics tied *The Good Lord Bird* to *The Adventures of Huckleberry Finn* (1884). Except for the negative comparison of the two novels rendered by Cartwright, reviews that link them stem from a fair grasp of the material. Both texts in fact employ humor to expose grave matters that give rise to human sorrow.

Akin to the novel *Middle Passage* (1990), a neo-slave narrative written by Charles Johnson, *The Good Lord Bird* won the National Book Award for Fiction. Also like the Johnson's work, McBride's book draws on a story by a white author. References to Herman Melville's novella *Benito Cereno* (1855) run through *Middle Passage*. There are allusions to *The Adventures of Huckleberry Finn* throughout *The Good Lord Bird*. Yet neither of the Black writers produced a mere copy of white literature. They revised renditions of Black life stories involving improvised escapes from slavery that uncovered a culture raised by Black bondage and pervaded by discreet behavior. Johnson compliments Melville and McBride pays tribute to Twain for capturing the heroic ideal of African Americans, extolling circumspection and distinctive from the central figures in classic slave narratives like the *Narrative of the Life of Frederick Douglass* (1845) in addition to *Incidents in the Life of a Slave Girl* (1861).

With regard to *The Good Lord Bird*, it is easy to tell that it commemorates Twain's *Huckleberry Finn* through its portrayal of Henry Shackleford, the protagonist. The hero of the novel is a pubescent boy, the same as Huck Finn. Henry likewise hails from a Midwestern state along the Mississippi River. Each of the characters is a motherless child with a negligent father. They both hit the road for an unusual reason and undergo a series of adventures that humor or horrify them. The two boys along the way to the end of their journey assume false identities.

Similar to Huck, Henry travels with an unexpected adult companion. Yet, instead of accompanying an enslaved Black man running from slavery, he goes with a free white man bent on ridding the nation of Black bondage. The imaginary Henry tours the country from Kansas and Missouri to Pennsylvania and Massachusetts with a figure torn from the pages of history.

He moves in the company of the famous abolitionist John Brown, whom Henry calls "the Old Man." On the trail, Henry witnesses savage battles between armed bands of white men over the practice of Black bondage, which evoke the bloody feud between the Grangerfords and Shepherdsons over the right of a daughter to choose a spouse in *Huckleberry Finn*.

Henry's adventures with the Old Man include a three-week layover at the Rochester estate of Frederick Douglass. On the property, the boy meets two women who bring to mind the Widow Douglas and her sister Miss Watson in Twain's novel, whose "pecking" at Huck "got tiresome" (10). The women at issue in *The Good Lord Bird* are Miss Ottilie, "a German white woman," and Miss Anna, "a colored woman from the South." Henry identifies the females as "Mr. Douglass's two wives." He is "uncouth in their eyes and needing barbering and learning of proper manners." The protagonist says, "I gave them a lot of work in that department." He relishes that they don't "have time to fool with [him] much" because they are obsessed with fussing over Mr. Douglass, trying "to outdo each other with the handling of him" (373–75).

Traces of the duke and dauphin, the shameless scoundrels in *Huckleberry Finn*, who desire to sell "Miss Watson's big nigger, named Jim" (13) back into slavery and also conspire to swindle young women out of money, surface in *The Good Lord Bird*. The counterparts to Twain's crooks are Chase and Randy. They accost Henry and fugitive slave "Nigger Bob" on the road to Pikesville. "Pro Slavers" who despise "Free Staters" against slavery, they are primed to treat Henry and Bob as merchandise for sale. Moreover, they have no qualms about bilking women out of cash. Chase and Randy act entitled to use females as well as Blacks for their personal benefit.

Nevertheless, it is a mistake to count Henry as a plain replica of Huck. Throughout McBride's novel, Henry performs a charade that renders him a clever reproduction of Twain's "nigger" Jim. Like the runaway in *Huckleberry Finn*, Henry represents a smooth operator, a deft dissembler, given to swift deployments of deception for the sake of an improvement in his lot. The protagonist in *The Good Lord Bird* follows a way of life to which Jim converts Huck. Henry in truth reflects a reality that McBride has known and come to understand from personal experience. Huck on the other hand embodies a vicarious sense of a lifestyle that Twain gathered from his association with Uncle Dan'l, the old enslaved Black man, who taught the white storyteller how to tell tall tales during his boyhood.

Henry exhibits the conduct of an African American who has realized that white people suffer from a form of blindness that prevents them from seeing him for whom he really is. The initial impression that John Brown forms of Henry underscores the visual impairment that disables whites to recognize Blacks as flesh-and-blood bodies with an array of hues and range of identities affected by social conditions. At first sight, the Old Man mistakes Henry for a girl and thinks that the boy's name is Henrietta. The historical abolitionist's misperception serves to prove that whites see Blacks as abstractions rather than varied, complex individual human beings. It is fair to say that *The Good Lord Bird* constitutes a meditation on the affliction of "blindsight," which has infected white people.

The social order established by Black bondage impeded the capacity of whites to picture Blacks as human equals. It classified visual features as vital signs of identity and worth. With Blacks confined to subservient roles, information about them that reached white eyes supported an unconscious feeling that dark skin signified an inferior character. Without a cognizant awareness, identification and recognition became detached processes in the minds of white people. In essence, whites were trained not to see what was before them when they looked at African Americans. The cultural positioning of Blacks on the lowest echelons in the country by and large caused whites to develop imaginations of them without a basis in reality, but which seemed factual to whites.

Ralph Ellison's *Invisible Man* (1952), another winner of the National Book Award for Fiction, exposes the persistence of blindsight among whites that leads them to see Blacks without seeing them. Successive white figures in the narrative fail to appreciate the person whom the narrator of the story actually is. The storyteller goes from striking a white crowd as a prizefighter to hitting one as a page before being seen by others as a peon, puppet, and philanderer in lieu of his philosophical self. A synopsis of the character's plight opens the prologue of the novel:

> I am an invisible man. No, I am not a spook like those who haunted Edgar Allan Poe; nor am I one of your Hollywood-movie ectoplasms. I am a man of substance, of flesh and bone, fiber and liquids—and I might even be said to possess a mind. I am invisible, understand, simply because people refuse to see me. Like the bodiless heads you see sometimes in circus sideshows, it is as though I have been surrounded by mirrors of hard, distorting glass. When they approach me, they see only my surroundings, themselves, or figments of their imagination—indeed, everything and anything except me. (3)

Henry in *The Good Lord Bird* confronts the same sort of blindness in white eyes, identifying him without recognizing him.

John Brown presumes to know the worth and wants of Black people. His attitude is evident in his relationship with Henry as well as his dealings with the boy's father. Pa, Henry's forebear, is an enslaved barber, illiterate Bible-thumper, and bootlegger of rotgut booze. The Old Man fails to recognize that Pa is resigned to his place in the social order where he entertains white men with his liquor and mangled secondhand quotes from Scripture. Pa declines to take flight into the wilderness with the Old Man because he has a good racket going in Dutch Henry's Tavern; he can "come and go as he pleased" (25), but Brown thinks the Black man is an oblivious victim of learned helplessness. "We've no time," asserts the Old Man, "to rationalize your thoughts of mental dependency, sir" (36). Proving the white man neither sees nor hears Blacks, Brown demands Pa along with his daughter (meaning Henry) let him carry the two of them to "safety." Pa's effort to tell the Old Man, "Henry ain't a" (36) girl is cut off by Brown, who believes that Pa means to say the name Henrietta.

About "how the Old Man's mind worked" (36), Henry remarks:

> Whatever he believed, he believed. It didn't matter to him whether it was really true or not. He just changed the truth till it fit him. He was a real white man. (36)

The given description epitomizes the two types of white racists generated by the institution of Black bondage. Both sorts of mentalities are depicted in *The Good Lord Bird*. The Old Man is the kind who is full of compassion for Blacks, who feels called to act as a guardian for them, who aspires to see them emancipated from subjugation to cruelty, but disbelieves in their true equality. His opposites are men like Chase and Randy in line with Dutch Henry Sherman, who owns Henry's father, his "aunt and uncle, and several Indian squaws, which he used for privilege" (25). Sherman and his ilk burst with contempt for people of color. White men with his frame of mind pack his tavern. They "drink, throw cards, tell lies, frequent whores, and holler to the moon 'bout niggers taking over the world and the white man's constitutional rights being thrown in the outhouse by the Yankees" (20). And the place's patrons shudder at talk of Blacks being freed from bondage and afforded social equality.

Across the board, socially conditioned white minds, McBride's novel demonstrates, believe whatever they are trained to believe about Blacks. It does not matter whether the belief is true or false. Such minds twist reality to meet their expectations. In the novel, the critical telltale sign of the delineated mentality is a character's perception of Henry. For the bulk of the narrative, the male figure dons a dress and bonnet. He does it to conform to the Old Man's expectations after he is snatched from Dutch Henry's tavern and taken on the road with the abolitionist. Every white person, save one, who witnesses the boy in the traditional female garb, mistakes Henry for a girl. The single exception is Frederick, the Old Man's son, who is portrayed as a person too soft in the head to keep an idea fixed in his mind.

Frederick serves as an excellent example of a white man whose mind has not hardened into a rigid perspective that cast everything in black-and-white terms. He is a "huge, strapping youth about twenty years old" (46). A ton of weapons hang off him so that when he makes a move, he sounds like metal jangling in "a hardware store." Henry observes, "His brains was muddy" (55). When Henry falls from a horse and his frock flies up, exposing his male genitals to Frederick, the Old Man's son is thrown for a bit. He wonders whether Henry is a "sissy," but he is confused about what it means to be gay, and he cannot think of a reason to make a fuss about Henry's sexual identity. So he lets the matter go without further mention. Henry decides that Frederick happens to be "as good a friend as a feller—or a girl who really was a feller—could want" (139).

William Chafe in *Women and Equality* laid a foundation on which to draw a comparison between the positions of women and Blacks in the national development. McBride achieved a similar end through his treatment of the protagonist in his novel *The Good Lord Bird*. Chafe warned against concluding that the given groups "have suffered comparable physical and material injury" (672). The researcher found a "parallel" that "consists of the way in which blacks and women have been given the psychological message that they should be happy" with their situation (665). He understood that judging people by their appearance is an entrenched social custom that has inclined the collections in question to practice "dissembling in order to conform to social preconceptions" (667) about their character, and to avoid being forced "into a form of physical or spiritual exile" (669) for a failure to uphold standards. Chafe offers "the coquette role" in women's history as food for thought on which to chew for a taste of "manipulative behavior" (668) incited by inequality. Henry plays the part in *The Good Lord Bird* when circumstances call for it.

The mind of the Old Man in the novel is too fixed to see Henry as anything other than as he first sees him, that is, as a Black girl in need of safekeeping. Brown exoticizes Henry; the white man regards the Black boy as a talisman, a lucky charm, sent by Providence to afford the abolitionist magical powers and bring him good fortune in his crusade to save enslaved blacks from the scourge of slavery. In the course of their travels from the prairies of Kansas to the plantations of Virginia, Brown never has a second thought about the sexual identity of Henry. The Old Man preaches to Henry and directs the boy, but he never bothers to gain any real knowledge of the youth, his thoughts and feelings, hopes and dreams, fears and anxieties. Brown's attitude toward Henry is reflective of a compassionate white man's stance on Black people, conducive to a messianic complex. The Old Man assumes that he knows the wants and needs of every African American whom he encounters, from Henry to legendary historical figures like Frederick Douglass and Harriet Tubman. While Dutch Henry, along with Chase and Randy, like the duke and dauphin in *The Adventures of Huckleberry Finn*, feel born to lord over Blacks and women, Brown harbors a sense of being made to shelter underdogs from harm.

Brown's fixed opinion of Blacks causes him to believe that Douglass and Tubman are willing to put their fortunes on the line and join him in his attack on the armory at Harper's Ferry. Although the two famous escaped slaves pledge to participate in Brown's violent venture, the renowned African Americans are no more honest with the Old Man than Henry and Nigger Bob are with Chase. Douglass and Tubman never come close to showing a reckless disregard for life and limb by joining Brown at Harper's Ferry, where the Old Man meets devastating defeat. The renowned African Americans just tell Brown what they sense he wants to hear. It is the same thing that Henry and Nigger Bob do with Chase; they tell the chauvinistic white man what they feel will make them agreeable to him. Chase is a contemptuous bigot; in his mind, Black people are born for his benefit. He holds in his head the idea that Blacks are subordinate to whites by nature, that they are made to occupy the substratum of the social order, that he has a natural right to use them as he pleases. Detecting how Chase pictures them causes Henry and Bob to play up to him, while the scoundrel plots to sell the Black boy into prostitution and the Black man into drudgery. The sole difference between Chase and Brown is that the latter figure has a misguided desire to help Blacks, while the former character has a malignant disposition to harm them; both white men hold a mistaken view of Black people.

W. E. B. Du Bois realized that the effect of Black bondage on the white imagination engendered a divided mind among African Americans. In *The Souls of Black Folk* (1903), Du Bois held that Black people were "gifted with second-sight in this American world" because the social order denied them "true self-consciousness" free from false public judgments. The system was designed, Du Bois observed, just for Blacks to envision themselves "through the revelation" of denigrating white opinions. African Americans, he indicated, were accustomed to "a peculiar sensation," which constituted a "double-consciousness," amounting to a "sense of always looking at one's self through the eyes of others, of measuring one's soul by the tape of a world that looks on in amused contempt and pity." They are forever subjected to a "twoness," being a Black American, consisting of "two souls, two thoughts, two unreconciled strivings." Their "dogged strength alone" kept them from "being torn asunder" (38). Du Bois concluded:

> The history of the American Negro is the history of this strife,—this longing to attain self-conscious manhood, to merge his double self into a better and truer self. In this merging he wishes neither of the older selves to be lost. He would not Africanize America, for America has too much to teach the world and Africa. He would not bleach his Negro soul in a flood of white Americanism, for he knows that Negro blood has a message for the world. He simply wishes to make it possible for a man to be both a Negro and an American, without being cursed and spit upon by his fellows, without having the doors of Opportunity closed roughly in his face. (39)

The Good Lord Bird makes it plain that the institution of Black bondage engendered a white mind full of compassion or contempt for blacks that left African Americans disposed to double consciousness. The Old Man exhibits that mind of a white man closed to ideas other than his own. For instance, about Brown, Henry says, "Anytime he said something about the will of God, it meant he weren't going to cooperate or do anything but as he saw fit" (167). In reference to white views of Blacks, Douglass tells Henry:

> "They know you as property. They know not the spirit inside of you that gives you your humanity. They care not about the pounding of your silent and lustful heart, thirsting for freedom; your carnal nature, craving the wide, open spaces that they have procured for themselves. You're but chattel to them, stolen property, to be squeezed, used, and occupied." (385)

Traveling as a boy clad as a girl, Henry resolves that whites "didn't no more take notice me of being a boy under that dress and bonnet than they would notice a speck of dust in a room full of cash" (401).

Furthermore, *The Good Lord Bird* illustrates that African Americans confronted by whites blind to their true humanity resorted to deft dissembling. Henry confesses that Blacks in bondage knew that honesty was not the best policy for them. The protagonist says:

> Truth is, lying come natural to all Negroes during slave time, for no man or woman in bondage ever prospered stating their true thoughts to the boss. Much of colored life was an act, and the Negroes that sawed wood and said nothing lived the longest. (53)

White racism, the novel proves, "made white folks subject to trickeration" (60). Henry asserts, "Colored was always two steps ahead of white folks" because the underdogs were required to think "through every possibility of how to get along without being seen and making sure their lies match up with what white folks wanted" (61).

Henry masquerading as a girl represents the prime example of a Black character who resorts to trickeration in *The Good Lord Bird* hoping to turn advantageous interactions with whites that are in essence fraught with danger. Nigger Bob is quick to admit a willingness to engage in deft dissembling to advance his self-interest. He confesses that he would be happy to trade places with Henry and put himself in a position to flee bondage with the assistance of Brown by assuming the identity of a girl. Bob declares:

> "If I could get Old Brown to favor me and carry me to freedom, why, I'd dress up as a girl every day for ten years. I'd be thoroughly a girl till I got weak from it. I'd be a girl for the rest of my life. Anything's better than bondage." (113)

The attitude of Bob is typical of the enslaved in *The Good Lord Bird*. Blacks in the book subject to slavery stay poised to put on a show for whites aiming to improve their lot.

Sibonia is the best example of the fact that the Black characters in the novel are dedicated to fooling whites by acting as if they are other than they really are. She first appears locked in a muddy stall for livestock, where she spends her nights at the end of a grueling day expended on dirty work with a gang of fellow Black slaves. Henry comes away from his initial encounter with her certain that she is a madwoman. He finds her "cackling and babbling like a chicken" (254). In truth, she is playing crazy to seem too senseless to whites to suspect that, akin to the real-life Nat Turner, she is using Bible meetings to plan a slave revolt.

The white characters in *The Good Lord Bird* indicate that identifying oneself as a white person leads to identification with the long list of positive connotations associated with the word "white." At heart, feeling white prompts individuals to presume that they are righteous, reputable, honorable, honest, stainless, spotless, innocent, impeccable, blameless, bright, and beautiful. Identifying as white induces individuals to grow full of hubris to a degree that blinds them to the merits of nonwhite people. The Old Man represents a perfect example of someone who feels white. He is so full of himself, so self-absorbed, so proud that he thinks that he knows Black people well, but he cannot distinguish between a Black boy and a black girl. And he is not alone in his blindness; he is just one of a host of white figures presented in *The Good Lord Bird* resembling one-eyed Jack in *Invisible Man*, looking to relieve Blacks from oppression, with a picture of African Americans that is delusional.

Time and again, black slaves in McBride's book display second-sight, which enables them to see what proud white characters miss. The vision possessed by the enslaved becomes apparent the instant they spot Henry disguised as a girl. They are no more misled by his outfit than the woman Judith Loftus is tricked by the sight of Huck dressed as a girl in *The Adventures of Huckleberry Finn*. McBride's story as well as the fiction of Twain makes it apparent that social underdogs like slaves and women in American society are indisposed to suffer the blindsight that disabled King Lear from seeing his daughters for who in essence they are. *The Good Lord Bird* illustrates that black bondage compelled past African Americans stuck in the system to figure out the true character of figures that they faced on sight for the sake of their well-being.

When Nigger Bob encounters Henry on the road, the black man is too busy trying to save himself from getting into trouble with the contemptuous white man Mr. Pardee to give Henry his full attention. Bob is hard-pressed to develop a good cover story for refusing to obey the wishes of the white tyrant. Nevertheless, the boy strikes the black man as odd at first sight, and once Bob settles his conflict with Pardee, he determines that Henry is a boy in the clothes of a girl. Then he advises Henry to continue playing the part of a girl in the interest of finding a way out of slavery. At that point, Nigger Bob professes, "If I could get Old Brown to favor me and carry me to freedom, why, I'd dress up as a girl every day for ten years" (113).

Henry never manages to pull the wool over the eyes of Pie, whose fortunes depend on sizing up and shaking down men. The boy says, "She was all class." He observed, "She surveyed the room slowly like a priestess." Pie is a "bundle of beauty" (229–30), an enslaved woman condemned to play the part of a *filles de joie* for the pleasure of depraved white men. Akin to Loftus in *Huck Finn*, Pie was quick to smell a rat. The black woman exhibits the personality of a smooth operator. Her white madam, Miss Abby, "let her choose her own customers more or less, and live as she wanted" (253). Pie takes one good look at Henry and tells him, "You's a lie" (244). Not caring to let white men "cut out them little grapes hanging between [his] legs and stick them down [his] gizzard" (224), she pledges to Henry that she will "girl you up" (248) just as Loftus showed Huck how to act like a girl so that he "might fool men" (Twain 85).

Sibonia is no less perceptive than Pie. The insurrectionist, who covers her cunning by pretending to be insane, knows right away that Henry is not a girl. She calls him a "mule-headed sissy" (259) who needs "more than a bonnet and some pretty undergarments" to dodge "the white man's evil" (260). Sibonia is more typical in her deportment and discernment. Attempting to recruit Black slaves to join the Old Man in his attack of the armory at Harper's Ferry, Henry finds one circumspect Black slave after another who recognizes his true identity despite his garments. He dupes neither the Coachman nor his spouse, who both mistrust him and keep him at arm's length without a bit of interest in becoming a part of Brown's guerrilla army.

It seems that pride, hubris, or chauvinism blind everyone who mistakes Henry for a pubescent girl. This no doubt is the case for the Old Man in particular and his white fellows in general. The rule applies to a solitary Black character, the figure representing the historical Douglass. Overweening and intoxicated, he makes the mistake of calling Henry "Harlot Shackleford" (385) and then seeks to seduce the boy, whom he mistakes for a girl. Freedom, it appears, has given the great Black orator the attitude of a self-absorbed white man.

Tubman on the other hand, ever circumspect, comes across as a former slave who maintains humility. Henry professes, "that woman had my number" (431). After alerting him to the fact that "We all got to die" (433), Tubman says:

"But dying as your true self is always better. God will take you however you come to him. But it's easier on us all to come to him clean. You are forever free that way. From top to bottom." (433)

Then, as a show of solidarity, without exposing the boy in front of Brown, the Black abolitionist and activist who escaped the slavery into which she was born and made thirteen excursions on the Underground Railroad to rescue almost six dozen Blacks from the bowels of bondage, remembered as "the Moses of her people," hands the boy "her beaten colorful shawl." Tubman instructs him, "Take that and hold it." She believes "it may be useful" (434), presumably in his efforts to keep white men in the dark about his true self.

The Good Lord Bird is a deft chronicle of historical fiction with bits of sidesplitting comedy charged by compelling dialogue and delightful characterization. It draws to its conclusion with Henry taking cover while the Old Man leads fewer than twenty whites and less than a handful of Blacks in the raid on the arsenal at Harpers Ferry. After the attack fails, the hero escapes to Philadelphia, where he spends the remainder of his days free from slavery. The paucity of Black support for Brown's campaign tells that enslaved African Americans frowned on open resistance to Black bondage. It vouchsafes that a culture grew among the enslaved that fostered artful dissembling to make the best of a bad situation. By the end of McBride's book, the protagonist exemplifies a member of African American society who has become a smooth operator, a Black person given to double consciousness and accustomed to devising strategies to turn to his advantage interactions with white people afflicted by a form of blindsight that impaired their vision of his humanity as male chauvinism has left men in the dark about sexuality.

# Postscript

On One's Game[1]

*If you dig grounds that others don't,
Bet you will strike gold where they won't.*

Fourteen days after I graduated from grade school at Our Mother of Sorrows, I met Oliver Brown. I was hired to be his summer assistant for six weeks. He was the groundskeeper at the Holy Redeemer Church located in the Cresheim Valley ward of the city. I pegged him on sight as no kind of hero.

My first morning on the job, Miss Mary, the business manager, welcomed me. While she detailed my hours and duties, the groundskeeper, a tall Black man, stepped two feet inside the office, stopped, and hunched up with a Titleist golf visor in hand and a big grin on his face. Mr. Brown was a stranger to me until the business manager, a white woman with strands of gray in a beehive, introduced him. She said his real name, but she stressed that everyone called him "Bud" around the church. The man wore a khaki shirt beneath blue overalls that appeared ironed. I placed the man close in age to my grandfather, who was a boy when Theodore Roosevelt occupied the White House. The Black man, I learned, had worked at the church since the Great Depression. He met Miss Mary after a Sunday service when she was a girl with her hair done in pigtails.

The man was a hoary old guy, yet sturdy and trim. His complexion was a tinge lighter than a Hersey chocolate bar. It was beyond me why he kept his shoulders arched and his head bowed. His posture grated on my

---

1. This narrative is based on a true story. The names of people and places are fiction.

nerves. He kept his eyes glued to the floor as Miss Mary spent a few more minutes reciting the terms of my employment and having me fill out forms. On one of the documents, I saw Miss Mary had typed in a misspelling of my name. When I pointed out her mistake, she raised an eyebrow. Mr. Brown darted a glance at me and rolled his eyes, as the business manager placed me in his custody with a request for him to show me the ropes.

"Yes, Ma'am," he responded.

"Thank you, Bud," she said.

He waved me out of the office in the Parish House to an archway outside connected to the church building where the groundskeeper spelled out what he expected of me. First, he instructed me to mind my manners at all times. Second, he ordered me to call him "Mr. Brown." He said the church cook, Mrs. Brooks, served breakfast at 8:00 sharp Monday through Friday in the kitchen. I had to arrive in the morning by then if I wanted to eat any food. He wanted me ready for work at half past the hour and not any later. In the main, he directed me to put my best foot forward with an eye to see that the property around the Holy Redeemer stayed spick and span. "Be sorry," he said, "to let a soul catch you idle."

I was amazed. He was acting high and mighty with me. In the sight of Miss Mary, he behaved like a boy. It hardly made any sense to me. His manners annoyed me so much I almost told him to shove it. I felt I should have nothing to do with him. Through mysterious means, my father's sister's husband, a chemistry teacher, who urged me to attend services at the New Bethlehem Baptist Church, set it up for me to work with Mr. Brown. I aimed to use my earnings from the six-week job to cover the cost of needed books, supplies, and carfare that would come with starting high school at the Prep in the fall. Nevertheless, I figured I could go hunt for another gig or just make do with what I earned from my paper route, which I was keeping anyway.

As I followed the groundskeeper on a tour, the scenery kept me from heading home. The environment enchanted me. From the back of the Holy Redeemer, the lawns of the Friendship Dell Country Club stretched farther than my eyes could see. The whole neighborhood seemed like the location of an old movie starring Katherine Hepburn and Cary Grant. Stone mansions sat in separate lots with black cast-iron or white picket fences backed by thick hedges. Shade trees lined the roads, and cool breezes swayed the leaves. I could not believe the area was located within the city limits.

By then in June, about the inner city, a smattering of trees, charred by fumes from heavy traffic, let temperatures rise to blood-boiling levels.

The houses on my block of Race Street were each attached to another one like units on a row of two-story zoo cages. The entire street went without air-conditioners. On the most sweltering nights, when homes baked with heat like ovens, families slept on their porch. It was a wonder a riot never broke out in the neighborhood. I felt I knew for sure why unrest had grown persistent in the summer among Black inner-city dwellers across the country. It came from overheating.

The day after I graduated from Our Mother of Sorrows, Blacks rioted in Cincinnati. Unrest soon followed in Tampa and Buffalo. The events recalled the Watts uprising that shook the city of Los Angeles with the shock of an earthquake two summers earlier. A long, hot season of urban furor awaited the nation. In a month, riots would ravage Black sections of Newark, Detroit, and Milwaukee.

Reckoning the job at the Holy Redeemer provided me with a way to escape some of the inner-city heat, I resolved to stay put and stomach Mr. Brown's conduct. So I allowed him to engage me in a rigorous routine that began right after the tour. For the day, he assigned me a lawn to mow and hedges to trim, as well as a garden to weed, a walkway to sweep, and trash to collect. It turned out that the bulk of my assignments exposed me to the sun. I got a fifteen-minute break in the morning and also in the afternoon. A half-hour was allotted for lunch at high noon. I finished my first day under the groundskeeper with my shirt dampened by sweat.

It took a lot of effort to get back to the Cresheim Valley site the next morning. I had to beat the sunup. Then it was necessary for me to deliver the newspapers on my route. Next, I needed to ride the Market Street subway to Penn Station. At the terminal, I had to catch the regional train to the Highland depot. From that juncture, I faced a block and a half walk.

At Penn Station, senior white men in blue or gray suits and solid or striped ties stepped from the cars of the Cresheim Valley train. Besides them, young white women in miniskirts and high heels left the vehicle. I boarded a car with Black women in housedresses and flats. Behind a Black man with a tool belt, I sat and gazed at the sights that appeared outside the window as the rail line rolled out of the terminal tunnel to my stop. Along the tracks, parks and pools replaced warehouses and factories. Congested arteries gave way to quiet lanes. By the Highland depot, I spotted a Black woman in a maid's uniform, who was walking a shaggy dog and pushing a white baby in a carriage.

I reached the Parish House kitchen fifteen minutes after 8:00 a.m. Mrs. Brooks, the Black cook, dressed like a nurse in a white gown and stockings, set a plate of eggs, bacon, and toast on the table beside a cup of coffee in front of Mr. Brown. She met my eyes, looking sorry for me. The groundkeeper viewed me with a frown. He told me to wait for him outside because I was too late for breakfast.

On the steps in back of the Parish House, I steamed while I waited for Mr. Brown. I grew anxious to give him a piece of my mind. But then I had second thoughts as I gave his conduct further consideration. He slouched in the company of Miss Mary, but straightened up out of her sight. Moreover, he bowed and scraped for her in a manner that reminded me of an African native from a Tarzan movie devoted to the king of the jungle. Anytime he had me alone he acted as if he believed I should bow down to him. I judged him a two-faced creep, like the preacher played by Burt Lancaster in *Elmer Gantry*.

I lost my train of thought when the shadow of the groundskeeper fell over me. He announced that he was going to give me a lesson on the smart way to cut grass. According to him, I made a mess of the small patch I had mowed the day before. He insisted I missed spots and left rough edges. My effort was sloppy, he argued. And, he added, if I wanted to stay on the job, I had better make a point of being tidy.

He stationed me in the middle of the backyard that abutted a hurricane fence belonging to the Friendship Dell Country Club. The lawn lay between the Parish House and a wooden shed where Mr. Brown stored tools and equipment. Barred from the hut by him, I waited in the sun while he fetched the lawnmower. Once he returned with it, he demonstrated how I should cut the grass in even rows. He challenged me to match his effort. The groundskeeper questioned if I had enough brains to pull off the trick.

Determined to prove him wrong, I took hold of the mower and began pushing it forward in a straight line. As I cut a few even rows, the old man went to supervise me from the shade of an oak tree. Two white men came from a nearby house. I guessed one of them in a black shirt with a white collar was the pastor. His companion seemed more important because he had on a blue suit with a white shirt and red tie. At their appearance, Mr. Brown hunched up and grinned. "Good morning, Pastor" and "Hello, Deacon," he said, before they glimpsed him.

The deacon noticed me first. I heard him mumble, "Those people," to which the pastor replied, "Not all of them." Turning to the groundskeeper, the deacon asked, "Keeping the new boy busy, Bud?" In reply, the pastor exclaimed, "Depend it!" Mr. Brown just nodded his head and widened his grin until the white men passed by him.

I won tentative approval from the groundskeeper for the completion of my assignment. My stomach growled. For a second, I felt dizzy and disoriented. Through the hurricane fence, I gazed at a spread of tennis courts laid out on the Friendship Dell property yards from the stairs of the establishment's big red brick clubhouse. Young people in white outfits occupied each quadrangle. Two pigtailed blond girls played on the nearest court. Seeming no older than me, one of them rushed the net to finish an intense rally with a drop shot, and she strutted back to her baseline looking less winded than I felt.

Mr. Brown allowed me to have lunch in the kitchen. The cook served me a sandwich of baloney and cheese on Wonder bread with chips and a Coke. From the meal, I gained the strength to get through the rest of the day. In all likelihood, I would have fainted otherwise while I balled and burlapped roots for protection until planted in a garden tilled by the groundskeeper. He stayed on my back to see that each wrapping was neat.

On the train ride home, Mr. Brown hung on my mind. My picture of him brought to mind the scheming skipper of the PT boat crew in *McHale's Navy*. The sitcom commander was always gracious and obliging in the face of Captain Binghamton. Behind the back of his superior officer, he plotted to take advantage of him. In essence, McHale put on shows designed to dupe his supervisor. It was the kind of relationship, I imagined, Mr. Brown had with white folks. However, McHale was sure to get something out of his pranks. I doubted the groundskeeper profited from his shenanigans.

By my calculations, Mr. Brown's trickery earned him basically a lifetime of being a flunky. It was apparent his manners around whites earned him their respect and trust. They regarded him as a treasure. I supposed that he was welcome to remain in service to the Holy Redeemer until the day he died. Nevertheless, the cost outweighed the benefit. It was not the sort of "Black Power" about which I heard Stokely Carmichael speak on the radio. The college student activist maintained Blacks should take up the right to act on their own terms, without charades to obtain the goodwill of whites.

During the following two weeks, I gathered the impression that Mr. Brown was held in high esteem by a bunch of Black workers employed in the vicinity of the church. The group included handymen along with maids engaged by owners of nearby mansions. It also consisted of guards, cooks, waitresses, janitors, and caddies on the Friendship Dell payroll. It seemed that they looked up to the groundskeeper on par with the admiration the Roman gladiators display for the title character played by Kirk Douglass in the movie *Spartacus*. The reason for their attitude toward Mr. Brown escaped me.

On my second Friday at the Holy Redeemer, rain poured through the morning. The groundskeeper had me work with him inside the church building to stay dry. We polished fixtures, dusted pews, and fixed a busted lever on a stained-glass window. Mr. Brown struck up a surprising conversation. He compared a happy life to a masterful round of golf. I had watched snippets of the game on television. But it never held my interest. I counted it as an excuse for old white men to hang out and exercise without breaking a sweat.

Mr. Brown made the sport sound like a science. He explained that the game was played on a course with fairways, rough patches, and traps. The obstacles in the field were natural and artificial. He told me the goal in golf was not a high amount of scores. Rather, the objective was a low number of miscues. Mr. Brown stressed that it took skill and ingenuity to manage the game. In truth, he contended, a steady hand and keen eye marked a champion.

Professing that an expert golfer appreciated geometry, he left me in the dark. I knew less than nothing about the branch of mathematics. He shed light on the matter with a reference to the pyramids of the Nile Valley. Listening to him credit Africans with developing geometry, I dropped my jaw. He went on, expounding on the importance of attention to points, lines, and angles in golf. A sharp player, Mr. Brown informed me, sized up a situation before a stroke.

I was flabbergasted by the story of the first Black man to play on the Professional Golfers Association tour. Named Charlie Sifford, the pioneer fell in love with golf as a teenage caddie in Charlotte and dreamed of a successful career in the sport. Yet Jim Crow laws in his hometown closed golf courses to Black players, so when he turned seventeen, he moved to Philadelphia, where he supported himself for a while with a humdrum job at the Nabisco factory on Roosevelt Boulevard. Finding the Cobbs Creek Golf Club open to Blacks, he proceeded to master the game through frequent rounds at the facility. A few years prior to my birth, Sifford began achieving fame with consecutive victories in the annual National Negro Open. By the time Mr. Brown began working at the Holy Redeemer, the golfer had been competing on the PGA tour for six seasons. Furthermore, Sifford had just won the Greater Hartford Open.

Mr. Brown finished telling me about Sifford at lunch. Afterward, the skies cleared. The sun blazed on my head. For the rest of the day, I worked beside the groundskeeper in the yards around the Holy Redeemer. At one point, the deacon crossed our path and said, "Keep up the good work, Bud." Mr. Brown nodded and smiled, and I followed suit.

Over the next week, the groundskeeper pulled out of me the fact that I had fallen in love with books. It was the start of the summer schedule for the business office. Miss Mary closed her doors for the week on Thursday at noon. She left Mr. Brown in charge of the remaining staff including only Mrs. Brooks and me. After Miss Mary departed, he sent me to help a construction crew hired to refurbish a house for a new assistant pastor due in the fall. The captain of the crew told me his team was wrapping up for the day, but I would find work for myself in the living room. And so I went there. On the bare waxed hardwood floor, I discovered the book *Manchild in the Promised Land* with a note signed by Mr. Brown that read, "Follow your bliss."

It crossed my mind Mr. Brown was somehow like the hero of *Hogan's Heroes*. The television figure was Robert Hogan, an American colonel imprisoned in a Nazi camp. Among a motley crew of captives from the Allied Forces, he was the ranking officer. With the aid of his comrades, he ran an underground espionage operation out of the prison compound. His German warden, Commandant Wilhelm Klink, never matched his wits. On a regular basis, Hogan advanced his own interests with false shows of deference for the commandant.

I contemplated Mr. Brown's words and deeds along with his standing among Black people who worked in the neighborhood. It was crystal clear that he put on shows for whites. Nevertheless, his regards for the feats of Sifford were loaded with personal and folk pride. After I added up what I knew of him, I suspected that he championed a secret organization, which worked for the good of Blacks. I meant to discover the whole truth.

Mr. Brown was keeping something up his sleeve. Whites around the Holy Redeemer never noticed it. They expected a fair deal from him. Their conduct around him said they trusted that he lacked the wiles to play any tricks on them. The pastor considered him above board beyond a shadow of doubt. In the deacon's view, Mr. Brown was a straight shooter. Parishioners of the Holy Redeemer sang his praises whenever they happened upon him. Diehard golfers, who played on the course at the Friendship Dell, addressed the groundskeeper as "Bud." They even picked up pointers about golf from him, in return for which they handed him tips.

It would have thrown the whites in the neighborhood for a loop to catch the sly side of Mr. Brown, which I missed at first. In the beginning, I held he had neither pride nor purpose. I imagined he amounted to a brainless drudge. His behavior in the face of whites embarrassed me. They virtually stayed poised to pat him on the head. And he looked ready to waggle for a stroke. The whites felt that they knew him. With a cool caginess, he kept his big secret hidden from them. After my third week under his supervision, I knew he vanished on Thursday before lunch and went unseen on Friday, but got his timecard punched anyway, and nobody noticed, it seemed, save me. It was the middle of my fifth week on the job before he came clean.

Mr. Brown caught me standing at rest in the field behind the Parish House. It was a hot August afternoon. I was tired of mowing. Sweat had to be mopped from my brow. My eyes peered through the hurricane fence at the nearest Friendship Dell tennis court, where the pigtailed blonde girl with the killer drop shot was running a stumped white boy ragged in a match. I was bitter that the boy was free to play with the girl while it was my job to cut the grass.

The groundskeeper surprised me. He snuck up behind my back and asked, "Ain't fair, huh?" His voice shook me.

I was unsure of how to answer him.

"We're locked in a game," he said. "Their folks started it. Son, you know the deal. They keep the field uneven. Don't sweat it? Turn tragedy into triumph. Bet on it." Poking my head with a finger, Mr. Brown whispered in my ear, "Win with this."

He lost me.

"Everyone has a dream," he said.

I granted that.

"It's hard for colored folks."

Of course, I agreed.

"I had a dream," he said.

I shrugged.

"Follow me."

Mr. Brown walked me to the shed from which I was banned since my first day on the job. He found the right key on his ring to unlock the door. His finger flicked on the light. He drew my attention to a corkboard and workbench. The fixtures were piled with pictures, plaques, and golf equipment.

The groundskeeper confessed that he was an avid golfer. He fell in love with the game around my age when he was employed as a caddy at the Friendship Dell Country Club. Mr. Brown dreamed of being a professional golfer. He ventured that he could have beaten Byron Nelson in the

1939 Masters Tournament, if the PGA had not barred Black players from competition. It was impossible for him to earn a living from playing golf, but he maintained a commitment to facing stiff competition in nearby open tournaments.

Mr. Brown lobbied a bygone pastor to become the groundskeeper at the Holy Redeemer. He saw that it afforded him a chance to work without anyone keeping tabs on him. Once Mr. Brown won everyone's trust, he developed a routine of slipping off to the Cobbs Creek Golf Club. He honed his grasp of the game to compete on the black professional circuit. The man was a contestant in the National Negro Open. On one occasion, he played a round at the Cobbs Creek Club with Sifford; Mr. Brown bragged that he let the legendary golfer have a good run for his money.

The groundskeeper had a whole lot of help. When Mr. Brown played golf, Mrs. Brooks watched her soap operas, *As the World Turns* before *Guiding Light*, in the kitchen, where she also kept an eye out for the pastor and deacon. The cook attended the New Bethlehem Baptist Church in the Powelton Village area, where the groundskeeper's cousin belonged to the congregation. Mr. Brown arranged for Miss Mary to hire Mrs. Brooks. During her youth, the business manager picked up golf from Mr. Brown. She felt it was a favor for which she could never repay the groundskeeper. Happy to accommodate Mr. Brown, she set the church office hours so that they did not conflict with his tee times. Miss Mary also served as a reference for job seekers directed to the Friendship Dell Country Club by the groundskeeper.

My last Friday at the Holy Redeemer, I hoped to see Mr. Brown. Yet I never saw him. The groundskeeper had bid me farewell two days earlier. He had handed me a gift. It was the novel *Invisible Man*. He said as well, "Follow your bliss." Hiking to the Highland station, in my mind, I pictured the groundskeeper lining up a tee shot.

Works Cited

Aesop. *Aesop's Fables*. Ed. Thomas James. Springfield: Farm and Fireside Company, 1881.
Aardema, Verna, and Jerry Pinkney. *Rabbit Makes a Monkey of Lion: A Swahili Tale*. New York: Dial Books, 1989.
Anderson, Sherwood. *Winesburg, Ohio*. New York: B. W. Huebsch, 1919.
Anderson, William. The *Life and Narrative of William J. Anderson*. Chicago: Daily Tribune Book and Job Printing Office, 1857.
Angelou, Maya. *I Know Why the Caged Bird Sings*. New York: Random House, 1969.
Arana, Marie "The Good Lord Bird." *Washington Post* 19 Aug. 2013 <https://www.washingtonpost.com/entertainment/books/the-good-lord-bird-by-james-mcbride/2013/08/19/e0759a98-05e1-11e3-88d6-d5795fab4637_story.html>.
Aristotle. *The Politics of Aristotle*. New York: Oxford UP, 1971.
Baldwin, James. *Another Country*. New York: Dial Press, 1962.
Bazin, Andre, "Adaptation, or the Cinema as Digest." *Bazin at Work*. Ed. Bert Cardullo and trans. Alain Piette and Bert Cardullo. New Brunswick: Routledge, Inc., 1997. 41-52.
Bibb, Henry. *Narrative of the Life and Adventures of Henry Bibb, an American Slave, Written by Himself*. New York: MacDonald & Lee, Printers, 1849.
Blassingame, John. *The Slave Community: Plantation Life in the Antebellum South*. New York: Oxford UP, 1979.
Bluestone, George. *Novels into Film*. Baltimore: Johns Hopkins UP, 1957.
Bradley, David. *The Chaneysville Incident*. New York: Harper & Row, 1981.
———. "On the Lam from Race and Gender." *New York Times* 3 Aug. 1986, sec. 7: 7+.
Bronte, Charlotte. *Jane Eyre*. London: Smith, Elder & Co., 1847.
Brown, Claude. *Manchild in the Promised Land*. New York: Macmillan & Co., 1965.
Brown, William Wells. *Clotel*. London: Partridge & Oakley, 1853.
———. *Narrative of William W. Brown, a Fugitive Slave. Written by Himself*. Boston: The Anti-Slavery Office, 1847.

Butler, Judith. "Performative Acts and Gender Constitution." *Theater Journal* 40.4 (1988): 519-31.
Butler, Octavia. *Kindred*. Boston: Beacon Press, 1979.
———. *Mind of My Mind*. New York: Doubleday, 1977.
———. *Patternmaster*. New York: Doubleday, 1976.
———. *Survivor*. New York: Doubleday, 1978.
Cable, George Washington. *The Grandissimes: A Story of Creole Life*. New York: Charles Scribner's Sons, 1880.
Calhoun, John C. "Speech on the Reception of Abolition Petitions." February 1837. *Speeches of John C. Calhoun*. New York: Harper & Brother's, 1843.
Cartwright, Justin. "The Good Lord Bird." *The Spectator* 25 Jan. 2014 <https://www.spectator.co.uk/article/the-good-lord-bird-by-james-mcbride---review>.
Chafe, William H. *Women and Equality: Changing Patterns in American Culture*. New York: Oxford UP, 1977. Rpt. in *Race, Class, and Gender in the United States*. Ed. Paula S. Rothenberg. New York: St. Martin's Press, 1998.
Chesnutt, Charles. *The Colonel's Dream*. New York: Doubleday, Page & Company, 1905.
———. *The Conjure Woman*. Boston: Houghton, Mifflin and Company, 1899.
———. *The House Behind the Cedars*. Boston; New York: Houghton, Mifflin and Company, 1900.
———. *The Marrow of Tradition*. Boston; New York: Houghton, Mifflin and Company, 1901.
———. *The Wife of His Youth and Other Stories of the Color Line*. Boston; New York: Houghton, Mifflin and Company, 1901.
Chesnutt, Helen M. *Charles Waddell Chesnutt: Pioneer of the Color Line*. New York: Van Rees Press, 1952.
Collins, Patricia Hill. *Black Feminist Thought*. New York: Routledge, 2000.
———. "Learning from the Outsider Within." *Social Problems* 33.6 (1986): 14–32.
Cousins, Paul. *Joel Chandler Harris: A Biography*. Louisiana State UP, 1968.
Craft, Ellen, and William Craft. *Running a Thousand Miles for Freedom*. Acton: Copley Publishing Group, 2000.
Davis, Angela. *Women, Race, & Class*. New York: Vintage Books, 1983.
de Cervantes, Miguel. *The Adventures of Don Quixote*. New York: Farrar, Straus, Giroux, 1986.
Delano Amasa, *Narrative of Voyages and Travels in the Northern and Southern Hemispheres: Comprising Three Voyages Round the World; Together with a Voyage of Survey and Discovery, in the Pacific Ocean and Oriental Islands*. New York: E. G. House, 1817.
DeVoto, Bernard. *Mark Twain at Work*. Cambridge: Harvard UP, 1942.
Dickens, Charles. *Great Expectations*. London: Chapman & Hall, 1861.
Douglass, Frederick. "The Heroic Slave." *Autographs for Freedom*. Ed. Julia Griffiths. Boston: John P. Jewett and Company, 1853.

———. *Life and Times of Frederick Douglass*. Boston: De Wolfe & Fiske Co., 1892.
———. *My Bondage and My Freedom*. New York: Miller, Orton & Mulligan, 1855.
———. *Narrative of the Life of Frederick Douglass: An American Slave, Written by Himself.* Boston: Bedford Books, 1993.
Dreisinger, Baz. "Marching On." *New York Times Book Review* 18 Aug. 2013, p. 1.
Du Bois, W. E. B. *The Souls of Black Folk*. Boston: Bedford Books, 1997.
Dumas, Alexandre. *The Count of Monte Cristo*. London: George Routledge and Sons, 1888.
Dunbar, Paul Laurence. *Lyrics of the Hearthside*. New York: Dodd, Mead and Company, 1899.
———. *Lyrics of Lowly Life*. London: Chapman & Hall, Ltd., 1897.
Edwards, Harry Stillwell. *Two Runaways and Other Stories*. New York: The Century Co., 1922.
Eliot, T. S. "An Introduction to *The Adventures of Huckleberry Finn*." London: Cresset Press, 1950.
Elkins, Stanley. *Slavery: A Problem in American Institutional and Intellectual Life*. Chicago: U of Chicago P, 1976.
Ellison, Ralph. "Change the Joke and Slip the Yoke." *Partisan Review* 25.2 (1958): 212-22.
———. *Invisible Man*. New York: Random House, 1993.
———. *Shadow and Act*. New York: Random House, 1964.
Equiano, Olaudah. *The Interesting Narrative of the life of Olaudah Equiano, Written by Himself.* Boston: Bedford Books, 1995.
Faulkner, William. *The Sound and the Fury*. New York: Jonathan Cape & Harrison Smith, 1929.
Fishkin, Shelley Fisher. *Was Huck Black?: Mark Twain and African American Voices*. New York: Oxford UP, 1994.
Franklin, Benjamin. *Observations Concerning the Increase of Mankind, Peopling of Countries, Etc. Perspectives in Biology and Medicine* 13.4 (1970): 469-75.
Gaines, Ernest. *The Autobiography of Miss Jane Pittman*. New York: Dial Press, 1971.
Gates, Henry Louis. *The Signifying Monkey*. New York: Oxford UP, 1988.
Giovanni, Nikki. "'Jane Pittman' Fulfilled My Deepest Expectations." *New York Times* 3 Mar. 1974, p. 115.
Haley, Alex. *Roots*. New York: Doubleday, 1976.
Harper, Frances. *Iola Leroy*. Boston: James H. Earle, 1892.
Harris, Joel Chandler. *Uncle Remus: His Songs and His Saying*. New York: Penguin Books, 1986.
Hartman, Saidiya. *Scenes of Subjection: Terror, Slavery, and Self-Making in Nineteenth-Century America*. New York: Oxford UP, 1997.
Hemenway, Robert. "Introduction: Author, Teller, and Hero." *Uncle Remus: His Songs and His Saying*. New York: Penguin Books, 1986.
Hemingway, Ernest. *Green Hills of Africa*. London: Jonathan Cape, 1936.

Henson, Josiah. *The Life of Josiah Henson, Formerly a Slave, Now an Inhabitant of Canada, as Narrated by Himself.* Boston: Arthur D. Phelps, 1849.

Hubbard, Ruth. *The Politics of Women's Biology.* New Brunswick: Rutgers UP, 1991. Repr. in *Race, Class, and Gender in the United States.* Ed. Paula S. Rothenberg. New York: St. Martin's Press, 1998.

Hurston, Zora Neale. *Their Eyes Were Watching God.* Philadelphia: J. B. Lippincott, 1937.

Hyman, Stanley Edgar. "The Folk Tradition." *Partisan Review* 25.2 (1958): 197–211.

Jacobs, Harriet. *Incidents in the Life of a Slave Girl.* New York: Harcourt Brace Jovanovich, 1973.

Jefferson, Thomas *Notes on the State of Virginia.* Philadelphia: Prichard and Hall, 1785.

Johnson, Charles. *Middle Passage.* New York: Atheneum Publishers, 1990.

Johnson, Allan G. *The Gender Knot: Unraveling Our Patriarchal Legacy.* Philadelphia: Temple UP, 1997. Repr. in *Race, Class, and Gender in the United States.* Ed. Paula S. Rothenberg. New York: St. Martin's Press, 1998.

Johnson, Sadeqa. *Yellow Wife.* New York: Simon & Schuster, 2021.

Jones, Edward P. *The Known World.* New York: Amistad Press, 2003.

Keckley, Elizabeth. *Behind the Scenes: Or, Thirty Years a Slave and Four Years in the White House.* Chapel Hill: U of North Carolina P, 2011.

Kennedy, John Pendleton. *Swallow Barn, or A Sojourn in the Old Dominion.* Philadelphia: Carey & Lea, 1832.

Kirkus Reviews. The Autobiography of Miss Jane Pittman 26 Apr. 1971 <https://www.kirkusreviews.com/book-reviews/a/ernest-j-gaines-4/the-autobiography-of-miss-jane-pittman/#>.

Levine, Lawrence. *Black Culture and Black Consciousness.* New York: Oxford UP, 1978.

Locke, John. *An Essay on Human Understanding.* London: Eliz. Holt, Thomas Basset, 1689.

Lorber, Judith. *Paradoxes of Gender.* New Haven: Yale UP, 1994.

Malcolm X. *The Autobiography of Malcolm X.* New York: Grove Press, 1965.

Mannheim, Karl. *Ideology and Utopia.* New York: Harcourt, Brace, 1936.

Marx, Leo. *The Machine in the Garden: Technology and the Pastoral Ideal in America.* New York: Oxford UP, 1964.

Melville, Herman. "Bartleby, the Scrivener." *The Piazza Tales.* New York: Dix & Edwards, 1856.

———. "Benito Cereno." *The Piazza Tales.* New York: Dix & Edwards, 1856.

McBride, James. *The Good Lord Bird.* New York: Riverhead, 2013.

Miller, Jean Baker. *Toward a New Psychology of Women.* Boston: Beacon Press, 1986. Repr. in *Race, Class, and Gender in the United States.* Ed. Paula S. Rothenberg. New York: St. Martin's Press, 1998.

Morrison, Toni. *Beloved.* New York: Alfred A. Knopf, 1987.

Morton, Samuel George. *Crania Americana.* Philadelphia: J. Dobson, 1839.

National Humanities Center. *On Slaveholders' Sexual Abuse of Slaves: Selections from 19th- & 20th-Century Slave Narratives*, pp. 1–7 <http://nationalhumanities center.org/pds/maai/enslavement/text6/masterslavesexualabuse.pdf>.

Northup, Solomon. *Twelve Years a Slave*. Auburn: Derby & Miller, 1853.

Nott, Josiah C., and George R. Gliddon. *Types of Mankind*. Philadelphia: Lippincott, Grambo and Co., 1854.

Omi, Michael, and Howard Winant. *Racial Formations in the United States*. New York: Routledge, 1986. Repr. in *Race, Class, and Gender in the United States*. Ed. Paula S. Rothenberg. New York: St. Martin's Press, 1998.

Page, Thomas Nelson. *In Ole Virginia or Marse Chan and Other Stories*. New York: Charles Scribner's Sons, 1895 [c. 1887].

Pennington, James W. C. *The Fugitive Blacksmith; or, Events in the History of James W. C. Pennington, Pastor of a Presbyterian Church, New York, Formerly a Slave in the State of Maryland, United States*. London: Charles Gilpin, 1849.

Petry, Ann. *The Street*. New York: Houghton Mifflin Company, 1946.

Phillips, Ulrich Bonnell. *American Negro Slavery: A Survey of the Supply, Employment and Control of Negro Labor as Determined by the Plantation Regime*. Delhi: Lector House, 2020.

Pickering, Charles, *The Races of Man and Their Geographical Distribution*. Boston: Little and Brown, 1848.

Reed, Ishmael. *Flight to Canada*. New York: Simon & Schuster, 1976.

Roberts, John W. *From Trickster to Badman: The Black Folk Hero in Slavery and Freedom*. Philadelphia: U of Pennsylvania P, 1990.

Rowell, Charles H. "An Interview with Octavia E. Butler." *Callaloo* 20.1 (1997): 47–66.

Rushdy, Ashraf. *Neo-Slave Narratives*. New York: Oxford UP, 1999.

Simms, W. Gilmore. *The Sword and the Distaff: Or, Fair, Fat, and Forty*. Philadelphia: Lippincott, Grambo, & Co., 1852.

Saint Augustine. *The Confessions of St. Augustine*. New York: Penguin, 1961.

Schneir, Miriam. *Feminist: The Essential Historical Writings*. New York: Vintage Books, 1972.

Shikibu, Murasaki. *The Tale of the Genji*. New York: Penguin, 2002.

Stampp, Kenneth. *The Peculiar Institution: Slavery in the Ante-bellum South*. New York: Vintage, 1964.

Stein, Gertrude. *The Autobiography of Alice B. Toklas*. New York: Harcourt Brace and Company, 1933.

Steinem, Gloria. *Outrageous Acts and Everyday Rebellions*. New York: Holt, Rinehart, and Winston, 1983.

Stowe, Harriet Beecher. *Uncle Tom's Cabin*. New York: W. W. Norton & Company, 1994.

Tate, Claudia. "Sherley Anne Williams." *Black Women Writers at Work*. New York: Continuum, 1983. 205–13.
Trilling, Lionel. "Introduction to *Adventures of Huckleberry Finn*." New York: Rinehart, 1948.
Truth, Sojourner. *Narrative of Sojourner Truth*. Ed. Olive Gilbert. New York: Penguin Classics, 1998.
Turner, Nat. *The Confessions of Nat Turner*. As told to Thomas R. Gray. Baltimore: Lucas & Deaver, 1831.
Twain, Mark. *The Adventures of Huckleberry Finn*. London: Charles L. Webster and Company, 1884. eBooks@Adelaide, 2014 www.openrightslibrary.com/the-adventures-of-huckleberry-finn-ebook/.
Vonnegut, Kurt. *Mother Night*. New York: Dell, 1984.
Voltaire. *Candide*. Paris: Cramer, Marc-Michel Rey, Jean Nourse, Lambert, et al., 1759.
Walker, Alice. *The Color Purple*. New York: Harcourt Brace Jovanovich, 1982.
———. "Coming Apart." *You Can't Keep a Good Woman Down*. New York: Harcourt Brace Jovanovich, 1981.
———. "Jane Didn't Stay in a Corner." *New York Times* 23 May 1971, sec. BR: 6.
Walker, Margaret. *Jubilee*. New York: Houghton Mifflin Harcourt, 1966.
Washington, Booker T. *Up From Slavery: An Autobiography*. Garden City: Doubleday & Company, Inc. 1901.
Wecter, Dixon. *Sam Clemens of Hannibal*. New York: Houghton Mifflin, 1952.
Whitehead, Colson. *The Underground Railroad*. New York: Doubleday, 2016.
Williams, Roland L. *African American Autobiography and the Quest for Freedom*. Westport: Greenwood Press, 2000.
Williams, Sherley Anne. *Dessa Rose*. New York: William Morrow, 1986.
Wilson, Harriet. *Our Nig*. Boston: Geo. C. Rand & Avery, 1859.
Wright, Richard. "The Ethics of Living Jim Crow." *Uncle Tom's Children*. New York: Harper & Row, 1965.
———. *Native Son*. New York: Harper & Brothers, 1940.

Index

Aardema, Verna, 84
abolitionism, 30, 128, 139, 144–49, 154
"Adaptation, or the Cinema as Digest" (Bazin), 114
The Adventures of Don Quixote (Cervantes), 107
The Adventures of Huckleberry Finn (Twain): *The Autobiography of Miss Jane Pittman* (Gaines) and, 107; Black bondage in, 61, 71–78; *The Good Lord Bird* (McBride) and, 144–46, 149, 152, 153; notions of race in, 67–78; reception of, 78–81; smooth operators in, 73; social satire in, 70–71; women and notions of gender in, 61, 63–67
Aesop, 84–85
African storytelling tradition: Black bondage and, 85–92; *The Conjure Woman* (Chesnutt) and, 83, 92, 94–101; Harris and, 83, 87–92, 94–95
"Ain't I a Woman" (Truth), 139
American Negro Slavery (Phillips), 21–22
Ancient Greece, 84
Anderson, Sherwood, 94
Anderson, William J., 120
Angelou, Maya, 106

Another Country (Baldwin), 25
Arana, Marie, 144
Aristotle, 61
Atlanta Constitution (newspaper), 87–88
Atlantic Monthly (magazine), 94
Augustine of Hippo, 106
The Autobiography of Alice B. Toklas (Stein), 107
The Autobiography of Miss Jane Pittman (Gaines): Black bondage in, 108–13; film adaptation of, 103–5, 114–16; grief in, 111–13; knowledge as power in, 107–11, 113–14, 116; as neo-slave narrative, 7, 24; notions of race in, 108–13; oak tree in, 103, 113–14; reception of, 107, 113; slave narratives and, 105–6; style and plot of, 105–7, 108–11
The Autobiography of Miss Jane Pittman (1974 film), 103–5, 114–16
Autographs for Freedom (Griffiths), 47–48

Baldwin, James, 25
Banneker, Benjamin, 31
"Bartleby, the Scrivener" (Melville), 47, 92
Bazin, André, 114
Behind the Scenes (Keckley), 22, 120–21

Beloved (Morrison), 14, 24, 25, 122
Benito Cereno (Melville), 45–47, 54–59, 144
Bibb, Henry, 120
Billy Budd, Sailor (Melville), 47
Black Arts Movement, 7, 24
Black bondage: abolitionism and, 30, 128, 139, 144–49, 154; in *The Adventures of Huckleberry Finn* (Twain), 61, 71–78; African storytelling tradition and, 85–92; in *The Autobiography of Miss Jane Pittman* (Gaines), 108–13; in *Dessa Rose* (Williams), 133–41; Du Bois on, 149–50; *The Good Lord Bird* (McBride) and, 150; in *Incidents in the Life of a Slave Girl* (Jacobs), 19–20, 41–43; in *Kindred* (Butler), 118, 122–29; knowledge as power in, 107–8; in *Narrative of the Life of Frederick Douglass* (Douglass), 17–18, 20, 39–41; notions of gender and, 5–6; origins of, 13, 28; *Roots* (Haley) and, 118–19; sexual abuse and, 117, 120–21; skin color as marker of character and, 13–24, 28–35, 104; in *Uncle Tom's Cabin* (Stowe), 18–20; in *Up from Slavery* (B. T. Washington), 122; white writers on, 45–47, 54–59, 94–95. *See also* neo-slave narratives; slave narratives; smooth operating
Black Culture and Black Consciousness (Levine), 85
Black Feminist Thought (Collins), 105
Black Power, 159
Blassingame, John, 22–23
blindness: as effect of Black bondage, 13; in *The Good Lord Bird* (McBride), 145–47, 151–52; in *Invisible Man* (Ellison), 146–47;
in *Kindred* (Butler), 128. *See also* racism and notions of race
Bluestone, George, 114
Bost, W. L., 119
Bradley, David, 24, 122, 132–33, 142
Bronte, Charlotte, 107
Brotherhood of Sleeping Car Porters, 2
Brown, John, 145, 146–47, 149, 154
Brown, Oliver (groundskeeper), 155–63
Brown, William Wells, 22, 24, 106
Butler, Judith, 61, 132
Butler, Octavia, 122

Cable, George Washington, 94–95
Calhoun, John C., 16–17, 19–20
Candide (Voltaire), 107
Carmichael, Stokely, 159
Cartwright, Justin, 144
Cervantes, Miguel de, 107
Chafe, William, 148
The Chaneysville Incident (Bradley), 24, 122
"Change the Joke and Slip the Yoke" (Ellison), 79–80
Chesnutt, Charles, 24, 92–94, 107–8. *See also The Conjure Woman* (Chesnutt)
Clotel (W. W. Brown), 24, 106
Cole, Nat King, 85–86
Collins, Patricia Hill, 5–6, 105, 117
The Colonel's Dream (Chesnutt), 94
The Color Purple (A. Walker), 106, 141–42
"Coming Apart" (A. Walker), 117–18
Confessions (Augustine of Hippo), 106
The Confessions of Nat Turner (Styron), 111
The Confidence-Man (Melville), 47
The Conjure Woman (Chesnutt): African storytelling tradition and,

83, 92, 94–101; knowledge as power in, 107–8; as neo-slave narrative, 7, 24
"The Conjurer's Revenge" (Chesnutt), 99
The Count of Monte Cristo (Dumas), 78–79
The Countryman (newspaper), 87
Craft, Ellen, 6, 23, 36–37, 93–94
Craft, William, 6, 23, 36–37
Crania Americana (Morton), 15
Creole (ship), 45, 48–49. See also *The Heroic Slave* (Douglass)

Davis, Angela, 121, 139
Declaration of Independence (1776), 13–14, 31
Delano, Amasa, 54–59
Dessa Rose (Williams): abolitionism in, 139; Black bondage in, 133–41; historical sources of, 142; as neo-slave narrative, 7, 24, 122, 133; notions of race in, 131–32, 142; reception of, 132–33, 142; smooth operators in, 137, 140–41; style and plot of, 132–40; women and notions of gender in, 131–32, 134–41, 142
DeVoto, Bernard, 78
Dickens, Charles, 107
"The Dog and the Wolf" (Aesop), 85
Douglass, Frederick: O. Butler and, 119, 122; in *The Good Lord Bird* (McBride), 145, 149, 150, 153; on sexual abuse, 120; as smooth operator, 49; on white women, 126. See also *The Heroic Slave* (Douglass); *Narrative of the Life of Frederick Douglass* (Douglass)
Dreisinger, Baz, 144
Du Bois, W. E. B., 149–50

Dumas, Alexandre, 78–79
Dunbar, Paul Laurence, 23–24, 62

Edwards, Harry Stillwell, 94–95
Eliot, T. S., 78
Elkins, Stanley, 22, 23
Ellison, Ralph, 7–8, 79–80. See also *Invisible Man* (Ellison)
Equiano, Olaudah, 6, 21, 22, 37–39
An Essay on Human Understanding (Locke), 131
"The Ethics of Living Jim Crow" (Wright), 4, 108

Faulkner, William, 110
Fishkin, Shelley Fisher, 81
Flight to Canada (Reed), 7, 24
"The Folk Tradition" (Hyman), 80
Franklin, Benjamin, 15, 28–30, 57
From Trickster to Bad Man (Roberts), 86
The Fugitive Blacksmith (Pennington), 35–36
Fuller, Margaret, 62

Gaines, Ernest, 111. See also *The Autobiography of Miss Jane Pittman* (Gaines)
Gates, Henry Louis, 86–87
gender. See women and notions of gender
The Gender Knot (A. G. Johnson), 62
geometry, 160
Giovanni, Nikki, 103–4
Gliddon, George, 15
golf, 160, 162–63
Gone with the Wind (1939 film), 23
The Good Lord Bird (McBride): abolitionism in, 144–49, 154; *The Adventures of Huckleberry Finn* (Twain) and, 144–46, 149, 152,

The Good Lord Bird (continued)
153; as neo-slave narrative, 7, 24, 143; notions of race in, 145–54; reception of, 143–44; smooth operators in, 145–46, 153–54; trickeration in, 151–52; women and notions of gender in, 148–49, 152–54
"The Goophered Grapevine" (Chesnutt), 94, 95–97
Graham, Blanche, 1
The Grandissimes (Cable), 94–95
"The Gray Wolf's Ha'nt" (Chesnutt), 100
Great Expectations (Dickens), 107
Griffiths, Julia, 47–48
Grimke, Sarah and Angelina, 139
griots, 83–84

Haley, Alex, 118–19
Harper, Frances, 24, 106
Harper's Weekly (magazine), 23
Harris, Joel Chandler, 83, 87–92, 94–95
Hartman, Saidiya, 5, 14–15, 104–5
Henry, Patrick, 50
Henson, Josiah, 18–19
Hercules, 34
The Heroic Slave (Douglass), 7, 24, 45–46, 47–54, 59
"Hot Foot Hannibal" (Chesnutt), 100
The House Behind the Cedars (Chesnutt), 94
Howells, William Dean, 23
Hubbard, Ruth, 62
Hurston, Zora Neale, 25, 106
Hyman, Stanley, 80

Ideology and Utopia (Mannheim), 6
In Ole Virginia (Page), 94–95
Incidents in the Life of a Slave Girl (Jacobs): Black bondage in, 19–20, 41–43; O. Butler and, 119, 122; as classic slave narrative, 7, 106, 111, 133, 144; on sexual abuse, 121; smooth operating in, 20
indentured servitude, 27–28
intellectual activism, 105, 114
The Interesting Narrative of the Life of Olaudah Equiano (Equiano), 6, 22, 37–39
interracial marriage, 122, 123, 126
Invisible Man (Ellison), 3–4, 32, 80, 106, 146–47, 152
Iola Leroy (Harper), 24, 106

Jacobs, Harriet, 119, 122. See also *Incidents in the Life of a Slave Girl* (Jacobs)
James I, King, 27–28
Jamestown, 27–28
Jane Eyre (Bronte), 107
Jefferson, Thomas, 30–33, 111
Johnson, Allan G., 62
Johnson, Charles, 122, 144
Johnson, Sadeqa, 7, 24
Jones, Edward, 24
Jubilee (M. Walker), 24, 122
Judge, Oney, 34

Keckley, Elizabeth, 22, 106, 119, 120–21
Kennedy, John Pendleton, 45–46
Kindred (O. Butler): abolitionism in, 128; Black bondage in, 118, 122–29; *Dessa Rose* (Williams) and, 133; historical sources of, 119–22; as neo-slave narrative, 7, 24, 25, 122; notions of race in, 117, 122–29; as science fiction, 119, 122; smooth operators in, 117, 125, 127; style and plot of, 118, 119, 123–29; womanism and, 117–18; women and notions of gender in, 117, 122–29

King, Martin Luther, Jr., 7
Kirkus (magazine), 113
The Known World (Jones), 24
Korty, John, 105, 114

"Learning from the Outsider Within" (Collins), 5–6
Lee, Billy, 33–34
Levine, Lawrence, 85
Life and Narrative of William J. Anderson (Anderson), 120
Life and Times of Frederick Douglass (Douglass), 49
Life of Josiah Henson (Henson), 18–19
"The Lion and the Mouse" (Aesop), 84–85
Locke, John, 131
Lorber, Judith, 131
Loving v. Virginia (1967), 122

Macks, Richard, 119
Madison, James, 49
Mannheim, Karl, 6
Mardi (Melville), 47
Mark Twain at Work (DeVoto), 78
The Marrow of Tradition (Chesnutt), 94
"Mars Jeems's Nightmare" (Chesnutt), 98–99
McBride, James. See *The Good Lord Bird* (McBride)
McQueen, Butterfly, 23
Melville, Herman, 45–47, 54–59, 92, 144
Middle Passage (C. Johnson), 122, 144
Miller, Jean Baker, 62–63
Mind of my Mind (O. Butler), 122
Moby-Dick (Melville), 47
monogenesis, 15
Morrison, Toni, 14, 24, 25
Morton, Samuel George, 15
Mother Night (Vonnegut), 66–67

"Mr. Rabbit Grossly Deceives Mr. Fox" (Harris), 89–90
Murasaki Shikibu, 107
My Bondage and My Freedom (Douglass), 120, 126

The Narrative of Sojourner Truth (Truth), 111
Narrative of the Life of Frederick Douglass (Douglass): Black bondage in, 17–18, 20, 39–41; Blassingame and, 22; O. Butler and, 119, 122; as classic slave narrative, 6, 106, 111, 144; on singing, 90; Stowe and, 18–19
A Narrative of Voyages and Travels, in the Northern and Southern Hemispheres (Delano), 54
Narrative of William W. Brown, a Fugitive Slave (W. W. Brown), 22
Narratives of the Life and Adventures of Henry Bibb (Bibb), 120
National Association for the Advancement of Colored People (NAACP), 94
National Book Award, 141, 144, 146
Native Son (Wright), 106
Negro, use of term, 29
neo-slave narratives, 6, 7, 24–25, 143. *See also specific novels*
Neo-Slave Narratives (Rushdy), 143
New Bethlehem Baptist Church, 2
New York Times (newspaper), 103, 107, 132–33, 142, 144
nigger, use of term, 29, 38, 70–71, 79
Northup, Solomon, 22, 106
Notes on the State of Virginia (Jefferson), 30–32, 111
Nott, Josiah Clark, 15
Novels into Film (Bluestone), 114

oak tree, 103, 113–14, 115

Observations Concerning the Increase of Mankind (Franklin), 15, 28–30, 57
Omi, Michael, 15, 131
Omoo (Melville), 47
Our Nig (Wilson), 24, 106
Outrageous Acts and Everyday Rebellions (Steinem), 142

Page, Thomas Nelson, 94–95
Paradoxes of Gender (Lorber), 131
passing, 37, 93–94
patriarchy, 61–63, 139
Patternmaster (O. Butler), 122
The Peacock Poems (Williams), 132, 141
The Peculiar Institution (Stampp), 22
Pennington, James, 35–36
Pennsylvania Abolition Society, 30
Pennsylvania Gazette (newspaper), 30
"Performative Acts and Gender Constitution" (J. Butler), 61, 132
Petry, Ann, 106
Phillips, Ulrich Bonnell, 21–22
Pickering, Charles, 15
"Po' Sandy" (Chesnutt), 97–98
The Politics of Women's Biology (Hubbard), 62
polygenesis, 15
postmodernism, 133
Pulitzer Prize, 141

Rabbit Makes a Monkey of Lion (Aardema), 84
Races of Man and Their Geographical Distribution (Pickering), 15
Racial Formation in the United States (Omi and Winant), 15, 131
racism and notions of race: in *The Adventures of Huckleberry Finn* (Twain), 67–78; in *The Autobiography of Miss Jane Pittman* (Gaines), 108–13; in *Dessa Rose* (Williams), 131–32, 142; in *The Good Lord Bird* (McBride), 145–54; in *Kindred* (O. Butler), 117, 122–29; Omi and Winant on, 15, 131; scientific racism and, 15–16. *See also* Black bondage; blindness
Randolph, A. Phillip, 2
Reed, Ishmael, 7, 24
Roberts, John, 86
Roots (Haley), 118–19
Roots (1977 miniseries), 118–19
Running a Thousand Miles for Freedom (E. Craft and W. Craft), 6, 23, 36–37, 93–94
Rushdy, Ashraf, 143

Sam Clemens of Hannibal (Wecter), 80–81
"Sambo" stereotype, 22, 23
Scenes of Subjection (Hartman), 5, 14–15, 104–5
science fiction, 119, 122
scientific racism, 15–16
sexual abuse, 117, 120–21, 138–39
Shadow and Act (Ellison), 7–8
Shakespeare, William, 61
Sifford, Charlie, 160, 162–63
The Signifying Monkey (Gates), 86–87
Simms, William Gilmore, 45–46
"Sis Becky's Pickaninny" (Chesnutt), 99–100
The Slave Community (Blassingame), 22–23
slave narratives: characteristics of, 6–7, 35, 105–6, 111; *The Autobiography of Miss Jane Pittman* (Gaines) and, 105–6; *Dessa Rose* (Williams) and, 133; knowledge as power in, 107, 111; sexual abuse in, 120–21. *See also* neo-slave narratives; *specific narratives*
slavery, 13, 28, 29. *See also* Black bondage

Slavery (Elkins), 22, 23
Smith, John, 27–28
smooth operating: concept of, 3–6, 7–8, 14–15, 20–21, 33–35; in *The Adventures of Huckleberry Finn* (Twain), 73, 145–46; Brown (groundskeeper) and, 155–63; in *Dessa Rose* (Williams), 137, 140–41; Douglass and, 49; in *The Good Lord Bird* (McBride), 145–46, 153–54; in *Incidents in the Life of a Slave Girl* (Jacobs), 20; in *Kindred* (Butler), 117, 125, 127; in neo-slave narratives, 24–25
The Souls of Black Folk (Du Bois), 149–50
The Sound and the Fury (Faulkner), 110
The Spectator (magazine), 144
Stampp, Kenneth, 22
Stein, Gertrude, 107
Steinem, Gloria, 142
"The Story of the War" (Harris), 90–92
Stowe, Harriet Beecher, 18–20, 23, 43, 45–46
"Straighten Up and Fly Right" (song), 85–86
The Street (Petry), 106
Styron, William, 111
suffrage movement, 139
Survivor (O. Butler), 122
Swallow Barn (Kennedy), 45–46
The Sword and the Distaff (Simms), 45–46
"Sympathy" (Dunbar), 62

The Tale of the Genji (Murasaki), 107
"Tar-Baby" (African American folktale), 86, 89
"Tar-Baby" (Harris), 88–89
Their Eyes Were Watching God (Hurston), 25, 106

Toward a New Psychology of Women (Miller), 62–63
trauma, 14
trickeration, 151–52
tricksters, 86–87, 88–89
Trilling, Lionel, 78
Truth, Sojourner (Isabella Baumfree), 139
Tryal (ship), 45, 54. See also *Benito Cereno* (Melville)
Tubman, Harriet, 5, 139, 149, 153–54
Turner, Joseph Addison, 87
Turner, Nat, 24, 50–51
Twain, Mark, 80–81. See also *The Adventures of Huckleberry Finn* (Twain)
Twelve Years a Slave (Northup), 22, 106
Two Runaways and Other Stories (Edwards), 94–95
Typee (Melville), 47
Types of Mankind (Nott and Gliddon), 15
Tyson, Cicely, 103

Uncle Remus, 83, 87–92, 94–95
Uncle Remus: His Songs and His Sayings (Harris), 88–92, 94–95
Uncle Tom's Cabin (Stowe), 18–20, 23, 43, 45–46
Uncle Tom's Children (Wright), 108
Underground Railroad, 5
The Underground Railroad (Whitehead), 24
United States Constitution (1787), 33
Up from Slavery (B. T. Washington), 25, 122

Virginia (colony), 13, 27–28
Voltaire, 107
Vonnegut, Kurt, 66–67

Walker, Alice, 106, 107, 117–18, 141–42
Walker, Margaret, 24, 122
Was Huck Black? (Fishkin), 81
Washington, Booker T., 1, 25, 106, 122
Washington, George, 30, 33–34, 49
Washington, Madison, 48–49. See also *The Heroic Slave* (Douglass)
Washington, Martha, 34
Washington Post (newspaper), 144
Watkins, Sylvia, 119
"We Wear the Mask" (Dunbar), 23–24
Wecter, Dixon, 80–81
Wheatley, Phillis, 111
Whitehead, Colson, 24
The Wife of His Youth and Other Stories of the Color-Line (Chesnutt), 94
Williams, Leander, 1–4
Williams, Sherley Anne, 132, 141–42. See also *Dessa Rose* (Williams)
Wilson, Harriet, 24, 106
Winant, Howard, 15, 131
Winesburg, Ohio (Anderson), 94
Woman in the 19th Century (Fuller), 62

womanism, 117–18, 141–42
Women, Race, and Class (Davis), 121, 139
Women and Equality (Chafe), 148
women and notions of gender: in *The Adventures of Huckleberry Finn* (Twain), 61, 63–67; Black bondage and, 5–6; J. Butler on, 61, 132; in *Dessa Rose* (Williams), 131–32, 134–41, 142; in *The Good Lord Bird* (McBride), 148–49, 152–54; in *Kindred* (Butler), 117, 122–29; Lorber on, 131; patriarchy and, 61–63, 139; sexual abuse and, 117, 120–21, 138–39; suffrage movement and, 139
Women's Liberation movement, 141–42
Works Progress Administration (WPA), 119–20
Wright, Richard, 4, 106, 108
Wynn, Tracy Keenan, 105, 114

Yellow Wife (S. Johnson), 7, 24

www.ingramcontent.com/pod-product-compliance
Ingram Content Group UK Ltd.
Pitfield, Milton Keynes, MK11 3LW, UK
UKHW041708180825
461986UK00017B/835